Eugene O'Neill

GARLAND REFERENCE LIBRARY
OF THE HUMANITIES (vol. 860)

LIBRARY
COLBY-SAWYER COLLEGE
NEW LONDON, NH 03257

Eugene O'Neill

An Annotated Bibliography

Madeline Smith
Richard Eaton

GARLAND PUBLISHING, INC.
NEW YORK & LONDON 1988

Z
8644.5
.S6
1988

103662

© 1988 Madeline Smith and Richard Eaton
All Rights Reserved

Library of Congress Cataloging-in-Publication Data

Smith, Madeline.
    Eugene O'Neill : a bibliography, 1973–1985 / compiled and
annotated by Madeline Smith and Richard Eaton.
      p.   cm. — (Garland reference library of the humanities ;
vol. 860)
    Includes indexes.
    ISBN 0–8240–0691–7
    1. O'Neill, Eugene, 1888–1953—Bibliography.
I. Eaton, Richard.   II. Title.   III. Series.
Z8644.5.S6 1988
[PS3529.N5]
016.812'52–dc19   88-11264
                               CIP

Design by Renata Gomes

This volume has been printed on acid-free,
250-year-life paper.

Printed in the United States of America

\# 1791292

ACKNOWLEDGMENTS

Whatever the weaknesses of this work, they are in no way the fault of the many who have helped us to acquire and present our materials. West Virginia University, its English department faculty and staff, the University librarian and his staff (ILL, reference, and periodicals) have all been especially generous with their time, expertise, support, advice, and patience--this last so necessary in the face of our often so cranky frustrations. And especially Mary Jacqueline Seymour (Jackie) who, when we needed her most, assumed the responsibility of seeing two novices through the mysteries of computer technology, typing, retyping, correcting, recorrecting, and yet maintaining her (and our) balance and humor through the whole process. Thank you all.

INTRODUCTION

This work was originally designed to update Jordan Y. Miller's <u>Eugene O'Neill and the American Critic: A Biographical Checklist</u>, 2nd ed., revised, 1973. But as our digging deepened our circumference expanded. Professor Miller, as his title book's indicates, focused his scope on the matter of American O'Neilliana and O'Neillians. That was appropriate, especially since Professor Miller's work was an outgrowth of activities begun in the early 1950s when O'Neill was almost exclusively the province of the American theater, or American theater historians, critics and scholars. But in the last thirty years American theater has become enmeshed in the international theatrical community. Several British productions of O'Neill plays were translated to the United States, one by way of television (and another within two months of our writing this). From American reviews of British productions in America to British reviews of the same before emigration, and the door was opened: our range became more a broad cast than a focus.

The range is still, <u>ab ovo usque ad mala</u>, 1973 to 1985 (though we have annotated a few dissertations of 1971 and 1972 that had eluded Professor Miller), but, discovering that O'Neill's was truly an international stature, we have tried to make our width international also. The <u>malum</u>, that is, covering through 1985, was decided upon because, even now in the spring of 1988, many of the bibliographical resources and indexes necessary for further coverage are still unpublished (<u>American Literary Scholarship</u>, for instance, or consider the plight of the <u>Index Translationum</u>). Better to stop with some semblance of completeness, than to give a wrong impression.

Professor Miller set the standard for this kind of work: that is, the territory includes not only books, dissertations and serial publications (conventional for any bibliography) but also productions and reviews. We have followed Professor Miller generally, but widened American to mean English language and then included in separate sections foreign language scholarship and criticism--as much as we could uncover (considerably accomplished through the good offices of Iu. G. Fridshtein [see entry no. D74a] a serendipitous find)--and some (surely not all) foreign language productions, with the occasional review (acquired, for French reviews, by a search through microfilms of the files, unindexed, of <u>Le Figaro</u> and <u>France-Soir</u>, and for other nations' reviews, by sheer, and very rare, luck).

Obviously on the matter of productions both in America and elsewhere much, possibly most, has escaped our notice: community theaters, summer stock, college and university theaters. And few newspapers that might review or, at the least, notice their productions publish indexes or preserve their fugitive lives in microfilm. But the conclusions capable of being drawn from production information we have garnered certainly should be, though in brief, representative of the O'Neill condition, in large, in America and, we hope, the world.

CONTENTS

ABBREVIATIONS

We have tried to avoid abbreviations except for the standard ones used
in conventional bibliographical entries (U for University, P for Press)
and therefore known to everyone--or, at least, everyone likely to use
this work. So most of our entries give the full names for the relevant
journals. The exceptions are The Eugene O'Neill Newsletter, EON,
because it appears so often here, and those serial publications,
especially eastern European ones, whose unabbreviated forms we have
been unable to discover or unravel. With these latter we have probably
made some serious (and, maybe, to the initiated even humorous) gaffes,
confusing ephemeral news items with more enduring matters, but we hope
our viewers will be charitable.

Because very frequent reference is made to O'Neill's plays we do
abridge most play titles of more than one word.

Ah, Wilderness!	Wilderness
All God's Chillun	Chillun
The Ancient Mariner	Mariner
Anna Christie	Anna
Before Breakfast	Breakfast
Beyond the Horizon	Horizon
Bound East for Cardiff	Cardiff
Chris Christopherson	Chris
Days Without End	Days
Desire Under the Elms	Desire
The Dreamy Kid	Dreamy
The Emperor Jones	Jones
The Great God Brown	Brown
The Hairy Ape	Ape
The Iceman Cometh	Iceman
In the Zone	Zone
Lazarus Laughed	Lazarus
Long Day's Journey into Night	Journey
The Long Voyage Home	Voyage
Marco Millions	Marco
A Moon for the Misbegotten	Misbegotten
Moon of the Caribbees	Caribbees
More Stately Mansions	Mansions
Mourning Becomes Electra	Electra
Strange Interlude	Interlude
A Touch of the Poet	Touch
Where the Cross is Made	Cross
A Wife for a Life	Wife

EUGENE O'NEILL

A Bibliography
1973 - 1985

1972

A1   Anniah Gowda, Hennur H. Dramatic Poetry from Mediaeval to
         Modern Times: A Philosophic Inquiry into the Nature of
         Poetic Drama in England, Ireland and the United States of
         America. Madras: Macmillan.

In a chapter entitled "Twentieth Century America: The
Progressives" (331-62) five pages are devoted to Lazarus, which
like O'Neill's other plays succeeds despite its language rather
than because of it. Complains that O'Neill lacks a mastery "of
any form of verbal expression." Lazarus is "remarkable for its
moving and poetic spectacle and for its reasoned and scholarly
statement." Says the work "demonstrates the power of even the
widely agnostic twentieth century to create admirable religious
and metaphysical drama." But O'Neill fails to give his actors
words with "poetic connotation" or grandeur equal to the poetic
stature of his play's goals.

A2   Sochatoff, A. Fred. "Two Modern Treatments of the Phaedra
         Legend." In Honor of Austin Wright. Eds. Joseph Baim,
         et al. Pittsburgh: Carnegie-Mellon UP. 80-86.

Both O'Neill's Desire and T. C. Murray's Autumn Five (1924) make
use of the Phaedre story but must modify it because of the
importance in the original of Hippolytus' devotion to Artemis
(purity, charity), ignoring Aphrodite (sensuality). To
modernize, O'Neill uses a keyword, desire, and variations on it
throughout the play: desire for the land, for security, for
revenge, sexual release, perpetuation of the family,
understanding. But, though a tragedy, Desire still offers a
note of exaltation at the end.

1973

A3   Aarseth, Inger. "A Drama of Life and Death Impulses: A
         Thematical Analysis of Mourning." Norwegian Contributions
         to American Studies Dedicated to Sigmund Skard. Ed. Brita
         Seyerstad. Oslo: Universitetsforlaget. 291-304.

Concerned with the "metaphysical aspect" of Electra: "the
mythical-religious and symbolic implications of the major
conflict"; "the grey puritanism" of the Mannons versus "the
green 'paganism' of the South Sea Islanders--conflicts between
characters and within Ezra and Lavinia. Implications of the
conflict include life-death-spiritual immortality versus life
here and now, with immortality found only in the life cycle.
The house as prison, the moon representing romance, love and

sexual freedom. Finds validity in O'Neill's assertion that
Electra is "the drama of the life and death impulses." Ape and
Brown are used to explicate themes.

A4   Atkinson, Brooks and Albert Hirschfeld. The Lively
             Years--1920-1973. New York: Associated.

         Eighty-two essays (between 800 and 1000 words each) introducing
         82 plays produced in New York during the period 1920-73.
         Includes essays on Anna, Ape, Interlude, Desire, and Iceman.
         Includes illustrations by Hirschfeld.

A5   Bermel, Albert. Contrary Characters: An Interpretation of
             Modern Theatre. New York: Dutton. 105-21.

         In the chapter "The Family as Villain" Bermel tries to establish
         who is ultimately responsible for the problems with the Tyrone
         family. After finding excuses for or redeeming features in
         Edmund, Jamie, and Tyrone, he opts for Mary. Says the play is
         Mary's tragedy, that she has inflicted the deepest wounds.

A6   Brockett, Oscar G. and Robert R. Findley. Century of
             Innovation: A History of European and American Theatre and
             Drama Since 1870. Englewood Cliffs, NJ: Prentice.

         A richly detailed and illustrated book of over 800 pages doing
         what its subtitle says. The sections on America during the
         appropriate period of O'Neill's career, though not oriented
         around O'Neill, do much to establish the context of his work.

A7   Falb, Lewis W. American Drama in Paris, 1945-1970: A Study of
             Its Critical Reception. Chapel Hill: U of North Carolina
             P. 7-23.

         Discusses the reception of Jones, Chillun, Desire, Electra, Ape
         Cardiff, Welded, and Journey. Says that the French are
         ambivalent about O'Neill. They recognize his stature, but the
         playwright has not been widely received. Says he has received
         universal acclaim with Journey, while earlier works received
         mixed reviews. Acknowledges that French exposure to O'Neill is
         limited.

A8   Frenz, Horst. "Alexander Tairov and the 1930 World Tour of the
             Kamerny Theatre." Studies in Theatre and Drama: Essays in
             Honor of Hubert C. Heffner. Ed. Oscar G. Brockett. New
             York: Humanities. 177-94.

Tairov's interest in experimental theatre attracted him early to
O'Neill's work. At the same time, he saw theatre as reflecting
the ideologies of its society. The two O'Neill plays that were
drawn into the Kamerny Theatre's 8-play repertory were Desire
and Chillun. Discusses the treatment Tairov's production of
Chillun received and the changes wrought in the two plays
(there was also a production of Ape which did not go on tour).
Tairov's comments are also in Frenz and Tuck's Eugene O'Neill's
Critics: Voices from Abroad, see no. A167, A201, and A202.

A8a   Frenz, Horst. "Notes on Eugene O'Neill in France." Texte und
            Kontexte: Studien zur deutschen und vergleichenden
            Litteraturwissenschaft. Eds. Manfred Durzak, et al. Bern:
            Francke, 1973. 59-72.

        Surveys the history of French productions of O'Neill's plays,
        from Jones (1923) to Iceman (1967). Also evaluates the
        translations of O'Neill's work (34 plays published between 1963
        and 1965). Nonetheless, finds the French slow to appreciate
        O'Neill.

A9   Geddes, Virgil. The Melodramadness of Eugene O'Neill. 1934.
            Folcroft, PA: Folcroft. 1973; Norwood, PA: Norwood, 1977.
            Library Editions, 1973. Reprint of the 1934 edition
            published by the Brookfield Players, Brookfield, CT.

A10   Gelb, Arthur and Barbara Gelb. O'Neill. 2nd ed. New York:
            Harper & Row.

        One of the two most important biographies of O'Neill, this was
        originally published in 1962. New material is added in an
        epilogue, which provides an account of Carlotta O'Neill's final
        years.

A11   Gelb, Barbara. So Short a Time: A Biography of John Reed and
            Louise Bryant. New York: Norton.

        The relevant chapters are 5, 6, 7, 8 (pp. 76-125) and 11
        (pp. 184-91), covering the period of Reed's and Bryant's
        connection with O'Neill. There is no documentation except for a
        short final acknowledgement page which refers to material Arthur
        and Barbara Gelb had covered in their O'Neill.

A12   Heilman, Robert Bechtold. The Iceman, the Arsonist, and the
            Troubled Agent: Tragedy and Melodrama on the Modern Stage
            Seattle: U of Washington P, 72-114.

        The characters of the book's title refer to types: the iceman
        is the victim who opts out, the arsonist is the aggressive,
        vengeful destroyer; and the troubled agent is the vigorous man
        who is troubled by what he does. Chapter four, which deal with
        O'Neill, is divided into sections on 15 plays: Iceman,
        Interlude, Electra, Touch, Journey, Misbegotten, Mansions,
        Horizon, Chillun, Jones, Desire, Brown, Lazarus, Days, and
        Dynamo. Says that Iceman is not a tragedy because of the men's
        weakness in not being able to live with self-knowledge. The
        other plays in varying ways and to varying degrees reflect the
        same view of man--Electra and Journey with Iceman being
        O'Neill's most characteristic. Says O'Neill's characters do no
        achieve tragic heights, not because they try and fail, but
        because they undertake too little.

A13   Houseman, John. On Stage: Selected Theater Reviews from the
            "New York Times," 1920-70. Eds. Bernard Beckerman and
            Howard Siegman. New York: Arno.

        Includes:
        Alexander Woollcott's reviews of Horizon, 4 Feb. 1920, pp. 7-8;
        Jones, 7 Nov. 1920, pp. 13-14; Anna, 3 Nov. 1921, pp. 23-24;
        Ape, 21 Feb. 1922, pp. 26-27.

        Stark Young's review of Desire, 12 Nov. 1924, pp. 48-49.

        Brooks Atkinson's reviews of Brown, 25 Jan. 1926, pp. 63-64;
        Interlude 31 Jan. 1928, pp. 85-87; Electra, 27 Oct. 1931,
        pp. 127-29; Wilderness, 3 Oct. 1933, pp. 142-43; Iceman, 9 May
        1956, pp. 377-78; Journey, 8 Nov. 1956, pp. 378-79.

        Howard Taubman's review of Interlude, 13 Mar. 1963, pp. 449-51.

A14   Manheim, Michael. Eugene O'Neill's Language of Kinship.
            Syracuse: Syracuse UP.

        Shows that characters in O'Neill's early works are variations c
        the playwright's family. Does not read biography into the play
        but extrapolates it from them. Also discusses the language of
        kinship--the alternating between affection and hostility which
        is so typical of family relations. Observes that in the
        playwright's middle period (the 1920's) the characters withdrew
        from each other, but in the late plays, when O'Neill had come t
        terms with his family, the language of kinship resurfaces.

A15   Miller, Jordan Y. <u>Eugene O'Neill and the American Critic</u>.
       2nd ed. Hamden, CT: Archon.

       A revision of Miller's 1962 <u>Eugene O'Neill and the American
       Critic: A Summary and Bibliographical Checklist</u>.

       Rather more than a checklist since Miller annotates the
       secondary bibliography.

       Miller omits in his revision the long essay "Eugene O'Neill and
       the American Critic" in order to allow room for the
       bibliographical increases of the period between his first and
       second editions. Covers O'Neill scholarship and criticism
       through 1972. The bibliography of secondary materials is nearly
       40 percent larger than that of the first edition. The index
       (most valuable) is 30 percent larger.

A16   <u>The New York Times Directory of the Theater</u>. New York: Arno.

       Lists all plays reviewed in the <u>Times</u> through 1970. Especially
       good index.

A17   Raleigh, John Henry. "Eugene O'Neill." <u>Sixteen Modern American
       Authors: A Survey of Research and Criticism</u>. Ed. Jackson
       R. Bryer. New York: Norton, 417-43.

       This is the second edition revised of what was originally
       <u>Fifteen Modern American Authors</u> (the work now includes William
       Carlos Williams). A chapter is devoted to each writer--O'Neill
       being the only one included who is primarily a dramatist.
       Original chapters are updated from 1967 to 1971 or in some cases
       1973. The O'Neill supplement includes 30 additions to the
       original.

A18   Reiter, Seymour. <u>World Theater: The Structure and Meaning of
       Drama</u>. New York: Horizon.

       Two pages in this book are relevant to O'Neill. The discussion
       of <u>Ape</u> notes that the play "is close to the traditional concept
       of tragedy." Yank is superior to those about him, has a tragic
       flaw, and undergoes a recognition before he suffers a
       catastrophe.

A19   Schevill, James. Break Out: In Search of New Theatrical
             Environments. Chicago: Swallow, 190-97.

        In recalling a visit to Tao House after O'Neill's death, the
        author decides the Chinese influence on O'Neill was a strong
        element in his last plays. Chinese philosophy helped him to
        control his dreadful illness and gave him the capacity to
        reconcile the "polarities of existence" exhibited by his
        characters in Journey, Iceman, and Hughie.

A20   Sheaffer, Louis. O'Neill: Son and Artist. Boston: Little.

        The second volume in Sheaffer's definitive biography. Carefully
        researched and documented. Uses letters, documents, and
        interviews. Focuses on O'Neill's psyche and his relationship
        with his family.

A21   Williams, Raymond. Drama from Ibsen to Brecht. 2nd rev. ed. of
             Drama from Ibsen to Eliot. Harmondsworth: Penguin.
             250-52 and 335-39.

        Fleeting references to Journey and Electra. Part I discusses
        the three major dramatists of the period: Ibsen, Strindberg,
        and Chekhov. Part II deals with the Irish dramatists: Synge,
        Yeats, and Joyce to O'Casey. In the third section, under
        experimental drama, O'Neill's work is discussed.

A21a   Wilson, Garff B. Three Hundred Years of American Drama and
             Theatre. Englewood Cliffs, N.J.: Prentice-Hall.

        Touches lightly on O'Neill's contribution to American theater
        history in this Cook's tour.

                                    1974

A22   Atkinson, Jennifer M. Eugene O'Neill: A Descriptive
             Bibliography. Pittsburgh: U of Pittsburgh P.

        Takes up where the Sanburn and Clark bibliography left off in
        1931. Appendices include all published acting scripts,
        O'Neill's contributions to newspapers and periodicals, promo
        blurbs, auction material and book dealer catalogues, and a
        listing of plays in anthologies and film, radio and musical
        adaptations.

A23   Clurman, Harold. <u>The Divine Pastime</u>. New York: Macmillan.

Reprint with additions of work first published in 1946.   Latest addition--on O'Neill--was a review, first printed 10 May 1971, of <u>Journey</u> film.

A24   Frazer, Winifred. <u>E.G. and E.G.O.:   Emma Goldman and The Iceman Cometh</u>. Gainesville: Florida UP.

Studies the ways in which the life of radical Emma Goldman touched and influenced O'Neill's plays and life.

A25   Goldstein, Malcolm. <u>The Political Stage: American Drama and Theater of the Great Depression</u>. New York: Oxford UP.

Scattered references to <u>Chillun</u>, <u>Anna</u>, <u>Days</u>, <u>Desire</u>, <u>Jones</u>, <u>Ape</u>, <u>Brown</u>, <u>Iceman</u>, <u>Journey</u>, <u>Misbegotten</u>, <u>Electra</u>, and <u>Interlude</u>, but the preface says "the two giants of the period, Eugene O'Neill and Thornton Wilder, receive only brief mention in relation to many of their inferiors whose dramatic themes fall within the range of the book."

A25a   Granger, Bruce.   "Eugene O'Neill: Man of the Theatre." <u>America - Austriaca: Beitrage zur Amerikakunde</u>.   3 Vols. Ed. Klaus Lanzinger.   Vienna: Wilhelm Braumuller, 1974. 3:   24-32.

Concentrates on the stage craft and theatrical techniques of O'Neill's plays.

A26   Quintero, José. <u>If You Don't Dance They Beat You</u>.   Boston: Little.

Quintero's autobiography.   In Chapter 14 Quintero recalls his first bout with <u>Iceman</u>, preparing it for the Circle in the Square.   Chapter 16 recalls a meeting with Shane O'Neill.   The chapter also covers <u>Misbegotten</u> and, briefly, <u>Desire</u>.   Chapters 18-21 deal with the <u>Journey</u> and <u>Hughie</u> productions.   Throughout are recollections of meetings with Carlotta O'Neill.   No index.

A27   Vogel, Dan. <u>The Three Masks of American Tragedy</u>.   Baton Rouge: Louisiana State UP.   41-54.

Discusses what is unique and what is cohesive about American tragedy.   Short discussions on <u>Desire</u> and <u>Electra</u> as American

tragedies. Says that the masks of American tragic heroes are
the masks of Oedipus Tyrannos (O'Neill's heroes), Christ or
Satan.

1975

A28   Bonin, Jane F. Major Themes in Prize-Winning American Drama.
            Metuchen, NJ: Scarecrow.

Scattered references to O'Neill's plays--Anna, Interlude,
Horizon, and Journey. The themes include: "Women and Marriage
(Anna Christie presupposes the inability of women to survive
outside marriage"; Strange Interlude "suggests that the role of
women is to give themselves to men, to live through men, and to
bear children"; Horizon presents marriage as "the spoiler of
hopes"). "Work and Material Rewards" (Interlude denigrates the
get-ahead gospel and upholds the need for vocation"; Tyrone in
Journey sacrifices his talent for money); Religion (Journey
"seems to underscore the impossibility of finding strength or
solace through religion").

A29   Egri, Péter. "The Social and Psychological Aspects of the
            Conflict in Eugene O'Neill's Mourning Becomes Electra."
            Studies in English and American. Eds. Erzsebet Perenyi and
            Tibor Frank. Vol. 2. Budapest: Dept. of English,
                L. Eotvos U, 1975. 171-214.

A loosely-structured discussion of a variety of motifs in
Electra (puritanism, Oedipal and Electra complexes and fate) and
of the structure of the (epic). Concludes that the characters
are "balanced"--eliciting neither approval nor condemnation.

A30   Goyal, Bhagwat S. The Strategy of Survival: Human Significance
            of O'Neill's Plays. Ghazibad [India]: Vimal, Prakashon.

A "revised version" of the author's 1970 doctoral dissertation
(Agra U, India), it sensitively and intelligently studies the
relationship between O'Neill's themes and techniques. The
revisions--the only parts of the book that fall within the scope
of this annotation--involve a slight increase in the number of
items in the bibliography and two quotations in Chapter 8,
neither of which alters, as the author admits, his original
thesis. Covers the whole range of O'Neill's plays.

A31   Manocchio, Tony, and William Petitt. "The Tyrone Family."
        Families Under Stress: A Psychological Interpretation.
        London: Routledge, 102-28.

Studies families as treated by Shakespeare, Rattigan, Arthur
Miller, Albee, and O'Neill, each as a case study. Says the
Tyrones form a closed family whose members' interaction is
realistically and accurately representative of real people and
suggests alternative behaviors that might have resolved their
problems.

A32   Miller, Jordan. "Expressionism: The Waste Land Enacted." The
        Twenties: Fiction, Poetry, Drama. Ed. Warren French.
        Deland, FL: Everett/Edwards. 439-54.

Surveys the appearance of expressionism. There are chapters
devoted to Jones, "the first genuinely expressionistic play in
this country," and Ape. Other plays which some might think
expressionistic, Miller sees as "stylized" because, apparently
by his definition, expressionism is concerned with the
contemporary, gives a sense of immediacy, and avoids realistic
themes.

A33   Miller, Jordon. "The Other O'Neill." The Twenties: Fiction,
        Poetry, Drama. Ed. Warren French. Deland FL:
        Everett/Edwards. 455-73.

The recurring motif in this collection of essays is the
waste-land, which for O'Neill meant the "sickly pale underside
of life." Treats the 20s as O'Neill's apprenticeship years,
years of experimentation which eventually led to Journey and
Iceman. Says the strongest sense in O'Neill's work at this time
was a sense of dismay at the world around him.

.34   Morse, David. "American Theatre: The Age of O'Neill."
        American Literature Since 1900. Ed. Marcus Cunliffe.
        The History of Literature in the English Language 9.
        London: Barrie and Jenkins. 73-103.

Surveys the drama of the 20s and 30s beginning and ending with
O'Neill, who dominates the era. Paragraphs on the major plays
(as seen from the present) of the period. Notes that important
drama was in the interstices of commercial American theatre--and
had little immediate impact.

A35   Pilkington, John, ed. Stark Young: A Life in the
           Arts--Letters, 1900-1962. Baton Rouge: Louisiana State
           UP.

        Scattered references to O'Neill.

A36   Roberts, Patrick. "Orestes in Modern Drama: Mourning Becomes
           Electra." The Psychology of Tragic Drama. Ideas and
           Forms in English Literature 5. London: Routledge.
           170-82.

        The book's primary interpretation is Freudian, so that when the
        author turns to twentieth-century literature, he must
        distinguish between unconscious insights explicable by Freud and
        consciously Freudian insights. Says that Mourning is "the most
        thoroughgoing and consistent attempt to date to interpret the
        Orestes myth in the light of Freudian psyche analysis." Points
        to the interest O'Neill had in the Orestian theme so that no
        character is judged: each is a victim of his personal
        compulsions. Says although Lavinia is at the center of the
        play, Orin is the most interesting character. Notes too that
        the play loses its force as tragedy because of the concern with
        myth and Freudian interpretation.

A37   Rosenstone, Robert A. Romantic Revolution: A Biography of John
           Reed. New York: Knopf. 235-77.

        Chapters 15 and 16 cover the period during which Reed's and
        O'Neill's lives crossed, dealing only glancingly with the
        Bryant-O'Neill affair. Though throughout the book Rosenstone
        uses much unpublished material, the O'Neill connections depend
        largely on established publications: Agnes Boulton's Part of a
        Long Story, the Gelbs' O'Neill, and Sheaffer's O'Neill: Son and
        Playwright (1968).

A38   Simon, John. Uneasy Stages: A Chronicle of the New York
           Theatre, 1963-1973. New York: Random.

        Reviews essays covering the season's productions (beginning with
        Spring 1963). The essays, which originally appeared in slightly
        different form in Commonwealth, The Hudson Review, and New York
        Magazine between 1963 and 1975, include reflections on the
        Actors Studio Interlude (Summer 1963), Misbegotten
        (Summer-Autumn 1968), Journey (Spring 1971), and Brown (Winter
        1972-73). The comments about both the plays and the productions
        themselves are brief (two to four paragraphs) and insightful.

A39   Wells, Arvin R. "Beyond the Horizon." Insight I: Analyses of
       American Literature. 2nd ed. Eds. John V. Hagopian and
       Martin Dolch. Frankfurt am Main: Hirschgraben-Verlag,
       186-93.

A study guide for use in German schools, which examines 50 works
of 31 American writers. O'Neill is represented by Horizon.
Summaries of O'Neill's career; slight analysis by a writer who
has a low opinion of O'Neill's work; then questions and answers
about the plays.

1976

A40   Andreach, Robert J. "O'Neill's Women in The Iceman Cometh."
       Eugene O'Neill: A Collection of Criticism. Ed. Ernest G.
       Griffin. New York: McGraw. 103-113.

A reprint. See entry no. A53.

A41   Asselineau, Roger. "Desire Under the Elms: A Phase of
       O'Neill's Philosophy." Eugene O'Neill: A Collection of
       Criticism. Ed. Ernest G. Griffin. New York: McGraw.
       59-66.

For annotation see no. A110.

A42   Avram, Rachmael ben. "Eugene O'Neill in the Divided Stream."
       Naturalisme Americain. Eds. Jean Cazemajou and Jean-Claude
       Barat. Bordeaux-Talence: Maisons des Sciences de l'Homme
       d'Aquitaine. 38-47.

A general assessment of O'Neill's place in American theater,
which concludes that his work "seemed to fail to arrive at the
promised end" (Journey being the exception). Referring to
Charles Walcutt's American Literary Naturalism, a Divided
Stream, Avram says that "O'Neill was reacting to the forces
which formed the naturalistic movement in the novel, by creating
a drama which embodied the very forms Prof. Walcutt describes"

A43   Baker, George Pierce. Dramatic Technique. 1919. New York:
       Capo.

A reprint.

A44   Bentley, Eric. "Eugene O'Neill's Pieta." Eugene O'Neill: A
       Collection of Criticism. Ed. Ernest G. Griffin. New
       York: McGraw. 136-138.

       A reprint. See no. A53.

A45   Birko, Alexander S., comp. Soviet Cinema: Directors and Films.
       Hamden, CT: Archon. 330.

       Mentions that the Soviet film Woman from the Fair (1928),
       directed by G. Makarov, was later banned. The story, which was
       based on O'Neill's Desire, concerned an Italian revolutionary
       movement.

A46   Bogard, Travis. "The Iceman Cometh." Eugene O'Neill: A
       Collection of Criticism. Ed. Ernest G. Griffin. New York
       McGraw. 92-102.

       A reprint. See no. A53.

A47   Carpenter, Frederic I. "Eugene O'Neill, the Orient, and
       American Transcendentalism." Eugene O'Neill: A Collection
       of Criticism. Ed. Ernest G. Griffin. New York: McGraw.
       37-44.

       A reprint. See no. A53.

A48   Chabrowe, Leonard. Ritual and Pathos: The Theater of O'Neill
       Lewisburg, PA: Bucknell UP.

       Expansion of an article, "Dionysus" in The Iceman Cometh."
       Considers O'Neill's theory of tragedy as ritual. Says that
       O'Neill's greatest works are cathartic in effect and move the
       audience to pathos.

A49   D'Andrea, Paul. "Thou Starre of Poets: Shakespeare as DNA."
       Shakespeare: Aspects of Influence. Harvard English
       Studies 7. Ed. G.B. Evans. Cambridge: Harvard UP.
       163-91.

       Deals with Tom Stoppard, Slowomir Mrozek, and Eugene O'Neill.
       The O'Neill section (pp. 179-88) says the two icons of Journey
       are the Virgin and Shakespeare. Points out the frequency of t
       Shakespeare allusions. Edmund's control is the sea, Mary's th
       Virgin, and James's is Shakespeare. Shakespeare appears to us
       as "living and life-giving power."

49a Dunning, John. Tune in Yesterday: The Ultimate Encyclopedia of
       Old-Time Radio 1925-1976. Englewood Cliffs, N.J.:
       Prentice-Hall.

     Several references to 1930s and 1940s radio dramatizations of
     O'Neill's plays.

50   Eddleman, Floyd Eugene, comp. American Theatre Criticism:
       Supplement II. Hamden, CT: Shoe String.

     Offers a highly selective list of readings and, where possible,
     reviews of major productions for each of O'Neill's plays.
     Organized alphabetically by play title. O'Neill material, pages
     119-29.

51   Engel, Edwin A. "Ideas in the Plays of Eugene O'Neill." Eugene
       O'Neill: A Collection of Criticism." Ed. Ernest G.
       Griffin. New York: McGraw. 21-36.

     A reprint. See no. A53.

52   Gillett, Peter J. "O'Neill and the Racial Myths." Eugene
       O'Neill: A Collection of Criticism." Ed. Ernest G.
       Griffin. New York: McGraw. 45-58.

     Sees the "Negro" plays--Thirst, Dreamy, Jones, Chillun, and
     Iceman--as showing progressive development in O'Neill's
     treatment of blacks. At first the black is primitive with only
     the superficial covering of civilization (Thirst), but by
     Iceman, we see in Joe Mott a black on equal terms with the other
     inhabitants of Harry Hope's. Most attention is paid to Chillun,
     which is seen as a play about racial relations in America. Says
     the play suggests that happiness is only gained when the black
     man surrenders to the white myths.

53   Griffin, Ernest G., ed. Eugene O'Neill: A Collection of
       Criticism. New York: McGraw.

     The editor contributes an introduction (pp. 1-20) to O'Neill's
     life and career. Reprints 13 essays, parts of books, and
     articles--two of which are not listed in Miller:

     1. Gillett, Peter J. "O'Neill and the Racial Myths."
         Twentieth Century Literature 18 (1972): 111-20.
         See no. A52.

2. Asselineau, Roger. "Desire Under the Elms: A Phase of
    O'Neill's Philosophy." Festschrift Rudolf Stamm.
    Eds. Eduard Kolb and Jorg Hasler. Bern: Franke. 59-66,
    277-83. See no. A110.

A54   Kauffmann, Stanley. Persons in the Drama: Theater Criticism
         and Comment. New York: Harper.

       A collection of reviews originally published in The New
       Republic, World, Performance, Horizon, and The American Scholar
       He reviews Journey, pp. 133-34 (12 June '71), Wilderness, pp.
       136-39 (11 Oct. '75), and Misbegotten, pp. 134-36 (26 Jan. '74)
       For scattered comments on productions see his index.

A54a   Korenev, Maya. "Eugene O'Neill and the Traditions of American
         Drama." 20th Century American Literature: A Soviet View.
         Trans. Ronald Vroon, Moscow: Progress, 1976.

       Sees the proper study of American drama as beginning with
       O'Neill. Says his contribution to drama was his experimenta-
       tion. Sees Miller, Albee, Green, and Hellman as expressing some
       diversity of form too.

A55   Olson, Elder. "Modern Drama and Tragedy: A View of Mourning
         Becomes Electra." Eugene O'Neill: A Collection of
         Criticism. Ed. Ernest G. Griffin. New York: McGraw.
         87-91.

       A reprint. See no. A53.

A56   Raghavacharyulu, D.V.K. "Waiting for Hughie." Studies in
         American Literature: Essays in Honour of William Mulder.
         Eds. Jagdish Chander and Narindar S. Pradhan. Delhi:
         Oxford UP. 43-51.

       Notes that the plotting of the action in Hughie is like that of
       Iceman or Journey--confessional. Says the play is also like
       Beckett's Waiting for Godot in its revelation of "human
       disjuncture and absurdity." Says, though, that O'Neill's play
       has "tidings of the miraculous" in that Charlie and Erie do
       succeed in establishing human contact in the face of void as
       Charlie is transformed into Hughie.

A57   Raleigh, John H. "Mourning Becomes Electra and A Touch of the
           Poet." Eugene O'Neill: A Collection of Criticism. Ed.
           Ernest G. Griffin. New York: McGraw. 81-86.

       A reprint. See no. A53.

A58   Tiusanen, Timo. "Through the Fog into the Monologue: Long
           Day's Journey into Night." Eugene O'Neill: A Collection
           of Criticism. Ed. Ernest G. Griffin. New York: McGraw.
           114-129.

       A reprint. See no. A53.

A59   Törnqvist, Egil. "Parallel Characters and Situations in Long
           Day's Journey into Night." Eugene O'Neill: A Collection
           of Criticism. Ed. Ernest G. Griffin. New York: McGraw.
           130-135.

       A reprint. See no. A53.

A60   Winchester, Otis W. "Eugene O'Neill's Strange Interlude as a
           Transcript of America is the 1920's." Eugene O'Neill: A
           Collection of Criticism. Ed. Ernest G. Griffin. New York:
           McGraw. 67-80.

       A reprint. See no. A53.

                                  1977

A60a   Blum, Daniel. A Pictorial History of the American Theatre:
           1860-1976. 4th ed. enlarged and revised by John Willis.
           New York: Crown.

       A coffee-table book which includes many pictures of O'Neill and
       his father and scenes from O'Neill's plays.

A61   Bogard, Travis, Richard Moody, and Walter J. Meserve. American
           Drama. The "Revels" History of Drama in English 8.
           London: Methuen.

       Bogard in Part 1, Chapters 2 (pp. 24-42) and 4 (pp. 66-76) deals
       with O'Neill and experimental theater under the rubric of "Art
       and Politics" and with O'Neill as at the center of the "thematic
       context of American theatre." Part III, Chapter 10

(pp. 219-26), surveys O'Neill's career, giving most attention to
the years from Horizon on.

The statements throughout are solid, but the scope of the book
precludes the possibility of its being more than a survey based
on received opinion.

A62   Bruccoli, Matthew J., and C. E. Frazer Clark, Jr. First
            Printings of Americans Authors: Contributions Towards
            Descriptive Checklist. Vol. 1. Detroit: Gale.

Lists first editions of plays and collections of plays and
non-dramatic works in England and America. Covers O'Neill,
pp. 291-96.

A63   Cerf, Bennett. At Random: The Reminiscences of Bennett Cerf.
            New York: Random House.

A construction, apparently by Phyllis Cerf Wagner and Albert
Erskine, based principally on a number of interviews as part of
the Columbia Oral History program. Scattered recollections of
contacts with the O'Neills by his publisher (see especially
pp. 81-89).

A64   Cronin, Harry C. Eugene O'Neill: Irish and American: A Study
            in Cultural Context. New York: Arno.

Originally a doctoral dissertation, "The Plays of Eugene O'Neill
in the Cultural Context of Irish American Catholicism." (U of
Minnesota, 1968). See Miller, p. 476.

Stresses those features traditionally associated with the Irish
(their Catholicism, their concern with family, their loquacity)
and applies them to the canon. Finds that although Irish
Catholicism is not the only, or necessary, consideration, it
adds a meaningful dimension to the appreciation of O'Neill.

A65   Erlich, Alan. "A Streetcar Named Desire Under the Elms: A
            Study of Dramatic Space in A Streetcar Named Desire and
            Desire Under the Elms." Tennessee Williams: A Tribute.
            Ed. Jac L. Tharpe. Jackson: UP of Mississippi. 126-36.

Says that the two plays have identical subjects--the threat to
"family unit by the presence of desire." An outsider appears
and tries to redefine the family unit--succeeds in Desire, fails
in Streetcar. In both, the family is defined visually as a
home.

A66   Evans, Gareth Lloyd. "American Connections--O'Neill, Miller,
         Williams, and Albee." The Language of Modern Drama.
         Totowa, NJ: Rowman and Littlefield. 177-204.

Says that the four playwrights in the title aspired to write a
"heightened" language. Says that now man is more aware of his
own deficiencies than when O'Neill wrote, but that the
playwright tried to be "pathetically eloquent" in his "dramatic
inarticulations," and like the others he succeeded with an
American rhetoric that is almost reminiscent of old fashioned
pulpit oratory--"bold in its calculated artistry and its assault
on the emotions."

A67   Geddes, Virgil. The Melodramadness of Eugene O'Neill. 1934.
         Norwood, PA: Norwood.

A reprint.

A68   Hahn, Emily. Mabel: A Biography of Mabel Dodge Luhan. Boston:
         Houghton.

A fairly hasty survey of Luhan's life. Chapters 5, 6, and 7
deal with her connection with John Reed and the artistic and
radical-political scene of New York in the second decade of the
20th century. Though the author acknowledges as sources
materials in the Beinecke Rare Book Collection at Yale, her
bibliographical notes refer only to published books. One
reference to O'Neill.

A69   Sabinson, Harvey. Darling, You Were Wonderful. Chicago: Henry
         Reguery.

The author recounts a meeting he had with Carlotta in August
1959 in order to get her permission for his client Lester
Osterman to rename his theatre, the Coronet, after O'Neill (pp.
33-40). Reprinted in the advertising supplement to The New York
Times 7 Sept. 1980: 12, 14, 17.

A70   Shipley, Joseph T. The Art of Eugene O'Neill. 1928.
         Philadelphia: Folcroft.

A reprint.

A71   Zucker, Wolfgang M. "The Return of Demons." Continuities and
            Discontinuities: Essays in Psychohistory. Ed. Shirley
            Sugerman. Madison, NJ: Drew UP. 44-57.

        Says in the paragraph devoted to Jones that the myth of demonism
        asserts itself when Brutus falls at the feet of the god he no
        longer believes in, the nomos, the reality he has accepted for
        most of his life.

                                   1978

A72   Bogard, Travis. "Dreams of Joy, Dreams of Pain." Eugene O'Neill
            [Program distributed by Milwaukee Repertory Theater Co. to
            the audience members of Midwestern and Western tour of
            Wilderness and Journey].

        Literary content supervised by Paul Voelker.

A73   Bryfonski, Dedria, and Phyllis Carmel Mendelson, eds.
            Twentieth-Century Literary Criticism. Vol. 1. Detroit: Gale.
            381-407.

        Reprints excerpts from a selection of criticism--both
        contemporary with O'Neill's career and posthumous--from
        Alexander Woollcott's 1920 review of Beyond to Carll Tucker's
        1976 review of Journey.

A74   Commins, Dorothy. What is an Editor? Saxe Commins at Work.
            Chicago: Chicago UP.

        Two chapters deal exclusively with the relationship between
        O'Neill and Commins. Some letters are included and insights
        provided into O'Neill's life with Carlotta and his writing of
        Journey.

A75   Humphrey, Robert E. Children of Fantasy: The First Rebels of
            Greenwich Village. New York: John Wiley.

        Psychobiographies of Max Eastman, Floyd Dell, John Reed,
        Hutchins Hapgood, and George Cram Cook.

A76   Josephson, Lennart. A Role: O'Neill's Cornelius Melody.
            Stockholm Studies in History of Literature 19. Trans. Al
            Blair. Atlantic Highlands, NJ: Humanities.

        Despite awkwardnesses in the prose style and frequent statement

of the obvious, the book carefully analyzes the whole play. As
the title indicates the focus is on Melody--sources in real
life, literary motivation, change at the end of the play.
Explains the influence of Adler on O'Neill's conception of Con.

[Originally published in Swedish at Stockholm: Almqvist &
Wiksell, 1977.]

77   Pradhan, Narindar S. Modern American Drama: A Study in Myth
       and Tradition. New Delhi: Arnold-Heinemann.

Originally a dissertation, U of Utah, 1972. Deals with the
Edenic or Adamic myth as it relates to the work of 20th-century
American dramatists--especially of MacLeish, Arthur Miller,
Odets, O'Neill, Wilder, Tennessee Williams. The chapter
headings are: "The Garden," "Innocence," "The Fall," "The
Fortunate Fall," and "Quest for Paradise." Wilderness! and
Dynamo are touched on in "Innocence." Seventeen other O'Neill
plays are dealt with in the last chapter (especially pp.
122-29), where the quest, for O'Neill, has become "almost a
cult, a force in human affairs that seems to dominate all other
aspects of life." It is a "dream or craving for the ideal," and
is "the strength and weakness" of O'Neill's characters. In the
early plays it is the dream of escape. In Ape, Brown and Marco
we see the ugliness of reality. The later plays, however, show
what would have happened if the dreams of the early plays had
been realized--tragic defeat. References to Cardiff, Caribbees,
Horizon, Voyage, Ape, Zone, Brown, Ile, Marco, Interlude,
Lazarus, Iceman, Journey, Touch, Wilderness, Dynamo, Desire, and
Electra.

78   Scanlan, Tom. "Eugene O'Neill and the Drama of Family Dilemma."
       Family, Drama, and American Dreams. Westport, CT:
       Greenwood.

Describes O'Neill as dealing "predominantly with domestic
drama." Says he is a playwright who "traces the warring
impulses of security and freedom in the American family."

9   Schwarz, Alfred. From Buchner to Beckett: Dramatic Theory and
       the Modes of Tragic Drama. Athens: Ohio UP. 132-40.

In the Chapter "Society and Human Passion as a Tragic Motive,"
the author treats of Iceman and Journey, as well as works by
Miller and Strindberg. Says these two O'Neill plays differ from
early O'Neill and from Strindberg in their "preoccupation with

guilt." Plays differ from each other in that they view time
differently. In Journey, unlike Iceman, past and present are
inseparable.

A80   Stanley, William T. Broadway in the West End: An Index of
            Reviews of American Theatre in London, 1950-1975.
            Westport, CT: Greenwood.

        Primarily a research tool, it is rich with information about
        Productions and offers occasional short but valuable insights
        into the popularity of English productions.

A81   Wilmeth, Don B. The American Stage to World War I: A Guide to
            Information Sources. Detroit: Gale.

        Items 253, 771, 1131, 1132, and 1133 concern James O'Neill, Sr.

1979

A82   Bergman, Ingrid. "A Meeting with O'Neill." Eugene O'Neill: A
            World View. Ed. Virginia Floyd. New York: Unger.
            293-95.

        Bergman recalls meeting O'Neill in 1941. She says he talked
        about his 9-play American-history cycle and his hope to find a
        company that could do all the plays. Such a company, O'Neill
        envisioned, would stay together for four years.

A83   Bermel, Albert. "Poetry and Mysticism in O'Neill." Eugene
            O'Neill: A World View. Ed. Virginia Floyd. New York:
            Unger. 245-51.

        Poetry in this case means the yearning of the characters in
        Journey. Mysticism refers to the union they yearn for. The
        stage imagery in the characters' speeches is used to support the
        author's thesis that O'Neill was a mystic.

A84   Brown, Arvin. "Staging O'Neill's 'Simple Play.'" Eugene
            O'Neill: A World View. Ed. Virginia Floyd. New York:
            Unger. 288-89.

        The author talks about the two productions of Journey he
        directed (1965 and 1971) and the evolution of his understanding
        of the play.

85   Carpenter, Frederic I. _Eugene O'Neill_. 2nd ed. Boston:
          Twayne.

      A revision of the 1964 edition in which the advances in
      scholarship and criticism of the preceding 15 years are mainly
      handled in endnotes and in a new critique of _Hughie_. The
      secondary sources in the bibliography section are a highly
      selective, annotated list of books (including collections of
      articles).

86   Chothia, Jean. _Forging a Language: A Study of the Plays of
          Eugene O'Neill_. Cambridge: Cambridge UP.

      Shows O'Neill's handling of a range of language: colloquial
      American in his early plays, standard American in the middle
      plays, and Irish dialect and Broadway slang in the later plays.
      Appendices contain a list of O'Neill's reading before 1914,
      notes on works that influenced his plays, and a good
      bibliography.

87   Choudhuri, A. D. _The Face of Illusion in American Drama_.
          Atlantic Highlands, NJ: Humanities. 74-93.

      Studies the manipulation of illusion in modern American
      drama--the great dream in conflict with the pursuit of
      materialism. Considers Elmer Rice's _The Adding Machine_; Eugene
      O'Neill's _The Iceman Cometh_; Arthur Miller's _Death of a
      Salesman_; Clifford Odets' _Golden Boy_; Tennessee Williams' _The
      Glass Menagerie_; and Edward Albee's _Who's Afraid of Virginia
      Woolf?_. Says of _Iceman_ that the play is a rejection of middle
      class values and aspirations. Play emphasizes the importance of
      illusions, minimizes the importance of truth.

88   Egri, Péter. "The Use of the Short Story in O'Neill's and
          Chekhov's One-Act Plays: A Hungarian View of O'Neill."
          Eugene O'Neill: A World View. Ed. Virginia Floyd. New
          York: Unger. 115-44.

      Says that although O'Neill was fond of reading Chekhov as a
      young man, the similarities his work shares with Chekhov are
      found in O'Neill's later work. The similarities are based on an
      intellectual and emotional rapport and a tendency to think in
      terms of the short story before dramatizing. Includes a list of
      Hungarian productions from 1928-78.

A89   Eldridge, Florence. "Reflections on Long Day's Journey into
         Night: First Curtain Call for Mary Tyrone." Eugene
         O'Neill: A World View. Ed. Virginia Floyd. New York:
         Unger. 286-87.

       Florence Eldridge, who played Mary in the American premiere of
       Journey, recalls preparing for her role.

A90   Fitzgerald, Geraldine. "Another Neurotic Electra: A New Look
         at Mary Tyrone." Eugene O'Neill: A World View. Ed.
         Virginia Floyd. New York: Unger. 290-92.

       Fitzgerald, who under Arvin Brown's direction played Mary in the
       1971 production of Journey, recalls her rather startling
       interpretation of the role.

A91   Floyd, Virginia, ed. Eugene O'Neill: A World View. New York
         Unger. Includes:

         1. Floyd, Virginia. Three Introductions. See no. A92.
         2. Olsson, Tom. "O'Neill and the Royal Dramatic." See
            no. A101.
         3. Tiusanen, Timo. "O'Neill's Significance: A Scandinavian
            and European View." See no. A106.
         4. Leech, Clifford. "O'Neill in England--From Anna Christie
            to Long Day's Journey into Night: 1923-1958." See
            no. A98.
         5. Törnqvist, Egil. "Platonic Love in O'Neill's Welded."
            See no. A107.
         6. Jařab, Josef. "The Lasting Challenge of Eugene O'Neill:
            Czechoslovak View." See no. A96.
         7. Sienicka, Marta. "O'Neill in Poland." See no. A105.
         8. Egri, Péter. "The Use of the Short Story in O'Neill's an
            Chekhov's One-Act Plays: A Hungarian View of O'Neill."
            See no. A88.
         9. Koreneva, Maya. "One Hundred Percent American Tragedy:
            Soviet View." See no. A97.
        10. Frenz, Horst. "Eugene O'Neill and Georg Kaiser." See
            no. A93.
        11. Raleigh, John Henry. "The Last Confession: O'Neill and
            the Catholic Confessional." See no. 103.
        12. Raleigh, John Henry. "The Irish Atavism of A Moon for th
            Misbegotten." See no. A102.
        13. Wilkins, Frederick. "The Pressure of Puritanism in
            O'Neill's New England Plays." See no. A108.
        14. Bermel, Albert. "Poetry and Mysticism in O'Neill." See
            no. A83.
        15. Jackson, Esther M. "O'Neill the Humanist." See no. A95.

16. Rich, J. Dennis. "Exile Without Remedy: The Late Plays of
    Eugene O'Neill." See no. A104.
17. Eldridge, Florence. "First Curtain Call for Mary Tyrone."
    See no. A89.
18. Brown, Arvin. "Staging O'Neill's 'Simple Play.'" See
    no. A84.
19. Fitzgerald, Geraldine. "Another Neurotic Electra: A New
    Look at Mary Tyrone." See no. A90.
20. Bergman, Ingrid. "A Meeting with O'Neill." See no. A82.

92   Floyd, Virginia. "Introduction." Eugene O'Neill: A World
         View. New York: Unger. 3-33, 189-211, 279-85.

Introductions for each section of this book serve as rehearsals
for what was to be done more fully in Eugene O'Neill at Work
(1981). There are three sections to the book: "The European
Perspective," "The American Perspective," and "Four People of
the Theatre."

93   Frenz, Horst. "Eugene O'Neill and Georg Kaiser." Eugene
         O'Neill: A World View. Ed. Virginia Floyd. New York:
         Unger. 172-85.

Says that despite O'Neill's denial, it is likely that the
expressionism of his early days was influenced by George Kaiser.

94   Fuhrmann, Manfred. "Myth as a Recurrent Theme in Greek Tragedy
         and Twentieth-Century Drama." New Perspectives in German
         Literary Criticism: A Collection of Essays. Eds. Richard
         E. Amacher and Victor Lange. Trans. David Henry Wilson, et
         al. Princeton: Princeton UP. 295-319.

Originally published in German in Vol. 4 of Poetik und
Hermeneutik (Munich: Wilhelm Fink, 1971).

Describes ancient Greeks' handling of myth in tragedy--"bound to
the traditional skeleton of the story" but "free as regards
motivation." Modern handling in one case assumes the audience
is "familiar with the classical model and its standard
interpretation . . . [even to] a scene-for-scene comparison with
the . . . original." Asserts that O'Neill's Electra, Anouilh's
Antigone and Medee, Giraudoux's Amphitrion 38 and Electra,
Sartre's Les Mouches, following this concept, form almost a
genre--1. by following the plot, and 2. by developing a unique
interpretation of motivation. These are "relative" dramas when
"the events of the myth are merely an external, visual
manifestation" while "each interpretation . . . is the actual
meaning "of the myth."

A95   Jackson, Esther M. "O'Neill the Humanist." Eugene O'Neill: /
        World View. Ed. Virginia Floyd. New York: Unger.
        252-56.

        Says that O'Neill's plays of the 20's and 30's reflect the New
        Humanist view of life as expressed in the works of Irving
        Babbitt, Paul Elmer More, and Jacques Maritain.

A96   Jařab, Josef. "The Lasting Challenge of Eugene O'Neill: A
        Czechoslovak View." Eugene O'Neill: A World View.
        Ed. Virginia Floyd. New York: Unger. 84-100.

        Covers O'Neill's Czechoslovakian career, the history of
        production and the shifting of attitudes about O'Neill. Gives
        partial list of productions from 1925-75.

A97   Koreneva, Maya. "One Hundred Percent American Tragedy." Euge
        O'Neill: A World View. Ed. Virginia Floyd. New York:
        Unger. 145-71.

        Treats of the reception of O'Neill's plays in Russia. Tairov
        the Kamerny Theatre found O'Neill's personal vision and dramat
        sense matching his own. O'Neill's social vision was, of cours
        instrumental in Russian appreciation of his work, but so was h
        handling of tragedy--his experiments culminating in the 100
        percent American tragedy, Journey.

A98   Leech, Clifford. "O'Neill in England--from Anne Christie to
        Long Day's Journey into Night: 1923-58." Eugene O'Neill
        A World View. Ed. Virginia Floyd. New York: Unger.
        68-72.

        An appreciation of O'Neill's English career as Leech saw the
        playwright's work being performed from the 1920s on. Leech di
        before completing the essay.

A99   Lind, Ilse Dusoir. "Faulkner's Use of Poetic Drama." Faulkne
        Modernism, and Film: Faulkner and Yoknapatawpha, 1978.
        Eds. Evans Harrington and Ann J. Abadie. Jackson: UP of
        Mississippi. 66-81.

        From the 1978 annual Faulkner conference. Makes a detailed
        comparison between Chillun and A Light in August indicating so
        influences on Faulkner.

100   Manvell, Roger. <u>Theatre and Film: A Comparative Study of the
       Two Forms of Dramatic Art, and the Problems of Adaptation of
       Stage Plays into Film.</u> Rutherford: Fairleigh Dickinson UP.
       106-19, 253-58.

       In one section he studies films made from plays by Shaw,
       Chekhov, O'Neill, Winter, Strindberg, Pinter, Albee, and Weiss.
       Considers Sidney Lumet's 1962 film adaptation of <u>Journey</u>,
       starring Katherine Hepburn, Ralph Richardson, Jason Robards,
       Jr., and Dean Stockwell. Article summarizes the play and
       discusses the innovations and alterations in the film.
       Concludes that <u>Journey</u> "seems the case of a play most
       efficiently rendered, rather than transmitted into film, thus
       losing some of its overwhelming quality in the process, though
       by no means all." Considers the cast "extraordinary," but finds
       the Irish family that O'Neill describes eludes the actors.

       In another section he reviews the John Frankenheimer film of
       <u>Iceman</u>. Says that casting is "superb" with the exception of Lee
       Marvin, who gives a "somewhat heavy performance." Applauds
       Robert Ryan's performance as "sensitive" and notes that the
       play's weakness lies in characterization of Hickey which
       "appears too schematic, too much of a dramatic device imposed on
       the other, more profound characters. . . ."

101   Olsson, Tom. "O'Neill and the Royal Dramatic." <u>Eugene O'Neill:
       A World View.</u> Ed. Virginia Floyd. New York: Unger.
       34-60.

       Surveys the history of O'Neill in Sweden, especially at the
       Royal Dramatic Theater in Stockholm, from the 1920s to the
       present.

102   Raleigh, John Henry. "The Irish Atavism of <u>A Moon for the
       Misbegotten</u>." <u>Eugene O'Neill: A World View.</u> Ed. Virginia
       Floyd. New York: Unger. 229-36.

       Says that Phil Hogan's personality, family relationships,
       situation are modeled on the archetypal Irish peasantry.

103   Raleigh, John Henry. "The Last Confession: O'Neill and the
       Catholic Confessional." <u>Eugene O'Neill: A World View.</u>
       Ed. Virginia Floyd. New York: Unger. 212-28.

       Explores the Catholic influence of O'Neill's early childhood
       religious training on his late plays--the need to confess and
       seek forgiveness.

A104   Rich, J. Dennis. "Exile Without Remedy: The Late Plays of
        Eugene O'Neill." Eugene O'Neill: A World View. Ed.
        Virginia Floyd. New York: Unger. 257-76.

        Says that in his last plays O'Neill "ceases his earlier search
        for transcendence or salvation, and the human effort becomes a
        search for a means of survival."

A105   Sienicka, Marta. "O'Neill in Poland." Eugene O'Neill: A Worl
        View. Ed. Virginia Floyd. New York: Unger. 101-14.

        A history of O'Neill productions in Poland. Says that though
        O'Neill is not an influence on Polish theatre, he is still a
        presence and an influence on Polish sensibility.

A106   Tiusanen, Timo. "O'Neill's Significance: A Scandinavian and
        European View." Eugene O'Neill: A World View. Ed.
        Virginia Floyd. New York: Unger. 61-67.

        Partly an argument that O'Neill be kept "alive" by being made
        part of classical theatre, partly an observation that O'Neill
        matured as a dramatist too fast for Americans to keep up.

A107   Törnqvist, Egil. "Platonic Love in O'Neill's Welded." Eugene
        O'Neill: A World View. Ed. Virginia Floyd. New York:
        Unger. 73-83.

        Argues that the title of Welded, which is usually interpreted
        pejoratively, is really to be taken as suggesting that O'Neill
        is celebrating love as bonding, not binding. In Welded, love
        an expression of a platonic concept as found in The Symposium.

A108   Wilkins, Frederick. "The Pressure of Puritanism in O'Neill's
        New England Plays." Eugene O'Neill: A World View. Ed.
        Virginia Floyd. New York: Unger. 237-44.

        Says the conflict in O'Neill as expressed in his New England
        plays is between his Irish Catholicism and the Puritan
        culture--the former allowing for redemption and the latter
        offering no consolation.

A109   Wilson, Robert N. "Eugene O'Neill: The Web of Family." The
        Writer as Social Seer. Chapel Hill: U of North
        Carolina P. 72-88.

        In Chapter 17 of his book, Wilson discusses Journey. Notes th

"isolation and inwardness of the family unit" in the play and
the characters' confusion about their roles and values. The
book contains eight essays by a sociologist whose thesis is that
literature can help one to understand society.

1980

110   Asselineau, Roger. "Eugene O'Neill's Transcendental Phase."
       The Transcendental Constant in American Literature. New
       York: New York UP. 115-23.

Though reference is made to Web, Lazarus, Brown, and Electra,
the central interest is Desire. Says that in Desire is found an
animalistic interpretation of human behavior in conflict with a
spiritual interpretation. Says that the desire between the two
changes from lust to spiritual love, something that transcends
the body.

This chapter was first published in Festschrift Rudolf Stamm.
Ed. Eduart Kolb and Jorg Hasler. Bern: Franke Verlag, 1969.
277-83.

111   Bernstein, Samuel J. The Strands Entwined: A New Direction in
       American Drama. Boston: Northeastern UP.

Some very slight references to O'Neill.

112   Brüning, Eberhard. "Relations Between Progressive American and
       German Drama in the Twenties and Thirties." Actes du VIIIe
       Congrès de l'Association internationale de Littérature
       Comparée/Proceedings of the 8th Congress of the
       International Comparative Literature Association. Eds.
       Bela Köpeczi and György M. Vajda. 2 vols. Stuttgart:
       Bieber. 1: 789-95.

Sees the German and American theaters of the 1920s and 1930s as
part of an international theatrical scene. The "relations" of
the title are the result of socio-economic experiences common to
the Western world that propel the various nations' theaters to
express similar values, using similar experimental techniques.
"The same kind of environment, the same kind of social
conditions, the same aims and ideological positions led to
similar themes and techniques, made an inspiring exchange of
material and experience possible and produced similar effects in
different places." Among many references are some to Jones,
Ape, Brown, and Chillun.

A113   Burns, Morris U. The Dramatic Criticism of Alexander Woollcott
        Metuchen, NJ: Scarecrow. 85-92.

        The 180-page text includes Woollcott's comments on some 18
        O'Neill plays. The 95-page appendix--a list of 1500-plus play
        reviews by Woollcott--includes citations for reviews of 14
        original O'Neill productions up to 1928. The appendix, arrange
        alphabetically by play title, is not covered by the index.

A114   Ditsky, John. "O'Neill's Evangel of Peace: The Iceman Cometh.
        The Onstage Christ: Studies in the Persistence of a Theme
        London: Vision. 93-110.

        Essays which discuss plays modern and contemporary which contai
        Christ-figures. Considers Iceman's biblical overtones and
        concludes that the Christhood is "diffused" in the play. Both
        Parritt and Hickey are in ways Christ-like.

A115   Eben, Michael C. "Georg Kaiser's Von Morgens bis Mitternachts
        and Eugene O'Neill's Emperor Jones: Affinities in Flight.
        Georg Kaiser: eine Aufsatzsammlung nach einem Symposium i
        Edmonton, Kanada. Eds. Holger A. Pausch and Ernest
        Reinhold. Berlin: Agora. 263-76.

        Compares Kaiser's play to O'Neill's Jones in terms of structure
        characterization, and use of expressionistic techniques.

A116   Egri, Péter. "The Epic Tradition of the European Drama and the
        Birth of the American Tragedy." Actes du VIIIe Congres de
        l'Association Internationale de Litterature comparee/
        Proceedings of the 8th Congress of the International
        Comparative Literature Association, I: Trois grandes
        mutations Litteraires: Renaissance, Lummieres, debut de
        vingtieme siecle/ Three Epoch-Making Literary Changes:
        Renaissance, Enlightenment, Early Twentieth Century. Eds
        Bela Kopeczi and Gyorgy M. Vajda. Stuttgart: Bieber.
        753-59.

        Sees Interlude as "indicative of the crystallization of a form
        pattern . . . whose operation is . . .laid down in Hegel's
        philosophy of history" wherein an "historical tendency is the
        sum total of individual behaviors," a sum, however, "different
        from the conflicting wishes of the individuals." In the
        foreground of Interlude, the concern is with alienation; in th
        background, we know that the "mass-character of alienation" ha
        its source in "the inhumanity of World War I."

117   Fink, Ernest O. "Audience Aids for Non-Literary Allusions?
        Observations on the Transposition of Essential
        Technicalities in the Sea Plays of Eugene O'Neill." The
        Languages of the Theatre: Problems in the Translation and
        Transposition of Drama. Ed. Ortrun Zuber. Oxford:
        Pergamon. 69-81.

        Says there are three voices in O'Neill's Sea plays--of men, of
        things, of nature. Says the voice of things needs to be updated
        to continue to make the play meaningful. That is, conditions,
        technicalities, situations must be given the assistance of stage
        machinery, which wasn't necessary when the plays were first
        produced, so that a contemporary audience can identify with
        them.

117a   Frenz, Horst. "Eugene O'Neill and the European Connection."
        Literary Communication and Reception. Ed. Zoran
        Konstantinovic, et al. Innsbruck: AMOE, 1980. 385-90.

118   Gálik, Marián. "O'Neill, Baker, and Hung Shen." Proceedings of
        the 8th Congress of the International Comparative
        Literature Association. Eds. Bela Köpeczi and György M.
        Vajda. Stuttgart: Bieber. 1980. 381-85.

        Centers on the Chinese playwright Hung Shen's relationships with
        George Pierce Baker, his teacher, and O'Neill, whose work
        influenced Shen. Points out, but does not analyze, the
        influence of Jones on Chao Ta. In the foreword to his plays,
        Shen enjoys a fictive conversation with O'Neill, wherein he
        expresses admiration for the latter's work but reproaches him
        for borrowing heavily from Aeschylus when writing Electra.

119   Ooi, Vicki. C. H. "Transcending Culture: A Cantonese
        Translation and Production of O'Neill's Long Day's Journey
        into Night." The Languages of Theatre: Problems in the
        Translation and Transposition of Drama. Ed. Ortrun Zuber.
        Oxford: Pergamon. 51-68.

        Speaks of the difficulties of translating Journey into Chinese.
        Says that the inseparability of any man from his culture
        (feeling, language, thought) militates against the simple
        translation of words. Says Western families' nuances are too
        foreign to the Chinese. Says ambiguously in conclusion that if
        it were possible to surmount these obstacles, O'Neill's play
        would appeal on the grounds of its universality.

A120   Sewall, Richard. _The Vision of Tragedy_. New Haven: Yale UP.
           161-74.

        Journey is seen as exploring an area of contemporary life rich
        with "tragic potential" and reaching out toward "cosmic
        concerns." The "Tyrones Become Every family."

1981

A121   Berlin, Normand. _The Secret Cause: A Discussion of Tragedy_.
           Amherst: U of Massachusetts P.

        A series of chapters ("essays") concerned with seeing the
        "essence" of tragedy--the operations of fate, the "force behind"
        which express to us the incomprehensible mystery at the core of
        things. Chapter 3, "Passion: _Hippolytus, Phaedra, Desire_,"
        (pp. 33-63) analyzes first Euripedes' play, then Racine's,
        comparing it with Euripedes', then O'Neill's, comparing _Desire_
        with the other two plays. _Desire_ "has captured the tragic
        spirit," because "necessity hangs over the play . . . in the
        'sinister maternity' of two large elms." Sees Eben as
        Hamlet-like in his role as avenger of the past.

A122   Elsom, John, ed. _Post-War British Theatre Criticism_. London:
           Routledge. 209-16.

        Includes excerpts of reviews of _Journey_ that opened at the Old
        Vic (National Theatre) 21 Dec. 1971, starring Laurence Olivier.

A123   Floyd, Virginia, ed. _Eugene O'Neill at Work: Newly Released
           Ideas for Plays_. New York: Unger.

        Gathers 25 of O'Neill's notes and ideas for plays and provides
        commentary on them. New information on O'Neill contained
        herein.

A124   Higgs, Robert J. _Laurel and Thorn: The Athlete in American
           Literature_. Lexington: Kentucky UP. 55-62.

        Considers Gordon Shaw of _Interlude_ as an athlete-hero, using
        Lord Raglan's characteristics to define the traditional hero.
        Concludes "O'Neill looks at the hero archetypically and appears
        to conclude that the hero has his real being in woman for whom
        he strives in all his undertakings, that the antipathy on the
        part of the mind man toward the hero is to some extent sour
        grapes, but that the hero with all his systems of honor is

rather inflexible, hence quite superficial and, possibly, . . .
a bore."

Also touches on Abortion.

124a Jensen, George H. "Eugene O'Neill." Twentieth-Century
      American Dramatists. Ed. John MacNichols. The Dictionary
      of Literary Biography 7. Detroit: Gale Research Company.
      139-65.

An overview of O'Neill's life, summaries of the plays, useful
lists of first productions and publications. The bibliography
("References") is solid though slightly eccentric.

125   Misra, K. S. Modern Tragedies and Aristotle's Theory. New
      Delhi: Vikas. 185-206.

Half the book discusses Aristotle's theory of tragedy. Half
applies the theory to modern practice, concentrating mainly on
Synge, Galsworthy, R. C. Sherriff, Masefield, O'Neill, and T. S.
Eliot. Chapter 10 concerns Ape, which is seen as reflecting
Aristotelian principles in every way except in Yank's lack of
"spiritual and mental stature" (compensated for by his "mental
tension and resolute opposition" to fate), and in the absence of
that "effect of exaltation which great tragedy produces"
(lacking because "O'Neill's conclusion . . . is pessimistic").
In his analysis of the play, Misra explicitly uses a Jungian
approach.

126   Mordden, Ethan. The American Theater. New York: Oxford UP.

Surveys the whole of American theatrical history in 340 pages of
text with scattered comments on O'Neill and O'Neill productions.

127   Orr, John. Tragic Drama and Modern Society: Studies in the
      Social and Literary Theory of Drama from 1870 to the
      Present. Totowa, NJ: Barnes and Noble.

Part IV, chapters 9, 10, and 11, "American Tragedy and the
American Dream," covers O'Neill, Arthur Miller, and Tennessee
Williams. Chapter 9 (pp. 165-82) "Eugene O'Neill I: The Living
Tragedy" deals with Ape, Jones, Anna, and Chillun wherein the
striking formal elements confirm that these plays, despite their
potential universality, are primarily social statements.
Chapter 10 (pp. 183-205) "Eugene O'Neill II: The Life
Remembered" stresses Iceman and Journey as tragedy which finds

its force in contemporary (or at least remembered) American
conditions--capitalism and the family and the failure of
American dreams.

A128   Sinha, C. P. Eugene O'Neill's Tragic Vision. Atlantic
            Highlands, NJ: Humanities.

Introduction tries to "evolve a modern aesthetic of tragedy wit
a view of studying the tragic vision of O'Neill in a new
perspective." In chapters two and three discusses O'Neill as a
artist who suffered and who then gave shape to suffering.
Fourth chapter says that the O'Neill tragic hero suffers, not
because of his pride, but because he fails to realize his ideal
Chapter 5 tries to establish that O'Neill responds to the
"dynamics of change. He moves from negation to affirmation,
rejection of God to acceptance." The last chapter puts this
study in a context.

A129   Styan, J. L. Modern Drama in Theory and Practice. 3 vols.
            Cambridge: Cambridge UP.

Vol. 1. Realism and Naturalism.

The chapter called "Realism in America: Early Variations"
(122-36) makes some comments about Iceman and Journey. Says
Iceman was patterned on Gorky's Lower Depths, but it is more
like Chekhov's works in its negligible and inconclusive plot.
Journey and Misbegotten show that O'Neill had settled into an
"intense, obsessed" realism.

Vol. 3. Expressionism and Epic Theater.

The chapter entitled "Expressionism in America: O'Neill"
(97-111) attempts to put O'Neill's expressionistic works in the
context of experimental theatre of the 1920s. Says Robert
Edmund Jones was the agent for O'Neill's experiments by keeping
the playwright abreast of what was happening abroad. Says of
Jones that Brutus achieves self-knowledge and observes that
Chillun is a "psychological study of a mixed marriage."
Ape, Brown, Lazarus, and Electra are also treated.

A130   Tornqvist, Egil. "Strindberg and O'Neill." Structures of
            Influence: A Comparative Approach to August Strindberg.
            Ed. Marilyn Johns Blackwell. Studies in the Germanic
            Languages and Literatures 98. Chapel Hill: U North
            Carolina P. 277-91.

Surveys the known evidence for Strindberg's influence on O'Nei

with reference to standard publications, theses, and
dissertations. Says that O'Neill's familiarity with Strindberg
was great even though he probably never saw Strindberg's plays
performed. Discusses plays from O'Neill's canon--both early and
later--in terms of the Strindbergian influence. Notes that
O'Neill said he saw his own situation in terms of Strindberg's
depiction of family relationships and that O'Neill admired
Strindberg's "power to deal with modern psychological problems
in a dramatically convincing and arresting way."

131   Weathers, Winston. "Eugene O'Neill and the Tragic Word." The
       Broken Word: The Communication Pathos in Modern
       Literature. New York: Gordon & Breach. 93-108.

This is a version of his article "Communications and Tragedy in
Eugene O'Neill." ETC: A Review of General Semantics, (July
1962): 148-60. The introductory chapters of the book observe
that the last century may be characterized by the growing
awareness of the breakdown in communication owing to the loss of
faith in old certain ties and a consequent loss of semantic
understanding. In chapter 6, pp. 93-108, Weathers says that
O'Neill's plays are chiefly concerned with problems of
communication.

                              1982

132   Berkowitz, Gerald M. New Broadways: Theatre Across America
       1950-80. Totowa, NJ: Rowman and Littlefield.

Useful in putting the O'Neill revival into a context of
Off-Broadway activities of the late 1950s and 60s.

133   Berlin, Normand. Eugene O'Neill. New York: Grove.

An introductory treatment touches lightly on biography in
analyzing O'Neill's major plays. Discusses first Journey as
O'Neill's greatest achievement and then considers his chief
works in chronological order in terms of achievement, art, and
tragic vision: especially Anna, Ape, Days, Desire, Horizon,
Iceman, Jones, Misbegotten, and Electra.

134   Bigsby, C. W. E. A Critical Introduction to Twentieth-Century
       American Drama. Vol. 1 (1900-1940). Cambridge: Cambridge
       UP.

Chapter 1 ("Provincetown: The Birth of Twentieth-Century

103662   LIBRARY
                           COLBY-SAWYER COLLEGE
                           NEW LONDON, NH 03257

American Drama," pp. 1-35) is especially useful in describing
the ground in which O'Neill had his roots. Chapter 2 ("Eugene
O'Neill," pp. 36-119) is a sensitive, thoughtful survey of
O'Neill's career with analyses of important works (and some
censuring). Though not tendentious, it contributes to the
understanding of the main themes of O'Neill's achievement.
Appendices 1, 2, and 3 list "Harvard 47 plays, 1913-17;"
"Washington Square Players' Productions, 1915-18"; and
"Provincetown Plays: 1915-27."

A135   Cooley, John R. Savages and Naturals: Black Portraits by Whit
            Writers in Modern American Literature. Newark: U of
            Delaware P. 59-72.

        Despite the praise heaped upon O'Neill for moving the depiction
        of a black man "beyond the level of the minstrel show" in Jones
        Cooley says the play still "exploits those stereotypes in the
        white imagination which associate blacks with the savage and a
        jungle landscape.

A136   Dahl, Liisa. "The Connective Links between the Dialogue and th
            Interior Monologue Passages in Eugene O'Neill's Strange
            Interlude." Studies in Classical and Modern Philology
            Presented to Y.M. Biese on the Occasion of this Eightieth
            Birthday 4.1. 1983. Ed. Iiro Kajanto, et al. Helsinki:
            Suomalainen Tiedeakatemia. 23-32.

        Builds on Tiusanen and a 1963 study by Y.M. Biese as well as on
        semantic studies by Erik Andersson, M.A.K. Halliday, R. Hasan,
        Nils Erik Enkvist, and Jan-Ola Ostman to examine "the connectiv
        links between the dialogue and the interior monologue passages
        and on those between the stage directions and the interior
        monologues of Interlude. Finds "a number of text-linguistic an
        stylistic features" functioning as such links and contributing
        to the "coherence of the text of the play."

A137   Falk, Doris. Eugene O'Neill and the Tragic Tension. 2nd ed.
            New York: Gordian.

        Only appreciable difference between the first and second
        editions is the inclusion in the second edition of an
        "Afterword," which reflects on changes in society which alter
        our reading of O'Neill, and a brief list of indispensible book
        on O'Neill.

LIBRARY
COLBY-SAWYER COLLEGE
NEW LONDON, NH 03257

A138   Gardner, Virginia. "Friend and Lover": The Life of Louise
            Bryant. New York: Horizon.

        Chapters 2-5 (pp. 29-67) cover the Provincetown and Washington
        Square period when Louise Bryant's life crossed O'Neill's. Over
        a dozen of the relevant resources come from unpublished
        materials: four interviews with Dorothy Day, one with Conrad
        Aiken, several with Andrew Dagsburg and Heaton Vorse; the
        Granville Hicks collection at Syracuse University, and the John
        Reed Collection at Harvard. O'Neill falls in love with Louise.
        Louise helps O'Neill to control his drinking. Louise falls in
        love with O'Neill, but won't forsake John Reed for him.

A139   Goyal, Bhagwat S. The Strategy of Survival: Human Significance
            of O'Neill's Plays. Atlantic Highlands, NJ: Humanities.

        A revised version of his doctoral dissertation, Agra U, 1970.
        Says O'Neill's strategy of survival was a quest for self
        discovery and for the meaning of life, motivated by his desire
        to belong somewhere. After a chapter surveying O'Neill's life,
        Goyal takes up, in chapters ordered chronologically, blocks of
        plays, eventually including all those published. The concluding
        chapters contain brief essays on O'Neill's "most significant"
        plays--Jones, Ape, Interlude, Electra, Iceman, and Journey--as
        well as essays on O'Neill as tragedian and O'Neill's philosophy
        (in a deterministic, godless world, only illusions preserve us
        from despair).

A140   Greenfield, Thomas Allen. Work and the Work Ethic in American
            Drama 1920-1970. Columbia: U of Missouri P.

        Scattered references on O'Neill. Though he wrote on the
        periphery of the issues of work and the work ethic, O'Neill
        avoided addressing them in Caribbees, Zone, and Ape, while
        Journey and Interlude (despite Jane Bonin's Major Themes, q.v.)
        "although concerned in part with materialism, do not take on the
        problem of work in any meaningful manner." The "dramatic
        tension of between home values and work values is exploited much
        more fully" in Mansions.

A141   Miller, William. Dorothy Day: A Biography. San Francisco:
            Harper. 103-19.

        Does not document his book; much comes from interviews with
        Dorothy Day and access to her personal journals and many family
        letters. Reacts to the Agnes Boulton and Malcolm Cowley views
        of Dorothy Day and suggests that Josie Hogan was in part based
        on her.

A142   Orlandello, John. <u>O'Neill on Film</u>. London: Associated UP.

Examines in nine chapters the film versions of nine O'Neill
plays: <u>Anna</u>, <u>Interlude</u>, <u>Jones</u>, <u>Ah, Wilderness!</u> (and the version
called "Summer Holiday"), <u>Voyage</u>, <u>Electra</u>, <u>Desire</u>, <u>Journey</u>, and
<u>Iceman</u>. An introduction briefly surveys O'Neill's connection
with films. The conclusion generalizes about the reasons for
Hollywood's failure in converting O'Neill to the screen--partly
because of irreconcilable differences between stage and screen,
partly because of different perceptions of what the plays meant.
Maintains that <u>Voyage</u>, <u>Iceman</u>, and <u>Journey</u> are effective as
films because of sympathetic directing and advances in
cinematography. Contains a "Filmography." Does not discuss <u>Ape</u>
or <u>Recklessness</u> ("The Constant Woman") because the film of the
first is not currently available and that of the second is not
well preserved.

A143   Robinson, James A. <u>Eugene O'Neill and Oriental Thought: A</u>
        <u>Divided Vision</u>. Carbondale: Southern IL UP.

Extensive study of how Eastern thought illuminates some aspects
of O'Neill's art. Says the western writers O'Neill most admired
either paralleled or drew upon Oriental mystical theories:
Emerson, Nietzsche, Schopenhauer, and Jung. Theorizes that
O'Neill attracted to it because he sought a faith to replace his
lost Catholicism. Concludes that O'Neill did not accept Eastern
thought; still it influences his works.

A144   Sarlós, Robert Karoly. <u>Jig Cook and the Provincetown Players:</u>
        <u>Theatre in Ferment</u>. Amherst: UP of Massachusetts.

This well-researched study deals with the beginnings of the
group from 1915-1922. O'Neill and his work figure prominently
in the book. Sarlos draws on interviews and published and
unpublished material. The bibliography is helpful as are
appendices A, B, and C, which comprise the chronology of
productions, a Who's Who of the theatre's history, and a
dictionary of the playhouse's physical structure.

A145   Yarrison, Betsy Greenleaf. "The Future in the Instant." <u>To</u>
        <u>Hold a Mirror to Nature: Dramatic Images and Reflections</u>
        Ed. Karelisa V. Hartigan. Vol. 1. Washington, D.C.: UP
        of America. 137-60. [Papers from the U of Florida Dept.
        of Classics Comparative Drama Conference].

The thesis that "dramatic tempo animates, measures out, and
gives meaning to the movement of dramatic action through time"
and "mediates between empirical reality and the virtual reality

of the stage world" is illustrated by special reference to Jones
and Uncle Vanya because their "maximal use of the potential
theatricality of the spoken word" makes "easy to document and to
measure" "the phenomenal existence of tempo."

1983

A146   Chatterji, Ruby. "Existentialist Approach to Modern American
        Drama." Existentialism in American Literature. Ed. Ruby
        Chatterji. Atlantic Highlands, NJ: Humanities. 80-98.

Papers read at, or subsequently contributed to, a seminar held
at Hindu College, Delhi U, in Oct. 1980. Deals with O'Neill,
Albee, and Arthur Miller, but gives most attention to O'Neill
and carefully analyzes Iceman and Journey. Sees both plays as
reflecting in many ways the existential vision--an illusionless
view of life. The concern of the plays is their structure. But
O'Neill does not make the final existential statement, feeling
that a recognition of a need for hope justifies belief in
illusions. However, Larry, in Iceman, and Edmund, in Journey,
both achievesome meaning of "authenticity of self and a mental
state of revolt"--a state the existentialists advocate.

A147   Durnell, Hazel B. "Eugene O'Neill and the Far East." Japanese
        Cultural Influences on American Poetry and Drama." Tokyo:
        Hokuseido. 147-64.

Introductory-level essay on O'Neill's interest in the Far East,
a mention of plays which refer to the area, and a look at
O'Neill's biography as it pertained to the orient. Mentions
O'Neill's interest in oriental philosophy by reference to
Mansions. Also refers to Touch, Journey, Electra, and Lazarus.

A148   Grawe, Paul H. Comedy in Space, Time, and the Imagination.
        Chicago: Nelson-Hall. 221-35.

A general discussion of Iceman, which is categorized as a sombre
comedy in this book. Says the play is a "social comedy," where
no character is central. Discusses the groups that the
characters belong to and the love/hate relationships between
them. Sees Hickey as a threat to the denizens' survival rather
than a saviour and comments on the parallels between Hickey and
Christ. Hickey's ministry, though, has the opposite effect of
Christ's.

A149   Hayashi, Tetsumaro, ed. Eugene O'Neill: Research Opportunitie
         and Dissertation Abstracts. Jefferson, NC: McFarland.

         Includes: (1) an essay on "Eugene O'Neill: Research
         Opportunities," pp. 3-21, by Robert L. Tener, in which are
         discussed the 139 dissertations on O'Neill, completed between
         1928 and 1980: here lines of research and schools of thought
         are seen to have emerged; the last 3+ pages note future possibl
         lines of research: the matter of O'Neill's artistry, studies i
         characterization, textual studies, the relationship between
         O'Neill and his contemporaries; his influence on others,
         adaptations of his work in other media, and (2) pp. 22-144 list
         with, where available, the abstracts, the dissertations
         completed between 1928 and 1980--139 of them, arranged
         chronologically. Hayashi's sources are Dissertation Abstracts
         International.

A150   Kennedy, Andrew K. Dramatic Dialogue: The Duologue of Persona
         Encounter. Cambridge: Cambridge UP. 180-93.

         Discusses the different shapes and conventions of dialogue in
         drama from Aeschylus to playwrights contemporary. Studies in
         detail the dialogue of personal encounter between protagonists.
         Says that in O'Neill's works Journey and Hughie the dialogue
         reflects the need for self-disclosure. Says that later O'Neill
         reflects "special gifts for personal idiom in 'the vernacular'
         and for embodying personal encounter in dialogue."

A151   Olson, Sara. The Eugene O'Neill National Site, California.
         Harpers Ferry, WV: National Park Service, US Department o
         the Interior.

         Government pamphlet.

A152   Perry, Thomas Amherst. A Bibliography of American Literature
         Translated into Romanian with Selected Romanian Commentary
         New York: Philosophical Library.

         Pages 124-25, 171, and 265 list 18 plays by O'Neill published i
         Romanian between 1939 and 1968, and include a secondary
         bibliography of 19 articles and one book in Romanian on O'Neil
         and his plays.

A153   Shurr, William H. "American Drama and the Bible: The Case of
        Eugene O'Neill's Lazarus Laughed." The Bible and American
        Arts and Letters. Vol. 3 of The Bible in American Culture.
        Ed. Giles Gunn: Philadelphia: Fortress. 83-103.

The theme of the book and of the series is taken through modern
American drama with special attention given to Lazarus. Treats
of the story as found in John and Luke; then discusses O'Neill's
handling of the story. Finds that O'Neill celebrates generic
rather than individual immortality. What vitalizes the play is
its merging of traditional material with modern
influences--Nietzsche and Whitman. (Sees echoes of Whitman in
Lazarus' language and sense of "cosmic consciousness").

A154   Yu, Beongcheon. The Great Circle: American Writers and the
        Orient. Detroit: Wayne State UP. 141-58.

Devotes a chapter to O'Neill's interest in the East. First
surveys the work done in this area; then discusses how the plays
of the early and middle periods reflect O'Neill's interest in
the Eastern vision. Asserts that mysticism did not cease with
Electra but "turned inward, nurturing his mystical vision
itself."

1984

A155   Ahuja, Chaman. Tragedy, Modern Temper and O'Neill. Atlantic
        Highlands, NJ: Humanities.

Carefully analyzes all O'Neill's published plays, usually
working chronologically, to demonstrate the thesis that though
O'Neill had "a noble conception of the theatre, and a noble aim
of reviving the spirit of Greek tragedy . . . in terms of
achievement his success was of such a modest level that it did
not satisfy even himself." Finds that though he was a colossus
in the modern theater--vital and strong--O'Neill lacked the
finesse that brings greatness," the reason lying in his
inability to reconcile his inclinations--towards modernism,
towards irony--with the demands of tragedy. True there are
masterpieces--Ape, Jones, Brown, Interlude, Electra, Iceman,
Journey, and Misbegotten--but not as tragedies. It is only when
they are approached as "plays" that O'Neill's "range, variety,
theatrical experiment and dramatic power" can be appreciated.

A156   Anikst, Alexander. "Preface to Russian Translations of
           O'Neill." Eugene O'Neill's Critics: Voices from Abroad.
           Eds. Horst Frenz and Susan tuck. Carbondale: Southern IL
           UP. 153-62.

        A reprint. See no. A167.

A157   Bloom, Steven F. "Empty Bottles, Empty Dreams: O'Neill's Use
           of Drinking and Alcoholism in Long Day's Journey into
           Night." Critical Essays on Eugene O'Neill. Ed. James J.
           Martine. Boston: G. K. Hall. 159-77.

        Applies some of the characteristics of alcoholism--self-hatred,
        denial, cyclical patterns of behavior--to the four Tyrones to
        show that there is "a vital connection between the [play's]
        repetitiousness, the vision, and alcoholism."

A158   Bryer, Jackson R. "'Peace is an Exhausted Reaction to Normal':
           O'Neill's Letters to Dudley Nichols." Critical Essays on
           Eugene O'Neill. Ed. James J. Martine. Boston: G. K.
           Hall. 33-55.

        19 letters and telegrams from O'Neill to Dudley Nichols, sent
        between 1932 and 1949. They reveal O'Neill's attitude toward
        film adaptations of his plays, which Nichols worked on: Voyage
        and Electra.

A159   Colburn, Steven E. "The Long Voyage Home: Illusion and the
           Tragic Pattern of Fate in O'Neill's S. S. Glencairn Cycle.
           Critical Essays on Eugene O'Neill. Ed. James J. Martine.
           Boston: G. K. Hall. 55-65.

        Finds in Caribbees, Cardiff, Zone, and Voyage unity in that they
        have the same central conflict, one between the forces of
        illusion and actuality. In each play the protagonist tries to
        preserve his illusion. Also notes the Nietzschean influence in
        these plays.

A160   Cunningham, Frank R. "Romantic Elements in Early O'Neill."
           Critical Essays on Eugene O'Neill. Ed. James J. Martine.
           Boston: G. K. Hall. 65-72.

        Discusses Horizon, Anna, Jones, Ape, Desire, and Mariner in
        terms of "Romantic motifs and mythic patterns: dynamic
        organicism, the creative imagination as the basic process of
        Romantic affirmation of the organic universe, man's archetypal

journey from stasis to the recognition of the existence of such
a universe, the concept of timelessness or Edenic time, and the
cyclical nature of existence."

161   Egri, Péter. "'Belonging' Lost: Alienation and Dramatic Form
         in Eugene O'Neill's The Hairy Ape." Critical Essays on
         Eugene O'Neill. Ed. James J. Martine. Boston: G. K.
         Hall. 77-111.

See no. C210a.

162   Egri, Péter. "European Origins and American Originiality: The
         Case of Drama." The Origins and Originality of American
         Culture. Ed. Tibor Frank. Budapest: Akademial Kiado.
         405-22.

Although he does not define terms, Egri uses epic synonymously
with large-scale; his article discusses O'Neill's Iceman,
Interlude, and "A Tale of Possessors Self-Dispossessed" as epic
works. Finds the roots of epic appreciation in European works
but says Americans "received and reshaped" these influences and
thereby provided inspiration to the Europeans.

163   Ervine, St. John. "Counsels of Despair." Eugene O'Neill's
         Critics: Voices from Abroad. Eds. Horst Frenz and Susan
         Tuck. Carbondale: Southern IL UP. 79-90.

A reprint. See no. A167.

164   Falk, Candace. Love, Anarchy, & Emma Goldman. New York: Holt.

O'Neill is not included in the index although Wilderness, the
Gelbses O'Neill, and Sheaffer's Son and Playwright are in the
bibliography.

165   Field, B. S., Jr. "Concrete Images of the Vague in the Plays of
         Eugene O'Neill." Critical Essays on Eugene O'Neill. Ed. James
         J. Martine. Boston: G. K. Hall. 188-96.

Says that "vagueness in O'Neill's style is not merely a
regrettable defect." Considers O'Neill's canon in terms of
setting, language, characterization, and use of jokes. Suggests
that when O'Neill became overly concerned with what he wrote, he
tended to shun words that communicated precisely what he meant,
opting for more ambiguous words, which he saw as less

melodramatic. These plays baffled the audiences. As he became
less preoccupied with the precise word (in his later plays), he
wrote less ambiguously.

A166   Frazer, Winifred L. Mabel Dodge Luhan. Boston: G. K. Hall.

A thorough survey of Luhan's life and publications based on
published materials. (Rudnick's book had not been published
yet, but her dissertation had been used). One reference to
O'Neill. Chapter 3 covers the New York City period when Luhan
moved in the relevant O'Neill ambiance.

A167   Frenz, Horst, and Susan Tuck, eds. Eugene O'Neill's Critics:
          Voices from Abroad. Carbondale: Southern IL UP.

Eclectic group of 26 essays about O'Neill's international
reputation, written 1922 on. Only three of the 26 fall within
this book's scope: They are: Catherine Mounier's "Notes on the
1967 French Production of The Iceman Cometh," (1975), see no.
A185; An Min Hsia's "Cycle of Return: O'Neill and the Tao,"
(1978), see no. A171; and Timo Tiusanen's "O'Neill and
Wuolijoki: A Counter-Sketch of Electra," (1980), see no. A206

A168   Hallström, Per. "Nobel Prize Presentation." Eugene O'Neill's
          Critics: Voices from Abroad. Eds. Horst Frenz and Susan
          Tuck. Carbondale: Southern IL UP. 57-63.

A reprint. See no. A167.

A169   Hofmannsthal, Hugo Von. "The Beggar and The Hairy Ape." Euge
          O'Neill's Critics: Voices from Abroad. Eds. Horst Frenz
          and Susan Tuck. Carbondale: Southern IL UP. 9-10.

A reprint. See Miller no. A167.

A170   Hofmannsthal, Hugo Von. "Dramaturgical Reflections." Eugene
          O'Neill's Critics: Voices from Abroad. Eds. Horst Frenz
          and Susan Tuck. Carbondale: Southern IL UP. 3-9.

A reprint. See no. A167.

171   Hsia, An Min. "Cycle of Return: O'Neill and the Tao." Eugene
           O'Neill's Critics: Voices from Abroad. Eds. Horst Frenz
           and Virginia Floyd. Carbondale: Southern IL UP. 169-73.

       Based on a dissertation and an earlier study (see no. C97a),
       this work grants that Doris Alexander is correct in pointing to
       the East to trace O'Neill's mysticism. Says, though, that it is
       Tao, Light on the Path, which influenced O'Neill (the underlying
       principle of Taoism is the return of all existence). Says we
       see Tao influence in O'Neill's Kukachin, Marco, Nina, Miriam,
       Lavinia, Mary, Iceman characters, etc.

172   Jennings, Richard. "Dramatist of Monomania." Eugene O'Neill's
           Critics: Voices from Abroad. Eds. Horst Frenz and Susan
           Tuck. Carbondale: Southern IL UP. 25-29.

       A reprint. See no. A167.

173   Kimbel, Ellen. "Eugene O'Neill as Social Historian: Manners
           and Morals in Ah, Wilderness!" Critical Essays on Eugene
           O'Neill. Ed. James J. Martine. Boston: G. K. Hall.
           137-45.

       A look at O'Neill's comedy in terms of how the play reflects
       traditional values (home, family, respectability, success) at
       the early part of the century. Says the play testifies as to
       how much we have lost.

174   Kimura, Toshio. "O'Neill's 'Whited Sepulchre.'" Eugene
           O'Neill's Critics: Voices from Abroad. Eds. Horst Frenz
           and Susan Tuck. Carbondale: Southern IL UP. 92-96.

       A reprint. See no. A167.

175   Laszlo, B. Nagy. "The O'Neill Legend." Eugene O'Neill's
           Critics: Voices from Abroad. Eds. Horst Frenz and Susan
           Tuck. Carbondale: Southern IL UP. 122-33.

       A reprint. See no. A167.

76   Le Breton, Maurice. "Eugene O'Neill and the American Theatre."
           Eugene O'Neill's Critics: Voices from Abroad. Eds. Horst
           Frenz and Susan Tuck. Carbondale: Southern IL UP. 64-69.

       A reprint. See no. A167.

A177   Lewis, Ward B. Eugene O'Neill: The German Reception of
          American's First Dramatist. German Studies in America 50.
          Berne: Lang.

        Shows how German productions of O'Neill's plays interpreted the
        in such a way as to "illuminate the cultural attitudes and
        national sensibilities both of the audience and the playwright
        himself." Claims to concentrate on performance and reception c
        plays, but covers scholarship as well--scrupulously. Treatment
        are chronologically arranged in order of their appearance in
        Germany: Anna, Jones, Ape, Desire, Chillun, Brown, Interlude,
        Electra, Wilderness, Iceman, Misbegotten, Journey, and Touch.
        O'Neill is seen early on as old-fashioned and derivative, thoug
        Desire and Chillun were modestly successful and Interlude very
        much so. After World War II Electra was triumphant. From 195:
        until the mid-1960s, O'Neill's reputation was at a peak,
        especially in regard to his four last plays. He still receives
        more attention than any other English language playwright with
        the exception of Shakespeare.

A177a   Lichtenberg, Joseph D. "The Late Works and Styles of Eugene
          O'Neill, Henry James, and Ludwig van Beethoven."
          Psychoanalysis: The Vital Issues. Eds. John E. Gedo, et
          al. Psychoanalysis as an Intellectual Discipline. New
          York: International Universities. 297-319.

A178   Macardle, Dorothy. "The Dual Nature of Man." Eugene O'Neill'
          Critics: Voices from Abroad. Eds. Horst Frenz and Susan
          Tuck. Carbondale: Southern IL UP. 54-56.

        A reprint. See no. A167.

A179   Manheim, Michael. "The Transcendence of Melodrama in O'Neill'
          The Iceman Cometh." Critical Essays on Eugene O'Neill.
          Ed. James J. Martine. Boston: G. K. Hall. 145-58.

        Discusses the Iceman characters' pasts and concludes that the
        stories we hear of the former lives of these characters are
        melodramatic in that they all "hint of intrigue, and they all
        assume a fixed ethical framework and a struggle between
        protagonists and antagonists." Hickey is like Parritt in that
        he "is living a single melodrama." Hickey sees himself as a
        protagonist, but in the course of the play confronts his
        contradictory selves and achieves self-recognition, which the
        other characters do not. Slade unlike others, recognizes that
        there is no absolute past but only conflicting interpretation:
        of it: he lives in the "unmelodramatizable" present.

180   Marcel, Gabriel. "Interpretations by a Philosopher." Eugene
       O'Neill's Critics: Voices from Abroad. Eds. Horst Frenz
       and Susan Tuck. Carbondale: Southern IL UP. 75-77.

       A reprint. See no. A167.

181   Martine, James J., ed. Critical Essays on Eugene O'Neill.
          Boston: G. K. Hall.

       Thirteen original essays, one reprint, and an introductory essay
       by the editor.
       1. Introduction: A solid bibliographical essay that comments
           on the items included, organized into sections:
           bibliography, editions, and criticism.
       2. Jackson R. Bryer, "'Peace Is an Exhausted Reaction to
           Normal': O'Neill's Letters to Dudley Nichols." See
           no. A158.
       3. Steven E. Colburn. "The Long Voyage Home: Illusion and the
           Tragic Pattern of Fate in O'Neill's S. S. Glencairn Cycle."
           See no. A159.
       4. Frank R. Cunningham. "Romantic Elements in Early O'Neill."
           See no. A160.
       5. Lisa M. Schwerdt. "Blueprint for the Future: The Emperor
           Jones." See no. A197.
       6. Péter Egri. "'Belonging Lost': Alienation and Dramatic
           Form in Eugene O'Neill's The Hairy Ape." See no. A161.
       7. June Schlueter and Arthur Lewis. "Cabot's Conflict: The
           Stones and the Cows in O'Neill's Desire Under the Elms."
           See no. A195.
       8. Joseph S. Tedesco. "Dion Brown and His Problems." See
           no. A203.
       9. Carl E. Rollyson, Jr. "Eugene O'Neill: The Drama of
           Self-Transcendence." See no. A192.
       10. Ellen Kimbel. "Eugene O'Neill: The Drama of
           Self-Transcendence." See no. A173.
       11. Michael Manheim. "The Transcendence of Melodrama in
           O'Neill's The Iceman Cometh." See no. A179.
       12. Steven F. Bloom. "Empty Bottles, Empty Dreams: O'Neill's
           Use of Drinking and Alcoholism in Long Day's Journey into
           Night." See no. A157.
       13. Laurin Roland Porter. "Hughie: Pipe Dream for Two." See
           no. A188.
       14. B. S. Field, Jr. "Concrete Images of the Vague in the Plays
           of Eugene O'Neill." See no. A165.
       15. Susan Tuck. "The O'Neill-Faulkner Connection." See
           no. A207.

A182   McArthur, Benjamin. <u>Actors and American Culture 1880-1920</u>.
        Philadelphia: Temple UP.

        Stresses the "show biz" world of Richard Mansfield, Edward H.
        Sothern, Edwin Booth, Julia Marlowe, Ethel Barrymore, Joseph
        Jefferson and James O'Neill. Carefully documents the careers,
        reputations, labors, and standing in the community of actors of
        O'Neill's youth.

A183   Mirlas, León. "The Scope of O'Neill's Drama." <u>Eugene O'Neill'</u>
        <u>Critics: Voices from Abroad</u>. Eds. Horst Frenz and Susan
        Tuck. Carbondale: Southern IL UP. 101-09.

        A reprint. See no. A167.

A184   Montale, Eugenio. "O'Neill and the Future of the Theatre."
        <u>Eugene O'Neill's Critics: Voices from Abroad</u>. Eds. Hors
        Frenz and Susan Tuck. Carbondale: Southern IL UP. 71-7.

        A reprint. See no. A167.

A185   Mounier, Catherine. "Notes on the 1967 French Production of <u>T</u>
        <u>Iceman Cometh</u>." <u>Eugene O'Neill's Critics: Voices from</u>
        <u>Abroad</u>. Eds. Horst Frenz and Susan Tuck. Carbondale:
        Southern IL UP. 163-68.

        Draws parallels between O'Neill's play and Ibsen's <u>The Wild Du</u>
        and O'Neill's play and Beckett's <u>Waiting for Godot</u>. Then
        discusses the production directed by Gabriel Garran. Notes th
        the production was intellectual and comments on how Garran mad
        his actors familiarize themselves with the Bowery. Garran
        wanted simple sets, a heavy atmosphere, and clothing as close
        O'Neill's description as possible.

A185a   Murray, Edward. "Eugene O'Neill." <u>The McGraw-Hill</u>
        <u>Encyclopedia of World Drama</u>. New York: McGraw-Hill.
        <u>5 vols.</u>

        Vol. 4, 22-40
        The story of O'Neill's life and career, an introduction to his
        works (finding five periods to his evolution), summaries of 24
        of the plays with dates of composition and first publication a
        dates and locations of first productions, and a bibliography
        that goes up to 1978.

186   Natanson, Wojciech. "O'Neill's Comeback." Eugene O'Neill's
          Critics: Voices from Abroad. Eds. Horst Frenz and Susan
          Tuck. Carbondale: Southern IL UP. 116-21.

       A reprint. See no. A167.

187   O'Casey, Sean. "Three Tributes to O'Neill." Eugene O'Neill's
          Critics: Voices from Abroad. Eds. Horst Frenz and Susan
          Tuck. Carbondale: Southern IL UP. 45-48.

       A reprint. See no. A167.

188   Porter, Laurin Roland. "Hughie: Pipe Dream for Two." Critical
          Essays on Eugene O'Neill. Ed. James J. Martine. Boston:
          G. K. Hall. 178-87.

       Ties Hughie to its predecessor Iceman and shows that both plays
       provide "cultural insights" and reveal O'Neill's "personal
       experiences." Notes that Erie Smith, like Hickey, is at least
       partially based on Jamie O'Neill, that in both plays family life
       is negatively depicted, and that both plays "search for
       transcendence, a strategy for breaking the stranglehold of
       time."

189   Ranald, Margaret Loftus. The Eugene O'Neill Companion.
          Westport, CT: Greenwood.

       Aimed at "both a general and scholarly audience," this book
       includes analyses of O'Neill's plays and characters, biographies
       of those closely associated with the playwright, and casts of
       original productions, as well as appendices listing a chronology
       of plays, and of film, musical, operatic, and balletic
       adaptations. Encyclopedic in nature, the book is an important
       reference tool.

190   Reger, Erik. "The Georg Kaiser of America." Eugene O'Neill's
          Critics: Voices from Abroad. Eds. Horst Frenz and Susan
          Tuck. Carbondale: Southern IL UP. 30-32.

       A reprint. See no. A167.

191   Robinson, Lennox. "Beyond the Horizon Versus Gold." Eugene
          O'Neill's Critics: Voices from Abroad. Eds. Horst Frenz
          and Susan Tuck. Carbondale: Southern IL UP. 11-15.

       A reprint. See no. A167.

A192   Rollyson, Carl E., Jr. "Eugene O'Neill: The Drama of
            Self-Transcendence." Critical Essays on Eugene O'Neill.
            Ed. James J. Martine. Boston: G. K. Hall. 123-37.

        Discusses Lazarus' laughter as a means of transcending self and
        history and of joining the universal. The Romans in the play
        represent modern man who is "bound by a linear, historical
        concept of movement from life to death, whereas archaic man,
        represented by Lazarus and his followers, sees that life and
        death are but part of the same life cycle.

A193   Rudnick, Lois Palken. Mabel Dodge Luhan: New Woman, New
            Worlds. Albuquerque: U of New Mexico P.

        Definitive study of the life of Luhan. Chapters 3 and 4 deal
        with her years in New York City and her association with the
        bohemian world of art and politics in the second decade of the
        20th century. Careful research--especially in the manuscript
        collections at the Beinecke, Bancroft, Houghton, and Huntingdon
        libraries. Based on a Ph.D. dissertation at Brown U in 1977.
        Only one reference to O'Neill, and that is speculative.

A194   Sastre, Alfonso. "On the Death of Eugene O'Neill." Eugene
            O'Neill's Critics: Voices from Abroad. Eds. Horst Frenz
            and Susan Tuck. Carbondale: Southern IL UP. 97-100.

        A reprint. See no. A167.

A195   Schlueter, June, and Arthur Lewis. "Cabot's Conflict: The
            Stones and the Cows in O'Neill's Desire Under the Elms."
            Critical Essays on Eugene O'Neill. Ed. James J. Martine.
            Boston: G. K. Hall. 111-14.

        Says that the cows and the stones with which Ephraim Cabot is
        identified represent two ways of living--the easy life (cows)
        and the hard life (stones). Both attract him and are a source
        of moral conflict. At the end Cabot is tempted to turn his co
        loose, but he opts for the harder life--to continue on the far

A196   Schuh, Oscar Fritz. "O'Neill's Dramatic Work: His Image of
            Humanity." Eugene O'Neill's Critics: Voices from Abroad.
            Eds. Horst Frenz and Susan Tuck. Carbondale: Southern I
            UP. 135-40.

        A reprint. See no. A167.

197   Schwerdt, Lisa M. "Blueprint for the Future: The Emperor
        Jones." Critical Essays on Eugene O'Neill. Ed. James J.
        Martine. Boston: G. K. Hall. 72-77.

      Studies the levels on which man interacts--the personal, the
      social, and the impersonal--in Jones and traces these levels in
      later O'Neill plays.

198   Schyberg, Frederick. "An American Tragedy of Fate." Eugene
        O'Neill's Critics: Voices from Abroad. Eds. Horst Frenz
        and Susan Tuck. Carbondale: Southern IL UP. 50-53.

      A reprint. See no. A167.

199   Shipley, Joseph T. The Crown Guide to the World's Great Plays:
        From Ancient Greece to Modern Times. New York: Crown.

      Brief notes, thumb-nail summaries, excerpts from critics'
      responses, histories of first productions of: Horizon, Jones,
      Anna, Desire, Interlude, Electra, Ah, Wilderness!, Iceman,
      Journey, Misbegotten, Touch, and Mansions. Includes personal
      responses to individual plays. In a section entitled "O'Neill's
      Posthumous Plays" (by which he means "A Tale of Possessors
      Self-Dispossessed"), he describes his own contribution to the
      Swedish productions of O'Neill.

200   Smith, Susan Valeria Harris. Masks in Modern Drama. Berkeley:
        U of California P.

      A wide ranging study of the use of masks in, mostly,
      twentieth-century theater, touching on some 200 plays, both
      European and American. Sees masks as stage devices or as
      textual metaphors. Since the organization of the study is
      thematic, remarks on O'Neill are scattered (here the index is
      very useful), but cover, briefly, Ape, Chillun, Jones, Mariner,
      Fountain, and Days, and, to a greater extent, Lazarus and Brown.
      Demonstrates that O'Neill "clearly knew the European experiments
      in masked subjective projection" and observes that Brown is "the
      most thorough, labored exploration of protective masking on the
      modern stage."

00a   Stein, Rita, and Friedhelm Rickert. "Eugene O'Neill," Modern
        American Dramatists: A Library of Criticism. New York:
        Frederick Ungar. 2 vols. Vol. 1, pp. 52-78.

      An "overview of the critical reception of the dramatist from the

beginning of his career up to the present time through excerpt
from reviews, articles, and books." Some 30 excerpts are
arranged chronologically, starting with one from Edmund Wilson
(1922) and continuing through selections from Chabrowe, Chothi
and Virginia Floyd.

A201   Tairov, Alexander. "The Creative Work of Eugene O'Neill."
        Eugene O'Neill's Critics: Voices from Abroad. Eds. Hors
        Frenz and Susan Tuck. Carbondale: Southern IL UP. 41-4

        A reprint. See nos. A8 and A167.

A202   Tairov, Alexander. "Director's Notes." Eugene O'Neill's
        Critics: Voices from Abroad. Eds. Horst Frenz and Susan
        Tuck. Carbondale: Southern IL UP, 34-41.

        A reprint. See nos. A8 and A167.

A203   Tedesco, Joseph S. "Dion Brown and His Problems." Critical
        Essays on Eugene O'Neill. Ed. James J. Martine. Boston:
        G. K. Hall. 114-23.

        Uses a Jungian approach to analyze Brown in contrast to the
        popular Nietzschean approaches of other critics.

A204   Tetauer, Frank. "Raw, Brutal Visions." Eugene O'Neill's
        Critics: Voices from Abroad. Eds. Horst Frenz and Susan
        Tuck. Carbondale: Southern IL UP. 16-20.

        A reprint. See no. A167.

A205   Tetauer, Frank. "The Tragic Wandering of a Great Dramatist."
        Eugene O'Neill's Critics: Voices from Abroad. Eds. Hors
        Frenz and Susan Tuck. Carbondale: Southern IL UP. 20-2

        A reprint. See no. A167.

A206   Tiusanen, Timo. "O'Neill and Wuolijoki: A Counter-Sketch to
        Electra." Eugene O'Neill's Critics: Voices from Abroad.
        Eds. Horst Frenz and Susan Tuck. Carbondale: Southern
        UP. 174-81.

        Identifies Hella Wuolijoki, female Finnish playwright and
        contemporary of O'Neill, who, after having viewed Electra in

1934, wrote a counter-sketch. Tiusanen discusses her work
Justiina in terms of its affinities with and departure from
O'Neill's play.

207   Tuck, Susan. "The O'Neill-Faulkner Connection." Critical
          Studies on Eugene O'Neill. Ed. James J. Martine. Boston:
          G. K. Hall. 196-206.

Speculates on where Faulkner may first have encountered
O'Neill's work, with which he was clearly familiar. Then she
traces the parallels between Faulkner's "The Sailor" and
O'Neill's Glencairn; "The Longshoreman" and Jones and Chillun;
"The Kid Learns" and Cardiff; The Sound and the Fury and
Interlude; As I Lay Dying and Jones; Santuary and Jones and Ape;
and Light in August and Chillun.

208   Tynan, Kenneth. "The Heights and the Depths." Eugene O'Neill's
          Critics: Voices from Abroad. Eds. Horst Frenz and Susan
          Tuck. Carbondale: Southern IL UP. 111-12.

A Reprint. See no. A167.

                              1985

209   Barlow, Judith E. Final Acts: The Creation of Three Late
          O'Neill Plays. Athens: U of Georgia P.

The product of 12 years of research, Final Acts analyzes Iceman,
Journey, and Misbegotten, utilizing O'Neill's notes, drafts, and
scenarios. The Introduction says the book is "not intended
simply as a technical account of O'Neill's composition method in
his later years," but also shows the extent of the changes and
when the changes were made. Suggests that knowing the
playwright's original ideas can explain why a play succeeds or
fails and can help us focus on what we might have overlooked in
the finished product.

10   Floyd, Virginia. Eugene O'Neill: A New Assessment. New York:
          Ungar. 1985.

The author calls the book an "introductory study designed to
bring contemporary students and general readers to an
understanding of Eugene O'Neill, the man and the playwright."
Analyzes 50 plays, approached in four chronological sections:
"Early Plays and Beginnings," "Experimental Plays and

Maturation," "'Self' Plays and the Cycle," and "The Late Great
Plays." Gives plot summary and some analysis, but is aimed, as
Floyd says, at the basic level.

A211   Maufort, Marc. "Communication as Translation of the Self:
        Jamesian Inner Monologue in O'Neill's Strange Interlude."
        Communiquer et Traduire: Hommages a Jean Dierick. Ed.
        Gilbert Debusscher and Jean-Pierre van Noppen. Brussels:
        Editions de l'Universite de Bruxelles. 319-28.

Finds in Interlude unacknowledged echoes of Henry James in the
use of "the realistic inner monologue as a medium to communica
the human flow of consciousness" and refers to The Portrait o
a Lady to exemplify the correspondences. Says O'Neill's
monologue "differs from its Jamesian equivalent as it is
separated from the dialogue by means of insets." Like James,
though, "O'Neill wishes to suggest, through oppositions and
alternating rhythms, the human flow of consciousness." Also,
like James's monologue, O'Neill's unifies the work by
"establishing the importance of a central consciousness." Bu
though "James is primarily concerned with psychological issues
O'Neill makes efforts to rise from the personal to the general
and to formulate a compelling statement on the metaphysical
predicament of mankind."

DISSERTATIONS

1971

Hambright, Jeanne K. "The Journey Out: Contributions of German Dramatic Expressionism in the Social Protest Plavs of Eugene O'Neill." Diss. Tufts U.

Studies Wedekind and O'Neill--the first as a contributor to Expressionism, the second as a borrower from. Says both were influenced by Nietzsche, Marx, and Freud and found in Expressionism a means of conveying their political and psychological ideas. Of O'Neill's plays, Jones, Ape, Chillun, Desire, Marco, Brown, Lazarus, Interlude, Dynamo, Electra, and Days are considered.

Hinden, Michael C. "Tragedy: the Communal Vision: A Critique and Extension of Nietzsche's Theory of Tragedy with Attention Devoted to the Early Plays of Eugene O'Neill." Diss. Brown U.

Concentrates on Nietzsche's ideas expounded in The Birth of Tragedy. His fourth and last chapter deals with the plays of O'Neill's "Nietzschean Period"--Jones, Ape, Chillun, Desire, and Brown.

Karadaghi, Mohamad R. "The Theme of Alienation in Eugene O'Neill's Plays." Diss. U of California.

Says alienation is the most consistent of O'Neill's themes. Says O'Neill sought a cure for this modern illness this side of the grave in liquor, pipe dreams, insanity, and regression into childhood. Analyzes Cardiff, Horizon, Anna, Jones, Ape, Chillun, Desire, Brown, Interlude, Dynamo, Electra, Iceman, Touch, Journey, Misbegotten. Finds in first 11 plays man's alienation from God is in the foreground of the play. In the last four it recedes to the background.

McNicholas, Mary V., O.P. "The Quintessence of Ibsenism: Its Impact on the Drama of Eugene Gladstone O'Neill." Diss. Indiana U.

Finds the influence of Strindberg on O'Neill to be much exaggerated and says that Ibsen's themes and techniques discussed in George Bernard Shaw's Quintessence, as well as Shaw's own ideas, reverberate throughout O'Neill's work from early plays to late.

B5   Pickering, Christine P.   "The Works of Eugene O'Neill: A Greek
          Idea of the Theatre Derived from the philosophy of Friedrich
          Nietzsche." Diss. East Texas State U.

Asserts that O'Neill's conception of drama was based on a Greek
concept of theatre which he derived from Nietzsche. Analyzes 45
O'Neill plays for Nietzschean influence.

                                    1972

B6   Anderson, Elizabeth L.   "Pathetic Elements in O'Neill's
          Characters." Diss. Florida State U.

Applies Aristotle's definition of tragedy to O'Neill's Desire,
Electra, Iceman, Journey. Concludes that the actions of the
characters are not noble and that the characters are, therefore,
pathetic.

B7   Fleming, William P., Jr.   "Tragedy in American Drama: The Tragic
          Views of Eugene O'Neill, Tennessee Williams, Arthur Miller,
          and Edward Albee." Diss. U of Toledo.

Tries to develop a modern concept of tragedy, specifically as it
relates to American drama. Says O'Neill's final plays present t
Force which makes life tragic, mysterious and different for eve
man.

B8   Jiji, Vera M.   "Audience Response in the Theater: A Study of
          Dramatic Theory Tested Against Reviewers' Responses to the
          Plays of Eugene O'Neill." Diss. New York U.

Studies the first night responses to O'Neill's plays produced
between 1920 and 1967 to determine if the responses were intrins
(based on what was in the play) or extrinsic (focused in the mi
of the viewer). Concludes that the societal importance of a pl
has a great effect upon its reception.

B9   Pampel, Brigitte C.   "The Relationship of the Sexes in the Work
          of Strindberg, Wedekind, and O'Neill." Diss.
          Northwestern U.

Studies the attitudes of Strindberg, Wedekind, and O'Neill towa
male-female relationships, focusing on marriage, prostitution,
sexual repression. Says that these writers differed from previ
writers because they underscored man's sexual nature. Says
O'Neill emphasized the psychological motivation and dwelled on

natural desires and the frustration resulting from an inability to fulfill desires. Although O'Neill reflected Strindberg's pessimism, his characters seek relationships of love and understanding.

1973

10 Butler, F. Jay. "Eugene O'Neill's Use of Symbolism in Eight Major Experimental Plays." Diss. Loyola U.

Studies the use of symbolism in Ape, Chillun, Desire, Interlude, Brown, Electra, Iceman, and Journey, and concludes symbolism is used to extend the boundary, scope, and meaning of O'Neill's plays beyond the limits of mere realism. Says symbols function to universalize the playwright's themes. Notes O'Neill used symbolism experimentally in three areas: setting, character, and plot.

1 Corrigan, Ralph L., Jr. "The Function of the Green World in Selected Plays by Eugene O'Neill." Diss. Fordham U.

Explores O'Neill's themes of disharmony with and alienation from the natural world. Says O'Neill's answer lies in man's attempt to find the peace and harmony of the primitive state. Man either dreams of a substitute for nature or journeys to a "sacred grove" to rediscover harmony. Chronological discussion of O'Neill's changing attitude about possibility of finding a simple, harmonious life.

2 Fleckenstein, Joan P. "Eugene O'Neill's Theatre of Dionysius: The Nietzschean Influence upon Selected Plays." Diss. U of Wisconsin.

Analyzes Jones, Ape, Fountain, Marco, Brown, and Lazarus in terms of Nietzschean influence--death of God, eternal recurrence, the will to power, the transvaluation of values, and the Superman.

3 Goodell, Diana Charlotte. "The Emperor Jones in Reading Theatre Style." M.A. Thesis. California State U.

Finds that to convey the "expressionistic feeling," it is necessary, even in Reading Theatre style, to use scenary and props that produce exaggerated effects.

B14   Hurley, Daniel F. "The Failed Comedies of Eugene O'Neill." Dis·
      Louisiana State U.

      Studies O'Neill's career--beginning, middle, and end--for the
      playwright's changing attitude toward his characters. Says his
      view was comedic but changed to pathetic. Humor in the later
      plays drains, and we're left with a residue of agony.

B14a Reid, John Louden. "On O'Neill's Own Terms: A Study of the
      Playwright's Last Dramas." Diss. U of California at
      Berkeley.

      Touch, Mansions, Iceman, Journey, Hughie, Misbegotten use the
      mythologizing technique developed in O'Neill's earlier plays.
      Each reflects a central mythic event: Touch (Narcissus), Mansion
      (a Kafkaesque fairy tale), Iceman (the Harrowing of Hell), Journ
      (the artist's soul conjured from incantatory natural rhythms),
      Hughie (classical elegy and Irish wake), Misbegotten (black Iris
      joke). Four of the plays--Iceman, Misbegotten, Touch, Journey--
      reproduce the four main movements of Greek tragedy and the four
      steps in the Catholic Sacrament of Penance. These four plays
      collectively imply a workable contemporary religious stance.

B15   Wolkowitz, Alfred David. "The Myth of the Atridae in Classic an·
      Modern Drama." Diss. New York U.

      Studies the development of the Atridae myth from its Homeric
      sources to its use in 20th-century adaptations. Deals with the
      works of eight 20th-century playwrights who treated of the
      myth--including O'Neill's Electra.

                                1974

B16   Bishoff, Robert E., Jr. "Changing Perspectives: An American
      Tragedy from Literature to Film." Diss. U of Massachuset·

      Tries to show that film can complement a writer's work. Compar·
      dramatic literature and film--how meaning is communicated in ea·
      medium--and compares written and film versions of Journey and
      Anna.

B17   Brennan, Joseph J. "The Comic in the Plays of Eugene O'Neill:
      Use of Characterization, Situation, and Language in Relati
      to Henri Bergson's Theory of Comedy." Diss. New York U.

      Uses Bergson's definition of comedy to show that Ah, Wilderness·

is not the only play in O'Neill's canon to be thought comic.
Analyzes plays with comic elements in early, middle, and late
periods in O'Neill's career.

18   Dennery, Thomas. "Social Reform and the American Theater,
        1880-1920." Diss. Michigan State U.

Surveys the extent of social concern in the American theater by
examining the plays of the period 1880-1920, the reviews in the
New York Times, New York Dramatic Mirror, and Theatre, other
reviews in popular and literary magazines and the works of such
figures as Walter Pritchard Eaton, Brander Matthews, and William
Winter, James Huneker, and George Jean Nathan and others. Finds
considerable interest in social issues from 1880-1900, a decline
of interest thereafter, for half a decade, then regrowth of
interest, owing to the influence of the Muckrakers, the
Progressive Party (organized in 1904) and efforts to establish a
socialist theater in New York. The eventual heirs of these
concerns were the Washington Square and Provincetown Players, who
rejected social reform, advocating more fundamental changes in
American society.

8a Medvedeva, N. P. "Tvorcheskie iskaniĩa ĩu. O'Nila 20-kh godov i
        stanovlenie amerikanskoĭ natsional'noĭ dramy." Diss. Gorki
        State U [Russia].

9   Poulard, Regina. "O'Neill and Nietzsche: The Making of a
        Playwright and Thinker." Diss. Loyola U.

Explains the influence of Nietzschean philosophy as expressed in
The Birth of Tragedy and Thus Spake Zarathustra on O'Neill.
Explains how O'Neill's acceptance of Nietzschean ideas changed
during the course of his career, that in O'Neill's last period,
the playwright fused Nietzschean thinking with the ideas of Thomas
a Kempis' Imitation of Christ.

)   Sweet, Harvey. "Eugene O'Neill and Robert Edmond Jones: Text
        into Scene." Diss. U of Wisconsin.

Studies the contribution of Jones to the form of American theater.
Tries to devise a vocabulary for discussion and a context for
evaluation. Three collaborations with O'Neill are considered.
Chapter I surveys O'Neill's career in New York theatre; Chapter II
studies Jones's development in professional theatre throughout
America. Chapters III-V consider designs for Desire, Electra, and
Iceman.

1975

B21   Barlow, Judith Ellen. "Three Late Works of Eugene O'Neill: The
        Plays and the Process of Composition." Diss. U of
        Pennsylvania.

      Discusses how O'Neill wrote during the period 1939-43, by
      examining versions of the final drafts of Iceman, Journey, and
      Misbegotten. The study reveals that characters are more
      sympathetic in the final versions. In Iceman and Misbegotten,
      characters become less biographical in final versions, but in
      Journey, they become more biographically accurate. Also, in fin
      versions, there is an increased emphasis on the major character,
      lessened emphasis on secondary characters.

B22   Brown, Susan Rand. "'Mothers' and 'Sons': The Development of
        Autobiographical Themes in the Plays of Eugene O'Neill."
        Diss. U of Connecticut.

      Traces O'Neill's development to its apex--the late plays which
      record his relationship with his mother without falsification.
      Considers the sea plays, Horizon, Straw, Welded, Diff'rent,
      Fountain, Marco, Lazarus, Dynamo, Days, Mansions, Iceman, and
      Journey.

B23   Lewton, E.P.T. "Form and Content in the Last Plays of Eugene
        O'Neill." M. Phil. Thesis. U of Warwick [England].

B24   Miller, Robert Royce. "Tragedy in Modern American Drama: The
        Psychological, Social, and Absurdist Conditions in Historic
        Perspective." Diss. Middle Tennessee State U.

      The object is to examine the major 20th-century dramatists as
      reflecting those same concerns that attract contemporary poets,
      novelists, and short story writers. Deals with O'Neill's Jones
      reflecting the 20th-century concern with self-identification.

B25   Nash, William Alan. "The Homecoming Motif in Selected Works of
        Eugene O'Neill." Diss. U of Utah.

      Says man has since earliest time sought to overcome his alienat
      from nature and has attempted through the archetypal pattern of
      withdrawal and return to integrate himself in nature. Discusse
      O'Neill's treatment of the theme in Horizon, Jones, Ape,
      Lazarus,Electra, Journey, and Misbegotten.

26 Ratliff, Gerald Lee. "An Examination of the Parabolic Nature of
        'Suffering' in Selected Plays of Eugene O'Neill 1913-23."
        Diss. Bowling Green State U.

    Considers O'Neill's work during the period specified and concludes
    that O'Neill's use of biblical allusion is less important than his
    use of biblical analogue, that O'Neill is a Christian
    playwright-prophet, which is implicit in his treatment of
    suffering as man's saving grace, and that O'Neill's unique
    contribution to the world of literature is his ability to focus on
    suffering as improving, leading to a gospel of salvation.

27 Robinson, James Arthur. "O'Neill's Expressionistic Grotesque: A
        Study of Nine Experimental Plays by Eugene O'Neill." Diss.
        Duke U.

    Discusses Jones, Ape, Chillun, Desire, Brown, Lazarus, Interlude,
    Dynamo, and Days in light of the grotesque. Also, surveys O'Neill
    biography for his early acquaintance with the grotesque and
    compares O'Neill's use of the grotesque with Ionesco's, Genet's,
    Beckett's, and others.

28 Ross, Gwendolyn DeCamp. "Comic Elements in the Late Plays of
        Eugene O'Neill." Diss. U of Tulsa.

    Shows how O'Neill employs comic elements in his late plays to
    intensify a tragic condition or to point out man's tragic
    condition in a real rather than an ideal way. Also asserts that
    although American by birth, O'Neill was imbued with the Irish
    comic tradition. Focuses on the use of language to create comedy,
    the use of character as vehicle for comedy, and the use of
    situation to create comic effect. Plays considered are Iceman,
    Touch, Mansions, Journey, Wilderness, and Misbegotten.

9   Voelker, Paul Duane. "The Early Plays of Eugene O'Neill:
        1913-1915." Diss. U of Wisconsin.

    Analyzes the early plays and concludes that from the beginning
    O'Neill saw his work as a combination of the literary and the
    theatrical. Also concludes that George Pierce Baker's influence
    was not negative and may have been salutary. Demonstrates that
    O'Neill developed increasing competence in the use of setting,
    lighting, sound effects, blocking, and in plot structure, pacing,
    and rhythm in early plays.

1976

B30   Merz, Linda Marie. "Eugene O'Neill: The Man and the Quest."
         M.A. Thesis. Pacific Lutheran U.

      Finds that the setting functions almost as a character, especiall
      with the use of light and sound, to make with dialogue a symphony
      in which all parts have important roles in portraying the plays's
      themes. Considers Jones, Ape, Anna, and Misbegotten.

B31   Orlandello, John Richard. "Stage to Screen: Film Adaptations of
         the Plays of Eugene O'Neill." Diss. U of Michigan.

      Studies the O'Neill plays which have been adapted for film and
      discusses the problems of adapting the material. Also considers
      the advantages and disadvantages of the star system.

B32   Reifield, Beatrice Ann. "A Theory of Tragicomedy in Modern
         Drama." Diss. Pennsylvania State U.

      Explores the theory of tragicomedy in modern drama. Distinguishe
      between the tragicomic moment and the tragicomic play. Plays by
      Chekhov, Pirandello, Beckett, and O'Neill are analyzed to show
      recurring patterns of plot structure, character depiction, and
      tone.

B33   Rich, J. Dennis. "Eugene O'Neill: Visions of the Absurd." Diss
         U of Wisconsin.

      Analyzes O'Neill's plays from the perspective of the absurd. Say
      the playwright's ideas were influenced by Kierkegaard, Nietzsche
      Sartre, Camus, as well as by the American literary and
      philosophical traditions of Emerson, Hawthorne, Poe, Melville,
      Thoreau, and Whitman. Studies Thirst, Cardiff, Jones, Brown for
      absurdist influence. Says that, in the final stage of O'Neill's
      career, the struggle to discern the transcendental principle
      appears to cease and living is affirmed.

B34   Roland, Laurin Kay. "Biography and Culture in the Later Plays o
         Eugene O'Neill." Diss. U of Detroit.

      Asserts that the two enterprises of O'Neill's late years--the
      cycle of 11 plays and the autobiographical works--were not
      separate endeavors but successive stages in O'Neill's effort to
      achieve salvation. The personae's search for transcendence in
      these plays is ultimately a religious quest reflecting the
      spiritual longings of O'Neill.

1977

335 Bernard, Kathy Lynn. "The Research Library of Eugene O'Neill."
     Diss. U of Massachusetts.

     Study concludes that O'Neill was a careful reader and researcher,
     with a strong interest in history, philosophy, religion,
     shipbuilding, sailing, and literature. Analyzes two unfinished
     plays to show the influence of his reading upon his
     creativity--"Shih Huang Ti" and "Don Juan-Philip II" and considers
     finished works to show how ideas came to fruition--Fountain,
     Marco, Lazarus, Touch, Mansions. Examines Touch and Electra to
     show how widely he used his library and shows the relevance of
     library to major words, Iceman, Misbegotten, Journey.

336 Boeltl, Sheldon Jerome. "Hofmannsthal's Elektra and O'Neill's
     Mourning Becomes Electra: The Nature of Life." M.A. Thesis.
     California State U.

     Though similar, the two plays are also importantly different in
     the worlds and views of life presented. In Hofmannsthal, life
     explodes, then burns out; in O'Neill, life is suffocating and
     gradually stifling.

337 Cutler, Janet Klotman. "Eugene O'Neill on the Screen: Love,
     Hate, and the Movies." Diss. U of Illinois.

     Analyzes Anna, Jones, Journey, Iceman, Voyage as movie adaptations
     and art. Concludes that the films, like O'Neill's plays, are
     uneven.

338 Diamond, George Saul. "The Ironic Use of Melodramatic Conventions
     of The Count of Monte Cristo in the plays of Eugene O'Neill."
     Diss. Lehigh U.

     Discusses the characteristics of melodrama in general and of The
     Count in particular. Analyzes early O'Neill--Cardiff, Zone, Rope,
     and Cross--for early melodrama influence.

339 Friedman, Lois M., O.S.F. "The 'Dark Night of the Soul' in
     Selected Dramas by Three Modern Catholic Authors." Diss.
     Purdue U.

     Describes the criteria for evaluating the depth and authenticity
     of the mystical experience. O'Neill's technique for conveying the

dark night is to use the divided self. Concludes that O'Neill
fails to portray deep and authentic spiritual experiences.

B40   Hunt, Doris Ann. "Dialects of the Black Characters in the Plays
         of Eugene O'Neill." Diss. U of Florida.

      The introduction to the dissertation raises the question of
      whether O'Neill's handling of dialects was accurate. The body of
      the paper examines O'Neill's use of dialect and concludes that
      O'Neill did use black dialect well--especially in Brutus Jones's
      speech.

B41   Jensen, George Henry. "The Eugene O'Neill-Theatre Guild
         Correspondence." Diss. U of South Carolina.

      Edits the correspondence between the Theatre Guild and O'Neill
      from 1927-51. The letters reveal O'Neill's attitude toward his
      contemporaries, and toward the theater, his relationships with his
      producers, and his instructions for Guild productions of Mansions
      Interlude, Dynamo, Electra, Days, Iceman, Wilderness.

B42   Lischer, Tracy Kenyon. "The Passive Voice in American Literature
         Vehicle for Tragedy in Brown, Hawthorne, O'Neill, Wharton,
         and Frost." Diss. Saint Louis U.

      Looks to O'Neill's Electra and other works by other American
      writers to show that Americans devalue the female capability. The
      result in literature is a divided self, a person who can't
      assimilate the intuitive female principle and the reflective
      masculine nature.   Says when the nourishing female principle is
      needed, the protagonist remains passive or weds action to passion
      only in death.

B43   Mandel, Josef Lorenz. "Gerhart Hauptmann and Eugene O'Neill: A
         Parallel Study of their Dramatic Techniques in Selected
         Naturalistic Plays." Diss. U of North Carolina at Chapel
         Hill.

      Discusses the parallels in three plays of O'Neill and three of
      Hauptmann and contrasts their techniques. Whereas O'Neill sees
      psychological forces as precipitating catastrophe, Hauptmann see
      sociological forces. But both used Naturalistic drama and both
      playwrights' characters are subject to a life of suffering and
      despair.

44   Mihelich, Christine, I.H.M. "The Rite of Confession in Five Plays
        by Eugene O'Neill." Diss. U of Pittsburgh.

        Discusses Electra, Interlude, Iceman, Journey, and Misbegotten as
        confessional plays, wherein the characters confess their guilt to
        persons they have injured or to sympathetic proxies. Study
        assumes that O'Neill's recollection of the ritual prompted him to
        use the technique.

45   Pahnichaputt, M.L. Ananchanok. "The Image of Home in Five
        American Literary Works." Diss. U of Denver.

        Concludes that often home is pictured in its negative effects--as
        a place of confinement, a threat to freedom. Unlike the English
        literary tradition which celebrates the warmth of home, American
        literature shows familial conflicts which result in alienation.
        Eventually the houses are burnt, sold, divided up into apartments,
        or abandoned. Works discussed include Nathaniel
        Hawthorne's The House of Seven Gables; Ole Rolvaag's Giants of the
        Earth; Faulkner's Absalom, Absalom!; O'Neill's Journey; and Arthur
        Miller's Death of a Salesman.

46   Phillips, Julien Lind. "The Mask: Theory and Practical Use in
        the Plays of Eugene O'Neill." Diss. U of Minnesota.

        Touches on Jones, Fountain, and Marco, but concentrates on Ape,
        Mariner, Chillun, Brown, Lazarus, Electra, and Days. The focus is
        on how masks indicate symbolic values. Concludes that O'Neill's
        masks were successful in providing a separate dramatic element, in
        reinforcing plot and theme, and in forcing the actor to expand his
        art, but says that the masks were only limited in their success as
        a tool for conveying meaning.

47   Ryba, Mary Miceli. "Melodrama as a Figure of Mysticism in Eugene
        O'Neill's Plays." Diss. Wayne State U.

        Points out that the sources of O'Neill's mysticism were the Roman
        Catholic Church, Nietzsche, and Oriental traditions, all of which
        agree on the pattern, if not the goal, of mysticism. The pattern
        of O'Neill's mysticism conforms more to the pattern of melodrama
        than to tragedy.

48   Snow, Steven Allen. "Self, Family, and Survival in Contemporary
        American Drama." M.A. Thesis. U of Louisville.

        Studies four plays including one by O'Neill--Journey--to
        illustrate the function of the family in modern drama. Finds that

the central character seeks strength to face the world from his
family, which in its failure to provide the needed strength break
down, leaving the central character with no support.

B49 Sturm, Clarence. "Scholarly Criticism of Eugene O'Neill in
        Periodicals, 1960-1975, with a Bibliographical Overview of
        the American and German Studies." Diss. Oklahoma State U.

     A research tool which contains four main divisions:
     1. An introductory essay reviewing the state of O'Neill studies
         as reflected in scholarly articles in English from 1960-75.
     2. Abstracts of articles mentioned in the introduction.
     3. A bibliography of scholarship about O'Neill in German since
         1920.
     4. Biographical data containing important dates in O'Neill's
         life.

B50 Swanson, Mary Stewart. "The Themes of Time and Mortality in the
        Dramas of Eugene O'Neill." Diss. U of Minnesota.

     Attempts to find some evolution of attitude about mortality and
     immortality in O'Neill's work. Finds that in the early plays
     (Thirst, Sniper, Cardiff), there is an obsession with dying, but
     in the later plays (Touch, Mansions, Iceman, Journey, Misbegotten
     and Hughie) O'Neill learns to accept dying.

B50a Tsimbal, I. S. "Teatr Iûdzhina O'Nila." Avtoref. Diss. na Sois
        ychën. step. kand. iskusstvovedeniîa. Leningrad.

                              1978

B51 Castro, Donald Frank. "A Phenomenological Approach to the Concep
        of Genre." Diss. Washington State U.

     Consists of four related essays--related in terms of their
     subject, genre, and their common perspective, phenomenology. The
     fourth essay, "Autobiographical Drama: A Phenomenological
     Deception," discusses Journey, Williams' The Glass Menagerie, an
     Arthur Miller's After the Fall as comprising a new or previously
     unrecognized genre--autobiographical drama.°

52 Gray, Cecilia Dolores. "Achievement as a Family Theme in Drama."
       Diss. Oregon State U.

    A dissertation in Sociology. Analyzes O'Neill's <u>Journey</u> and
    Arthur Miller's <u>Death of a Salesman</u> to test propositions regarding
    family achievement theme--what sustains it.

53 Hagy, Boyd Frederick. "A Study of the Changing Patterns of
       Melodramas That Contributed to American Playwriting From
       1920-50." Diss. Catholic U.

    Contends that 19th-century melodrama made valuable contributions
    to 20th-century American playwriting. Fourteen 20th-century plays
    are discussed to prove his thesis, among them <u>Horizon</u> (1920) and
    <u>Desire</u> (1924).

54 Hanson, Eugene Kenneth. "Earth Mother/Mother of God: The Theme
       of Forgiveness in the Plays of Eugene O'Neill". Diss.
       Claremont U.

    Says O'Neill's plays deal with a quest for forgiveness from a
    woman, usually a mother, who represents O'Neill's rejected
    Catholicism. O'Neill's protagonists want a restoration of the
    relationship they once knew with the Virgin. The Mother-figure,
    like O'Neill's mother, fails, and the hero turns to other women,
    often prostitutes. They too fail, and the hero joins the
    misbegotten. The only hope of salvation is through art.

54a Knežević, Debora Julii. "Eugene O'Neill na pražském jevišti."
       Thesis. Charles U [Prague].

54b Peyrouse, John Claude, Jr. "The Use of Stagecraft in the Plays of
       Eugene O'Neill." Diss. U of Nebraska.

55 Walker, Herbert Kenneth, III. "Symbolism in the Later Plays of
       Eugene O'Neill." Diss. Ball State U.

    Tries to account for the disparity between the early and later
    plays by examining the simplicity of action and the unity of
    symbol and action in <u>Touch</u>, <u>Iceman</u>, and <u>Journey</u>. Agrees with Eric
    Bentley that O'Neill's early plays are ineffective and attributes
    this to the pretentiousness of his ideas, symbols, and themes.
    <u>Iceman</u> and <u>Touch</u> are successful because characterization is
    developed, plots are simple, and theme arises from action and
    character. Concludes that in <u>Journey</u> O'Neill perfected the use of
    symbol.

B56   Williams, Julia Willa Bacon. "Eugene O'Neill: The Philos-Aphilo
       of a Mother's Eternal Son." Diss. U of Michigan.

       Maintains that the effects on O'Neill of learning of his mother's
       addiction were several--alcoholism, guilt, death-wish, Jeckyll an
       Hyde personality, obsession with cathartic writing, and exorbitan
       demands on wives. Traces the intensity of his angst as it
       reverberates throughout his canon, and the philos-aphilos
       relationship in his plays.

                                   1979

B57   Lichtman, Myla Ruth. "Mythic Plot and Character Development in
          Euripides' Hippolytus and Eugene O'Neill's Desire Under the
          Elms: A Jungian Analysis." Diss. U of Southern California.

       Analyzes Euripides' and O'Neill's plays utilizing Jung's
       psycho-philosophical concepts of "myth" and "symbol." Each play
       is studied in terms of the playwright, the historical time of the
       play's conception, and the psychological climate of the time.
       Analysis reveals that both plays, in reflecting the psychological
       climates of their times, reflect man's quest for savage power.

B57a   Pinaev, S. M. "Khydozhestvennaiā Struktura dram Īu. O'Nila: K
          probleme Konflikta i ego dramaturgicheskogo voploshcheniiā.'
          Avtoref. Diss. na soisk. uchën. step. kand. filol. nauk.
          Moscow.

B57b   Shamina, V. B. "Mif i amerikanskaiā drama: Īu. O'Nil.
          Traur--uchast' Elektry; T. Uil'iams. Orfeĭ spuskaetciā v
          ad." Avtoref. Diss. na soisk. uchën. step. kand. filol.
          nauk. Leningrad.

B58   Smith, Susan Valeria Harris. "Masks in the Modern Drama." Diss
          Northwestern U.

       Points out that since Jarry's Ubu Roi, 1896, about 225 Western
       plays by playwrights such as Brecht, Cocteau, Genet, Ionesco,
       O'Neill, Pirandello, and Yeats have used masks. Categorizes the
       uses of the masks: to satirize; to suggest ritual and myth and
       invest the theatre with a communal spirit; to suggest man's inne
       life, to suggest the public or false face. Appendix lists some
       200 modern plays using masks.

859   Swanson, Margaret Millen. "Irony in Selected Neo-Hellenic Plays."
          Diss. U. of Minnesota.

       Studies works by O'Neill, Eliot, Sartre, Gide, Cocteau, and
       Ionesco, all derived from Greek drama. In Greek drama, the
       tension is between God and man, but in contemporary drama the
       tension is between conflicting aspects of man. Contemporary
       writers see no definite solutions, so they offer only tentative
       ones. Also, finds that in contemporary theater, judge and victim,
       who are distinct in Greek drama, may merge into a single character
       or protagonist.

                                    1980

860   Dakoske, Mary B. "Archetypal Images of the Family in Selected
          Modern Plays." Diss. U of Notre Dame.

       Draws on both British and American drama to study familiar
       archetypes in modern drama. Discusses O'Neill's Journey among
       others in terms of Jungian archetypes.

861   Hsia, An Min. "The Tao and Eugene O'Neill." Diss. Indiana U.

       Asserts that O'Neill's mysticism is essentially Taoist. Lists the
       basic tenets of Taoism and discusses Marco, Lazarus, Interlude,
       Fountain, and Brown as illustrating these tenets.

862   Jordan, John Wingate. "An Examination of the Plays of Eugene
          O'Neill in Light of C. G. Jung's Collected Works and Recorded
          Conversations." Diss. U of Houston.

       Compares Jung's writing with the most experimental O'Neill dramas
       written between 1916 and 1931. Notes that in certain instances
       O'Neill's stage directions and dialogue coincide verbatim with
       Jung's words. Finds Jungian influence in Thirst, Fog, Warnings,
       Horizon, Anna, Jones, Ape, Desire, Marco, Dynamo, Fountain,
       Lazarus, Interlude, and Electra.

863   Pike, Frank. "Confession as an Implicit Structuring Device in the
          Plays of Eugene O'Neill." Diss. U of Minnesota.

       Studies confession as a structuring device in Cardiff, Jones,
       Brown, Dynamo, Wilderness, Days, Touch, Hughie, Journey, Iceman,
       and Misbegotten.

B64 Watkinson, Sharon Anne Onevelo. "An Analysis of Characters in
       Selected Plays of Eugene O'Neill According to Erik H.
       Erikson's Identity Theory." Diss. New York U.

     Discusses Touch, Mansions, Iceman, Hughie, Journey, and
     Misbegotten in terms of Erikson's theory of identity. Notes that
     when he wrote Journey, O'Neill dispersed identity disorders among
     all four characters.

                                  1981

NONE

                                  1982

B65 Bloom, Steven Frederic. "Empty Bottles, Empty Dreams: O'Neill's
       Alcoholic Drama." Diss. Brandeis U.

     Examines the "realistic details with which the dramatist depicted
     the effects of habitual heavy drinking" and considers "the
     significance of alcoholism as a central feature of O'Neill's
     mature dramaturgy." Finds that O'Neill's portrayal of alcoholism
     and alcoholics in Iceman, Touch, Misbegotten, and Journey is
     consistent with "clinical observation" made subsequent to the time
     of the plays' composition. Holds, however, that O'Neill goes
     farther than verisimilitude by integrating the idea of alcoholism
     "into his vision" and by capturing the "despairing paradox of the
     human condition" in the contrast between "the romantic myth" about
     drinking and its reality.

B66 Como, Robert Michael. "The Evolution of O'Neill's Tragic Vision."
       Diss. U of Toledo.

     Maintains that Nietzsche's influence on O'Neill went beyond the
     thematic (the concern of most previous critics). Finds the formal
     implications in Nietzsche's tension between the Apollonian and
     Dionysian forces in life manifest in O'Neill's writing, from the
     early sea plays through Iceman. To "suggest primitive man's
     intimate relationship to the ebb and flow of life," "O'Neill set
     many of his early dramas away from civilization"--in the jungle
     on the sea. Settings for Ape and Iceman suggest the estrangement
     of modern man from the reality of his existence.

866a Hart, Doris. "An Historical Analysis of Three New York
          Productions of <u>Long Day's Journey into Night</u>." Diss. NYU.

367 Herzog, Callie Jeanne. "Nora's Sisters: Female Characters in the
          Plays of Ibsen, Strindberg, Shaw, and O'Neill." Diss. U of
          Illinois (Urbana).

     Sees Nora as the source of Strindberg's, Shaw's, and O'Neill's
     women. Women characters are described as types. Each playwright
     blends several types to produce major characters. But though the
     creative methods are similar, their aims are different: whereas
     Ibsen, Strindberg, and Shaw write to challenge conventional
     attitudes about women, O'Neill creates to reaffirm the
     conventional attitudes.

868 Kemper, Susan C. "The Novels, Plays, and Poetry of George Cram
          Cook, Founder of the Provincetown Players." Diss. Bowling
          Green U.

     Studies the philosophical ideas and literary techniques of George
     Cram Cook in two novels, two full-length plays, and a book of
     poetry--excludes collaborations and deals only with published
     work.

869 Smith, Madeline Catherine. "Eugene O'Neill and Sacramental
          Ritual." Diss. West Virginia U.

     Contends that O'Neill used rituals of the Roman Catholic Church to
     structure his plays. Ritual of Baptism is discussed in <u>Anna,
     Fountain</u>, and <u>Dynamo</u>; Communion, in <u>Lazarus</u>, <u>Iceman</u>, and <u>Journey</u>;
     Confession, in <u>Jones</u>, <u>Electra</u>, <u>Misbegotten</u> and <u>Iceman</u>; and
     Marriage, in <u>Welded</u>, <u>Days</u>, <u>Chillun</u>, and <u>Servitude</u>.

870 Sproxton, Birk Ernest. "Subversive Sexuality in Four Eugene
          O'Neill Plays of His Middle Period." Diss. U of Manitoba.

     Sees the period 1926-32 as needing special attention because
     O'Neill was then involved in a "sex research study" and in
     "analyzing conflicts in his family background" as well as writing
     plays. Of the plays of the period, <u>Lazarus</u>, <u>Interlude</u>, and <u>Dynamo</u>
     are for various reasons artistic failures, but these together with
     his one success--<u>Electra</u>--bring O'Neill to the forefront "as a
     major figure in the sexual revolution in American literature and
     an incisive critic of his culture."

B70a Szabó, K. "O'Neill tragédiafelfogása a kortársi elméletek
      tükrében." [The Tragic Theory of Eugene O'Neill, in Light o
      Other Contemporary Ideas]. Diss. Jozsef Attila
      Tudomanyegyetem [Hungary].

                              1983

. B71 Arai, Anuar Mohd Nor. "The Journeying Souls: The Verbal and
      Visual Quest in Metaphysical Theater and Film." Diss. U
      Southern California.

      Terms the modern theater of Strindberg, O'Neill, Ionesco, and
      Beckett, and the films of Bergman "pilgrimage dramas," wherein is
      evidenced a concern with "the abyss of fate," "the authors' own
      doubles," and the "dance of nostalgia." The authors in their
      works confront despair and "fears of life and death" through a
      metaphorical journey into self--a journey that may result in an
      exorcism of demons and in illumination. The journey, then, is a
      form of confession and therapy.

B72   Kobernick, Mark. "Semiotics of the Drama and the Style of Eugene
      O'Neill." Diss. U of Michigan.

      Discusses the "non-verbal signifying systems" in Eugene O'Neill'
      plays--Anna, Desire, Interlude, Electra, Journey, and Touch. Sa
      the study "theoretically grounds, then illustrates, the collecti
      of the data and their interpretation at three structural levels:
      the segment, the whole play, and the selected corpus." Says tha
      six semiotic dimensions have been found inherently valuable and
      adaptable to a controlled form: theatrical semiotic systems,
      motifs, dramatis personae configuration, personal awareness leve
      communicative functions, and Aristotelian divisions.

B73   Lloyd, David William. "The Tragic Sense of Eugene O'Neill." M.
      Thesis. U of South Africa.

      Surveys O'Neill's plays to show the movement of his tragic sense
      from crude melodrama to optimistic vision to disillusionment and
      despair (though with a "tentative element of hope" showing throu
      Journey "because some monumental meaning is proffered"). Specia
      attention is paid to Iceman and Journey.

B74   Schroeder, Patricia Richards. "The Presence of the Past in Mode
      American Drama." Diss. U of Virginia.

      Examines four modern American playwrights, including O'Neill, ir

their attempts to experiment with "dramatic structures in order to
portray a past that influences and partly constitutes present
stage reality." O'Neill experimented with methods of exposition
to define the relationship between past and present. The early
plays use "antimimetic expository techniques--to explore the
nature of a character's past"; in the later plays the "past
becomes an obsession of the characters and the exposition
itself . . . the central dramatic action."

1984

75 Hemmeter, Gail Carnicelli. "Eugene O'Neill and the Languages of
        Modernism." Diss. Case Western Reserve U.

    Studies language in O'Neill's work, which, Hemmeter says, has
    often been ignored or denigrated as stilted, repetitious. Says
    that O'Neill was experimenting with language as he was with
    form--creating a new language out of the remnants of melodrama,
    naturalism, and expressionism.

76 Shea, Laura. "Child's Play: The Family of Violence in Drama of
        O'Neill, Albee, and Shepard." Diss. Boston U.

    Examines six plays by three playwrights including Journey as
    representing a peculiarly modern feature in American
    drama--violence in the family. Sees violence as signifying a
    cultural system's attempting to "reassert its own integrity and
    difference, and thus its identity."

77 Shim, Jung Soon. "Self vs. Tradition: Images of Women in Modern
        American and Korean Drama." Diss. U of Hawaii.

    Three Korean and three American playwrights (including O'Neill) of
    the 1920's through 1970's represent two societies' "perceptions of
    and attitudes towards women, their changing roles, morality and
    values. . . ." Concludes that "most of the female characters
    examined . . . experienced an identity crisis because of the
    conflict between their own self-aspirations and traditional role
    expectations"; that male playwrights reflect "culturally
    stereotypical ideas about women"; and that American playwrights
    show women as having a "relatively stronger sense of
    individuality. . . ."

B78   Tuck, Susan. "Eugene O'Neill and William Faulkner." Diss.
         Indiana U.

      Asserts Faulkner's enthusiasm for O'Neill and studies the latter's
      influence on the novelist. Points out the similarities in the two
      writers' work, the impact of the Glencairn plays, Ape, and Jones
      on Faulkner's New Orleans tales, "analyzes expressionistic
      elements borrowed from O'Neill in As I Lay Dying," discusses black
      characterization in Chillun and Light in August, and compares
      Electra with Absalom, Absalom! and The Sound and the Fury with
      Journey.

B79   Vena, Gary A. "Eugene O'Neill's The Iceman Cometh: A
         Reconstruction of the 1946 Theatre Guild Production." Diss.
         New York U.

      Reconstructs the first performance of the Theatre Guild's Iceman,
      at the Martin Beck Theater 9 Oct. 1946. Uses interviews with some
      of the principals, promptbooks, photographs, newspaper accounts,
      rehearsal texts, and groundplans as sources. An appendix "offers
      a line-by-line account of the modifications of O'Neill's original
      text in relation to the script which emerges in performance" and
      "synopsizes more than forty-five reviews of the premiere
      performance."

B80   Wainscott, Ronald H. "A Critical History of the Professional
         Stage Direction of the Plays of Eugene O'Neill, 1920-1934."
         Diss. Indiana U.

      "Traces the development of stage direction" in O'Neill's plays
      from 1920-34. Considers 22 productions, beginning with Horizon
      and concluding with Days. "Study describes and evaluates what was
      most difficult for the directors, as well as what was most
      unusual, innovative, and historically significant." Concludes
      that there was a maturation in directing in that period, which
      corresponded with the development of serious drama.

                                    1985

B81   Mahmoud, Mahamed A. "A Stylistic, Sociolinguistic, and Discourse
         Analysis of Linguistic Naturalism in Selected Plays of Arthur
         Miller and Eugene O'Neill." Diss. U of Delaware.

      Suggests that language used by Miller and O'Neill, which has been
      largely ignored by scholars, bears a strong likeness to the
      language used by the uneducated classes they depict. Says their
      characters' language is orally-based, so it is often fragmented,
      repetitive, and formulaic.

1 Aarseth, Inger. "A Drama of Life and Death Impulses: A
     Thematical Analysis of Mourning Becomes Electra."
     Americana Norvegica [Oslo Universitetsforloget] 4:
     291-304.

An analysis of Electra concentrating "mainly on the
mythical--religious and symbolic implications of the underlying
conflict, which seems to originate in different religious
beliefs." Discusses the two impulses--adherence to a belief in
a just but severe Christian God and the attraction to a "pagan,
pantheistic belief." The pagan philosophy emphasizes the here
and now while the Christian (Mannon) philosophy looks to the
future.

Basney, Lionel. "Eugene O'Neill: Earthbound Aspiration."
     Christianity Today 23 Nov.: 17-22.

A 2,000-word introductory essay on O'Neill's themes, career,
reception, and techniques with short summaries of Marco, Brown,
Lazarus, and Electra that focus on O'Neill's religious
orientation. Finds O'Neill's religious statements
insubstantial. Says O'Neill sees tragedy as resting in the
failure of man's aspirations to find the truth he so mistakenly
seeks.

Booth, Willard. "Haunting Fragments from Eugene O'Neill." Adam
     39: 37-40.

The article occurs in a section entitled "Views and Reviews" and
suggests that O'Neill may have preserved Touch and Mansions for
a later trilogy. Stresses that O'Neill's thesis was that we are
what we are because our parents were what they were.

Coy, Stephen C., and Barbara Gelb. Letters. New York Times 8
     Apr.: II 21.

Exchange of letters between Coy and Gelb about her 4 Mar. 1973
article in the Times. Gelb said she thought James Tyrone
custodial yet resentful of Mary; Coy disagrees.

C5   Cunningham, Frank R. "The Great God Brown and O'Neill's
            Romantic Vision." Ball State U Forum 14.3: 69-78.

        The aim of society (Brown) to destroy Dion Anthony's creativity
        and the psychic conflict in Dion create the tension of the play
        Notes that the source of O'Neill's thought--Nietzsche's doctrir
        of eternal recurrence--is reflected in the play's structure and
        technique, and in the similarities between the prologue and the
        epilogue.

C6   Frazer, Winifred L. "O'Neill's Iceman--Not Ice Man." Americar
            Literature 44 (1973): 677-78.

        Asserts that O'Neill would have known the slang of the
        underworld of 1912--the period in which Iceman is set. Iceman
        meant an inmate whose promises were not to be relied upon or
        someone who bore worthless or trivial gifts, according to the
        Dictionary of American Underworld Lingo. Shows how these
        definitions are applicable to Hickey in Iceman.

C7   Gelb, Barbara. "Written in Tears and Blood. . ." New York
            Times 4 Mar.: II 19-20.

        Points out that when Journey was first performed, the
        recognition that it was about O'Neill's own family led to a
        reconsideration of his other plays--especially Chillun, Desire
        Brown, Electra, and Touch--and recognition of the
        autobiographical elements in them.

C8   Guruprasad, Thakur. "Experimentation with Dramatic Technique
            O'Neill's The Hairy Ape." Indian Journal of English
            Studies 14: 44-54.

        A "bird's-eye view of the multifarious [and long-noted] types
        experimentation involved in Ape.

C9   Hinden, Michael. "Liking O'Neill." Forum 2.3: 59-66.

        Evaluates O'Neill's strengths and weaknesses. Says that O'Ne:
        was a self-acknowledged "stammerer." His handling of languag
        was often inept--"language fails to meet our expectations."
        Notes that the language often improves as play progresses and
        that language of the middle-class is often plodding, but that
        the vernacular can be effective. Recognizing his limitations
        O'Neill concentrated on characterization and construction.
        Acknowledges that O'Neill's plays are not plays of ideas but

ritual, "a place for illumination of inner life." They are not
mere social diatribes.

10   Hinden, Michael. "The Birth of Tragedy and The Great God
            Brown." Modern Drama 16: 129-40.

Maintains that Nietzsche's interest in a fundamental unity
principle underlying all phenomena fascinated O'Neill
continually--even in his darker years when the vision had
slipped through his grasp. Thinks O'Neill responded to the
influence of Birth even in his sea plays, although some critics
think O'Neill had not mastered the book by the time he wrote
Brown, which elaborates most on Birth.

11   Josephs, Lois S. "The Women of Eugene O'Neill: Sex Role
            Stereotypes." Ball State U Forum 14.3: 3-8.

Contends that O'Neill never reached beyond traditional sex roles
after Beyond. Women in O'Neill plays belong to men and serve
their needs.

12   Kauffmann, Stanley. "Notes on Some New York Theaters."
            Performance 1.6: 82-87.

Some comments on the inadequacies of the new location of the
Circle in the Square company for staging Electra, a play "that
was dead before the playwright finished writing it."

12a   Kaul, R. K. "Tragedy and O'Neill." Jadavpur Journal of
            Comparative Literature 11: 93-106.

Sets O'Neill against the whole tradition of tragedy--Greek,
Renaissance, and modern--and then briefly comments on how
Electra, Lazarus, Brown, Interlude, Desire, and Journey fit
within the genre. Finds that O'Neill gives too much attention
to explanation, leaves too little room for inference. Still "in
fairness it must be added that he falls short because he aims
too high."

13   Labelle, Maurice M. "Dionysus and Despair: The Influence of
            Nietzsche upon O'Neill's Drama." Educational Theatre
            Journal 25: 436-42.

Discusses the Apollonian-Dionysian conflict, which is seen to
deepen in Desire.

C14   McLaughlin, Bruce W. "Strange Interlude and The Divine Comedy."
       The Theatre Journal [Albany] 12.2: 20-30.

       The author finds support for this thesis, that The Divine Come
       influenced O'Neill's Interlude, in Robert J. Andreach's work,
       which found a relationship between O'Neill's plays Ape and
       Fountain and Dante's work. Finds parallels in the structuring
       of the two works, in the use of the symbolic number three, in
       their concern with broken commandments, in their ethical
       concern, in their dependence upon characters who do not appear
       (Gordon Shaw and Beatrice).

C15   Mullaly, Edward. "O'Neill and the Perfect Pattern." Dalhousi
       Review 52: 603-10.

       Analyzes Mansions in terms of what O'Neill called the perfect
       pattern--an upright man gains power, abuses it, and this abuse
       leads to his downfall. Such is Simon Harford's lot.

C16   Nethercot, Arthur H. "The Psychoanalyzing of Eugene O'Neill:
       P.P.S." Modern Drama 16: 35-48.

       A second P.S.--he had published an article in two parts in
       Modern Drama in 1960 and 1961 and a postscript to them, after
       the Gelb biography, in 1965. Charming search for a book
       mentioned by Malcolm Cowley that O'Neill may have read by
       1923--which contains case histories in psychoanalysis. Survey
       briefly the building of the Yale collections of O'Neill's
       library. Also surveys the scholarly treatment of the influenc
       on O'Neill of modern psychology.

C16a   New York Times 14 Oct. 1973: VII 1.

       Article on house in Marblehead, MA, that once belonged to Eug
       O'Neill (1948-51).

C17   Reinhardt, Nancy. "Formal Patterns in The Iceman Cometh."
       Modern Drama 16: 119-28.

       Says aural and visual patterns and "purposeful patterning" he
       one to understand better O'Neill's play. Visual patterns
       include the symbolic positioning of tables and chairs and
       characters, and aural patterns include the repeated choral
       refrains, barroom songs, and antiphonal dialogue. These
       patterns reflect the play's paradoxical theme.

18   Rothenberg, Albert, and Eugene D. Shapiro. "The Defense of
            Psychoanalysis in Literature: Long Day's Journey into
            Night and A View from the Bridge." Comparative Drama 7:
            51-67.

        Contrasts the simple tension of Miller's play with the complex
        defensive sequence of O'Neill's.

19   Sayre, Nora. "Iceman Film does Justice to the Play." New York
            Times 30 Oct.: 36.

        Says that Marvin "has the salesman's slick authority, the talent
        for hustling . . . for invading privacy but lacks the necessary
        touch of the maniac spellcaster." Observes that the film
        close-ups destroy the ensemble impact of the group.

20   Scheibler, Rolf. "Hughie: A One-Act Play for the Imaginary
            Theatre." English Studies 54: 231-48.

        Comments on the difficulties of staging the play. Says play can
        reach its full development only in the imaginary stage of the
        reader's mind.

                                1974

1   Blesch, Edwin J., Jr. "O'Neill's Hughie: A Misconceived
            Experiment?" The Nassau Review: The Journal of Nassau
            Community College Devoted to Arts, Letters, and Sciences
            2: 1-8.

        Says that the problem with the play is that is is more like a
        monologue than a drama.

2   Cooley, John R. "The Emperor Jones and the Harlem Renaissance."
            Studies in the Literary Imagination 7: 73-83.

        Says that although O'Neill has a considerable interest in the
        subject of blacks from 1914-24, the roles were usually played in
        blackface. Cooley reevaluates Jones in terms of the Harlem
        Renaissance New Negro Movement (which celebrated black
        achievement and declared freedom from white myths and
        stereotypes of blacks). In this context he sees O'Neill's
        picture of Jones as a combination of a number of white
        stereotypes.

78

C23   Corey, James. "O'Neill's The Emperor Jones." American Notes
        and Queries 12: 156-57.

        A line-for-line comparison of how O'Neill patterned his witch
        doctor scene in Jones after Conrad's Heart of Darkness.

C24   Ditsky, John M. "All Irish Here: The 'Irishman' in Modern
        Drama." Dalhousie Review 54: 94-102.

        Discusses characteristics of the Irish in plays by Miller,
        Pinter, and O'Neill (Ape, Touch and Iceman). Irishman is
        displaced, a wanderer, a dreamer-poet, interpreter of life, a
        fighter, a drinker, and a loser. He is incompatible with the
        American success ethic. He is part of our heritage, and we al
        identify with him.

C25   Filipowicz, Halina. "Dream and Death in Gerhart Hauptmann's V
        Sonnenaufgang and Eugene O'Neill's Beyond the Horizon."
        Acta Universitatis Wratislaviensis 233: 69-83.

        Compares Hauptmann's and O'Neill's use of nonverbal
        devices--gesture, movement, music, lighting, coloring, and sta
        design, etc.--in two plays that are similar in their interchan
        of indoor with outdoor scenes throughout. Finds that O'Neill
        more visually than verbally oriented and that his dialogue
        rather supports or interprets what his settings, stage design,
        and lighting have already suggested.

C26   Fukushima, Osamu. "The Tragic Tone of Mourning Becomes
        Electra." Kyushu American Literature 15: 1-9

        A general discussion of alienation in Electra and of the
        symbolic tension created by the references to the South Sea
        Islands and the Mannon residence.

C27   Gelb, Barbara, and Tony Randall. Letters. New York Times
        24 Feb.: VI 70.

        Exchange of letters between Gelb and Randall concerning her
        "Jason Jamie Robards Tyrone" article in 20 Jan. 1974 issue of
        the New York Times.

28   Gelb, Barbara. "Jason Jamie Robards Tyrone." New York Times
            20 Jan. VI: 14-15, 58, 64-66, 72, 74.

        Covers Robards' career and points out similarities between him
        and James O'Neill, Jr., and between Robards and Eugene O'Neill.
        Includes his response to Lee Marvin's being chosen for the film
        Iceman.

29   Grecco, Stephen R. "High Hopes: Eugene O'Neill and Alcohol."
            Yale French Studies 50: 142-49.

        Contends that O'Neill's early drinking kept him from
        understanding himself. After he conquered his alcoholism, he
        wrote more understandingly and more strongly. Some observations
        about Caribbees and Iceman.

30   Gussow, Mel. "Jose Quintero's Long Journey Back." New York
            Times 28 Jan. 134.

        Recounts the peaks and valleys of Quintero's career--now at a
        peak with the success of Misbegotten.

31   Highsmith, James Milton. "The Personal Equation: Eugene
            O'Neill's Abandoned Play." Southern Humanities Review 8:
            195-212.

        Summarizes the play and shows how echoes of this early O'Neill
        reverberate in later plays. Draws parallels between the
        characters of Equation, its themes and concerns, and numerous
        other O'Neill plays.

32   Hinden, Michael. "Ritual and Tragic Action: A Synthesis of
            Current Theory." The Journal of Aesthetics and Art
            Criticism 32: 357-73.

        O'Neill and Jones, Electra, and Desire receive a couple of
        mentions but only in the company of other playwrights and a
        dozen other plays, as illustrations.

3   Krimsky, John. "The Emperor Jones: Robeson and O'Neill on
            Film." Connecticut Review 7: 94-99.

        Provides insights into the troubles O'Neill faced with
        censorship and racial prejudice during the 1933 film production
        of Jones.

C33a   New York Times   29 April 1974:   48.

        Note on the purchase of Monte Cristo Cottage by the Eugene
        O'Neill Memorial Theater Center.

C33b   New York Times   5 May 1974:   II 1.

        Comments on the controversy over the disposition of O'Neill
        estate.

C33c   Pavlov, Grigor. "Structure and Meaning in Eugene O'Neill's
             Mourning Becomes Electra." Annuaire de l'Université de
             Sofia: Faculté des lettres 68.1 (1974): 213-85.

        Begins with a survey of criticism since 1931 that is seen as
        reflecting two approaches: O'Neill's concern with the relation-
        ship between man and God and O'Neill's social-economic
        criticism, but usually developed by comparison and contrast
        between O'Neill's trilogy and the Oresteia. Concludes that
        O'Neill's play is too complex for "at and ready formulae."
        Then, devoting a section to each, analyzes the three parts of
        O'Neill's Electra. Finds in the three plays a pattern of
        repetition of situation, dialogue, and speech that in Homecomi
        grows naturally out of character and situation and focuses on
        socio-economic factors, but that in The Haunted because of his
        Freudian conception" "leads him to a mechanistic treatment of
        his characters . . ." that "runs counter to the complex
        dialectic conception of human nature he achieves dramatically
        Homecoming." In effect, a failure in the attempt to fuse the
        social, moral, and psychological.

C34   Richardson, Jack. "O'Neill Reconsidered." Commentary Jan.
             52-54.

        Uses the occasion of the publication of Sheaffer's second volu
        to elaborate on O'Neill's career. Finds O'Neill's work prior
        Journey, Iceman, and Misbegotten lacking because of O'Neill's
        desire to be a poet, his hope to restore antique forms of
        tragedy for modern use, and his desire to make "dramatically
        compelling" the prevailing philosophical and scientific notion
        Success in later plays due to some distance between O'Neill a
        his subject.

35   Scanlan, Tom. "The Domestication of Rip Van Winkle: Joe
          Jefferson's play as Prologue to Modern American Drama."
          Virginia Quarterly Review 50 (1974): 51-62.

          Argues that Jefferson's adaptation of Irving's story so softens
          and sentimentalizes as to give greater emphasis on the
          importance of the family structure thus prefiguring the family
          of O'Neill, Arthur Miller, and Tennessee Williams.

1975

36   Berkvist, Robert. "Hello, Columbus: A Playwright Explores
          Wonder and Terror." New Catholic World 218: 23-27.

          A general essay with two references to O'Neill. Of no
          importance to O'Neill scholarship.

37   Clarity, James F. Review of the Great Soviet Encyclopedia. New
          York Times 9 Jan.: 4.

          Comments that in the most recent volume of the Great Soviet
          Encyclopedia, O'Neill is treated without moral or social
          comment, whereas in the 1954 edition he was described as a
          "decadent American playwright." Iceman is no longer viewed as
          "a complete degradation."

38   Cunningham, Frank R. "Lazarus Laughed: A Study in O'Neill's
          Romanticism." Studies in the Twentieth Century 15: 51-75.

          Argues the difficulty of imagining in dramatic literature, "save
          Goethe's Faust II, such an attempt to create the Transcendental
          ideal . . . [the] ideal image of man" and of bringing "to
          fruition" his fusion of Nietzsche and Buddha begun in Brown.

9   Curran, Ronald T. "Insular Typees: Puritanism and Primitivism
          in Mourning Becomes Electra." Revue des Langues Vivantes
          [Belgium] 41: 371-77.

          The allusions to Typee and to the Blessed Isles in Electra are
          O'Neill's attempts to re-employ "in various forms the
          conventional image of exotic islands in order to gain a
          universally-conditioned response from his audience--escape from
          unpleasant reality . . . ." But whatever the islands mean to
          the audience, there is no escape for O'Neill's characters. For
          them, escape (the islands) is not only freedom but sexual
          license as well, and any suggestion of the latter revivifies the
          curse of their ancestral New England puritanism.

C40   Fiet, Lowell A. "O'Neill's Modification of Traditional America
        Themes in A Touch of the Poet." Educational Theatre
        Journal 27: 508-15.

        Goes back to James Steele MacKaye's Hazel Kirke and James A.
        Herne's Shore Acres to point out that O'Neill was still linked
        to nineteenth-century concepts, particularly in regard to the
        nuclear family.

C41   McDonough, Carole, and Brian McDonough. "Mourning Becomes
        Electra: A Study of the Conflict between Puritanism and
        Paganism." English Review 3: 6-19.

        Discusses pagan and Puritan elements in the play--the house,
        the Mannon ancestors, and the Mannons themselves. Says that t
        trilogy pits the "devastating effects of Puritanism"
        against the "free-seeking, life-loving forces of paganism."
        Concludes that the play's ending--Lavinia's reversion to
        Puritanism--"demonstrates O'Neill's admiration for the Puritan
        character" . . . "though he may not have agreed with its
        principles.

C42   Nethercot, Arthur H. "Madness in the Plays of Eugene O'Neill.
        Modern Drama 18: 259-79.

        In 42 of 45 published plays there is some form of mental
        instability. Both O'Neill's life and works indicate mental
        instability. Categorizes sources of the disorders in O'Neill'
        plays.

C43   Nethercot, Arthur H. "O'Neill's More Stately Mansions."
        Educational Theatre Journal 27: 161-69.

        O'Neill's themes of madness, loneliness, and mysticism are we
        developed in this last rough play.

C44   Novick, Julius. Review of Arvin Brown's artistic direction.
        New York Times 12 Oct. 1975: II 1, 5.

        Says that Brown has so invigorated the Long Wharf Theater
        company (New Haven, CT) that two of their productions have be
        viewed nationwide on public television and six have been
        transferred to New York, including Wilderness!

44a   Saqqaf, Abdulaziz Yassin. "The Nature of Conflict in The Hairy
          Ape." Journal of English [Sana'a Univ.]: 77-84.

44b   Sinha, C. P. "Eugene O'Neill and the Tragic Vision." Journal
          of the Bhagalpur University 6.2: 89-95.

       Argues that O'Neill's vision ws tragic and ties his vision to
       his biography. Says only in Lazarus and Wilderness did he
       strike a hopeful note. Says Misbegotten and Journey expresses
       his "eternal anguish." Nonetheless, says that to O'Neill, as to
       Nietzsche, tragedy is an affirmation, a celebration of life.
       Concludes O'Neill both wrote and lived tragedies.

5   Wharton, Don. "Eugene O'Neill: The Man Behind the Genius."
          Readers Digest May: 112, 176-78, 184.

       Strings together predictable glimpses of O'Neill--from O'Neill's
       own words and those of family, wives, and acquaintances.

1976

6   Adler, Thomas P. "'Through a Glass Darkly': O'Neill's Esthetic
          Theory as Seen through his Writer Characters." Arizona
          Quarterly 32: 171-83.

       Alluding to nine O'Neill writer-characters, Adler shows that
       from the poet Fog to Edmund in Journey, O'Neill demonstrated
       that writers can lift man from confusion to truth.

7   Cranston, Alan. "A Living Monument to Eugene O'Neill." New
          York Times 24 Oct.: II 7-8.

       Cranston (U.S. Senator from California) describes O'Neill's
       association with Tao House and the six-year struggle to get
       government support for the landmark.

7a   Frenz, Horst. "Eugene O'Neill: A Contemporary American
          Playwright."Eigo Seinen [Tokyo] 122 (1976): 34-39.

       Originally a paper delivered before the American Literary
       Society of Japan (Kagoshima, 26 Oct. 1975). Appreciative.
       Stresses O'Neill's universality. O'Neill, open to
       experimentation, strives to express his deepest fears in order
       "to cope with the basic questions of existence--problems and
       questions . . . which are still relevant today."

C48   Gabbard, Lucina P. "At the Zoo: From O'Neill to Albee."
        Modern Drama 19: 365-74.

        Says Ape and Zoo Story are both plays about men imprisoned
        within themselves--men who recall animals caged in a zoo.
        Ultimately ends up stressing the differences between the plays

C49   Gálik, Marián. Chao-the King of Hell and The Emperor Jones:
        Two Plays by Hung Shen and O'Neill." Asian and African
        Studies 12: 123-31.

        Hung Shen studied under George Pierce Baker in 1919-20.
        He probably saw Jones in the US; certainly he read it.
        Its influence shows in Chao-the King of Hell (1923) in
        scenic structure, character roles, forest setting, visions,
        sound effects, and in the finale. Says the difference is
        that Hung's expressionism was purely technical, not like
        O'Neill's. And so, his attempt to bring O'Neill to
        China--through imitation--failed.

C50   Going, William T. "Eugene O'Neill, American." Papers on
        Language and Literature 12: 384-401.

        Makes a well-documented case for O'Neill as a playwright in th
        mainstream of American authors, which include Frost, Melville,
        and Hawthorne. Describes O'Neill's plays as romantic in theme
        techniques, and setting and finds some of the romantic in
        O'Neill's life. Ultimately, though, decides that O'Neill's
        orientation was American and 20th-century--American in his
        rootlessness, in his need to dissolve family ties, in his sear
        for a moral center to replace lost religion, and in his
        themes--miscegenation, concern with prostitutes, with the sea,
        with New England, with the decline of urban life.

C50a   Hamilton, J. W. "Early Trauma, Dreaming and Creativity: the
        Works of Eugene O'Neill." International Review of
        Psychoanalysis Pt 3: 340-64.

C51   Levitt, H.N. "Comedy in the Plays of Eugene O'Neill." Player
        Magazine 51: 92-95.

        Analyzes O'Neill's plays according to Alan Reynolds Thompson's
        classification, in The Anatomy of Drama, 1942, of the six
        sources of laughter: comic taboo, physical movement and
        slapstick, plot, verbal, characters, and ideas. Charts 45
        plays.

2   Oliver, R.W. "From the Exotic to the Real: The Evolution of
       Black Characterization in Three Plays by Eugene O'Neill."
       Forum 13: 56-61.

    Illustrates the playwright's progress toward realism from Brutus
    Jones through Jim Harris to Joe Mott.

3   Powers, Dennis. "The Russians Said Hello to Dolly Levi." New
       York Times 5 Sept.: II 5, 24.

    Talks about the reception given to the American Conservatory
    Theater in Russia. Its two productions including Desire (Lyubov
    pod Viasami)--were excerpted in film for Soviet TV. Played the
    Lensoviet Palace of Culture in Leningrad. Mentions that two
    O'Neill plays are in rehearsal in Russian theaters.

4   Robinson, James A. "O'Neill's Grotesque Dancers." Modern Drama
       19: 34-49.

    Covers Jones, Ape, Desire, Brown, and Lazarus. Says all dances
    and choreographed movements within the plays enforce or define
    the themes of the plays.

a   Sheaffer, Louis. "O'Neill's Way." Confrontation 17: 169-70.

    Says that in reconstructing conversations between O'Neill and
    others in his biography on O'Neill, he "invented nothing" and
    "borrowed everything" and took an attitude of skepticism toward
    the playwright's own claims about himself.

    Stroupe, John H. "The Abandonment of Ritual: Jean Anouilh and
       Eugene O'Neill." Renascence 28: 147-54.

    Claims that the renunciation of rituals is the renunciation of
    life itself. Whereas Anouilh's characters, Antigone, Becket,
    Orpheus, perish when they refuse to yield to rituals which
    violate their ethics, O'Neill's characters accept social
    programming and survive. For O'Neill the stress is not on the
    quality of life but living.

C56   Törnqvist, Egil. "Miss Julie and O'Neill." Modern Drama 19:
       351-64.

       Points out similarities between the Electra trilogy and Miss
       Julie. Also considers in much detail the influence of
       Strindberg on O'Neill's early works.

                                    1977

C57   Berkvist, Robert. "Liv Ullmann's Love Affair with Eugene
          O'Neill." New York Times 10 Apr: II 1, 9.

       Interviews Liv Ullmann in Washington, D.C., while Anna is on
       tour before going to Broadway. Ullmann sees Anna as a stronger
       woman than is Ibsen's Nora--and sees Anna as rather like Josie
       Hogan--and says O'Neill's success in Scandinavian countries is
       the result of their people's capacity to accept symbols.
       Ullmann says the play reflects a modern attitude about
       women--Anna is seeking freedom "in the face of terrible male
       chauvinism."

C58   Berkvist, Robert. "Theater." New York Times 25 Dec: II 2.

       Briefly describes the relationship between Touch and the cycle
       that was to be called The Calms of Capricorn.

C59   Bogard, Travis. "C.W.D.'s at Tao House." EON 1.1: 3-5.

       Tao House, where O'Neill worked from 1937-1944, was setting o
       O'Neill's most intense work. At the end of each month O'Neill
       would note in his journal "C.W.D. 30," which meant 30 creative
       working days. Only breaks in creativity were caused by illne
       Here he wrote Touch, Mansions, Journey, Misbegotten, Hughie,
       Iceman, as well as worked on the 11-play cycle. Traces the
       history of the house to its presently becoming a historic sit

C60   Burke, Tom. New York Times 15 May: II 5, 22.

       Burke writes on Mary McCarty, who plays Marthy Owen in
       Quintero's Anna.

61   Carpenter, Frederic I. "The Enduring O'Neill: the Early Plays."
       <u>EON</u> 1.1: 1-3.

       Defends O'Neill's early plays, which he saw in the original
       performances and which moved and continue to move him strongly.
       <u>Desire</u>, <u>Beyond</u>, <u>Anna</u>, <u>Interlude</u>, <u>Jones</u>, and <u>Wilderness</u>, are
       enduring works.

62   Chabrowe, Leonard. "An Open Letter to John Henry Raleigh." EON
       1.2: 8-10.

       Chabrowe defends his book <u>Ritual and Pathos--the Theater of
       O'Neill</u> against Raleigh's review in <u>American Literature</u> (March
       1977).

3   Eder, Richard. Article on Liv Ullmann. <u>New York Times</u>
       26 Jan.: C15.

       Says of the upcoming production of <u>Anna</u> that when Quintero is
       directing, he suffers and imposes that suffering on his actors.

3a   Egri, Péter. "Eugene O'Neill: <u>The Iceman Cometh</u>." <u>Hungarian
       Studies in English</u> 11: 95-105.

       Drawing comparisons between Ibsen's <u>The Wild Duck</u> and Gorky's
       <u>The Lower Depths</u> and O'Neill's <u>Iceman</u>, Egri concludes that
       <u>Iceman</u> is a tragi-comedy of illusion and despair. Also
       discusses <u>Iceman</u> in terms of Goeth's progressive/retrogressive
       motifs, the former furthering the action and the latter
       retarding it.

4   Egri, Péter. "O'Neill in Hungary: A Letter." <u>EON</u> 1.1:
       15-16.

       Notes there is a great deal of interest in O'Neill in Hungary.
       Mentions the works by O'Neill which have been translated into
       Hungarian and comments on some scholarly treatments of O'Neill,
       including his own book.

       Floyd, Virginia. "Behind Life Forces in Eugene O'Neill." <u>EON</u>
       1.1: 5-13.

       Summarizes papers presented at the 1976 MLA session on Irish
       Catholicism, New England Puritan and Humanistic concerns in the
       plays of O'Neill. Papers by: John Henry Raleigh, "Irish
       Catholicism in O'Neill's Later Plays"; Frederick Wilkins,
       "'Stones Atop O' Stones,' the Pressure of Puritanism in

O'Neill's New England Plays"; Esther M. Jackson, "O'Neill the Humorist"; and Albert Bermel. "Theatre Poetry and Mysticism in O'Neill."

C66   Garzilli, Enrico F. "Long Day's Journey into Night (Mary) and Streetcar Named Desire (Blanche): An Inquiry into Compassion." The Theatre Annual 33: 7-23.

Says Journey and Streetcar are plays which reflect a decade's sensibilities. Still, though, they are able to "elicit in us . . . compassion and pity." Compares the two plays for the influence of the past on the characters Mary and Blanche, thei lost innocence, the elusiveness of affection and protection, a their homelessness.

C67   Gelb, Barbara. "Touch of the Tragic." New York Times Magazin 11 Dec.: 43-45, 118, 120, 122, 124-128, 130, 132-38.

As Quintero and Robards prepare for Touch's opening (25 Dec. 1977), Barbara Gelb interviews them. Stresses Quintero's identification with O'Neill.

C68   Hill, Philip G. "A New Look at Mary Cavan Tyrone." Southern Theatre 21.1: 11-17.

Argues that a close reading of Journey and careful study of O'Neill's relations with his own mother suggest that Mary Tyr was not the "sweet but victimized, saintly and long suffering lovable old lady" as usually portrayed but was "in fact . . . twisted, bitter, vicious woman who is herself the cause of mo of her family's troubles." Evidence of O'Neill's feelings toward his mother is derived from Sheaffer's biography.

C69   Innes, Christopher. "The Salesman of the Stage: A Study in Social Influence on Drama." English Studies in Canada 3 336-50.

Discusses Arthur Miller's Death of a Salesman, O'Neill's Icem and Jack Gelber's The Connection as plays dealing with salesn and materialism.

C70   Jackson, Esther M. "O'Neill the Humanist." EON 1.2: 1-4.

Sees O'Neill as following in the tradition of New Humanists (Babbitt, P.E. More) treating the same themes of democracy,

freedom, and crisis of faith and eventually exhibiting the same
"tragic humanism." Surveys plays from Thirst to Journey.

71   Kennedy, Joyce D. "O'Neill's Lavinia Mannon and the Dickinson
         Legend." American Literature 49: 108-13.

Suggests that Emily Dickinson and her sister Lavinia served as
models for Lavinia Mannon. Draws numerous parallels between the
sisters and O'Neill's character.

72   Kennedy, Joyce D. "Pierre's Progeny: O'Neill and the Melville
         Revival." English Studies in Canada 3: 103-17.

Compares Melville's Pierre to O'Neill's Electra and concludes
that O'Neill was influenced by Melville's work, but admits there
is no proof that O'Neill owned or had read the book.

73   Lucow, Ben. "O'Neill's Use of Realism in Ah, Wilderness!"
         Notes on Modern American Literature 1: Item 10.

Sees an implied criticism of the small town in the play. Says
that Richard must give up the wilderness for civilization, the
individual for society.

4   OhAodha, Michael. "O'Neill and the Anatomy of the Stage
         Irishman." EON 1.2: 13-14.

Suggests that the early O'Neill Irishmen were stage Irishmen but
that later Irish characters, such as the Tyrones, were more
real.

5   Quinby, George H. "O'Neill in Iran." EON 1.2: 10-12.

Comments on the performances of O'Neill plays in Farsi and
English in Iran when Quinby was there in 1956-57 and 1962-63.
Explains what Iraninans could and couldn't understand of
O'Neill. Lists the O'Neill plays translated into Farsi: Sea
Plays, Wilderness, Journey, and Straw.

6   Raleigh, John H. et al. "The Enduring O'Neill: Which Plays
         Will Survive?" EON Preview: 2-15.

Based on a panel discussion of 27 Dec. 1975. Discusses what
criteria should be used to judge the best of O'Neill's plays.
In addition to Raleigh, panelists include Doris Falk, Virginia

Floyd, Esther M. Jackson, and Frederick C. Wilkins. Some of the
considerations for judging O'Neill suggested by the panelists
are his use of dramatic technique, his ability to translate his
own life into drama, and his adherence to more conventional
European stage forms.

C77   Ryan, Pat M. "Stockholm Revives O'Neill." Scandinavian Review
          65.1: 18-23.

Narrates the circumstances leading to Karl Ragnar Gierow's
production of Journey in Stockholm, 1956, and, subsequently, to
other dramatic productions of Touch, Hughie, and Mansions.
Information rests, in part, on an interview between the author
and Gierow and on letters from Carlotta O'Neill in the archives
of the Royal Dramatic Theater.

C78   Sarlós, Robert K. "Response to the Preview Issue: A Letter."
          EON 1.1: 14-15.

Unhappy about the panel evaluation of O'Neill's plays. See
Raleigh, et al., in Jan. 1977 EON. Asserts that plays should
seen and evaluated in terms of potential for production. Find
merit in Interlude, Electra, Cardiff, Caribbees, and Rope.

C79   Scheick, William J. "The Ending of O'Neill's Beyond the
          Horizon." Modern Drama 20: 293-98.

Says Robert Mayo is articulate about his dreams at the beginning
of the play, but he dies inarticulate. Loss of verbal gift is
result of his dying away from his family and friends. Movement
toward silence is a result of disillusionment rather than
illumination.

C80   Scrimgeour, James R. "From Loving to the Misbegotten: Despair
          in the Drama of Eugene O'Neill." Modern Drama 20: 37-53.

Discusses O'Neill's treatment of the despairing human
consciousness throughout his career, showing the characteristic
of the human being in despair that changed and those that
didn't. O'Neill shows despair as a result of pride, anger and
self-contempt, which may lead to suicide. John Loving, Dion
Anthony, Caligula, characters in Iceman, and Jamie are
characters who despair.

81   Thompson, Leslie M. "The Multiple Uses of the Lazarus Motif in
         Modern Literature." Christian Scholar's Review 7: 306-29.

      Ranges widely over the literature of the 19th and 20th
      centuries. Pages 311-19 are on plays; pages 312-14 on O'Neill's
      Lazarus. Sees Lazarus as illustrating "the complexity of modern
      life and the existential leap of faith necessary for belief in
      the miraculous" and reflecting "not only the increasing
      secularization and demythologization of Christianity, but
      also . . . man's perennial concern with death and the variety of
      his responses to it. . . ."

82   Törnqvist, Egil. "O'Neill's Work Method." Studia
         Neophilologica: A Journal of Germanic and Romance
         Languages and Literature 49: 43-58.

      "A slightly different version" of his essay in Swedish:
      "O'Neill's arbetssat," Drama och Teater. Ed. Egil Tornqvist
      (Stockholm: Almqvist and Wiksell, 1968). Describes what
      writing means to O'Neill; where he does it best; when and for
      how long at a time; the evolution of a play from draft to draft;
      overlapping creativity; the differences between the production
      and the published version, etc.

83   Voelker, Paul D. "Eugene O'Neill and George Pierce Baker: A
         Reconsideration." American Literature 49: 206-20.

      Counters the prevailing notions about Baker's influence on
      O'Neill (especially Travis Bogard's) by suggesting that Baker's
      influence on O'Neill was a positive one.

84   Voelker, Paul D. "O'Neill and George Pierce Baker." EON 1.2:
         4-6.

      Abstracts Voelker's dissertation "The Early Plays of Eugene
      O'Neill, 1913-1915." See entry no. B29.

85   Wasserstrom, William. "Notes on Electricity: Henry Adams and
         Eugene O'Neill." Psychocultural Review 1: 161-78.

      Says Dynamo reveals the playwright's attractive to the optimism
      of Walter Lippman and Charles Beard in contrast to the pessimism
      of Henry Adams and D.H. Lawrence concerning the effect of modern
      mechanization on the human psyche. Wasserstrom reflects on the
      play after a production at Syracuse University. Says that
      O'Neill's theme in the play is betrayal; ultimately, O'Neill
      renounced an easy faith in progress.

C86   Weixlmann, Joe. "Staged Segregation: Baldwin's Blues for
            Mister Charlie and O'Neill's All God's Chillun Got Wings."
            Black American Literature Forum 11: 35-36.

        Says that Baldwin's play, blending symbolism and setting in an
        effort to point out the separation of white and black people,
        finds its inspiration in O'Neill's Chillun. But, where Baldwin
        most generally makes his points "with words instead of actions,"
        O'Neill "allows physical effects to substitute for verbal ones."
        Chillun is seen as a failure because 1) "racial attitudes . . .
        cause the play to crumble at the end," 2) O'Neill did not know
        enough of Negro life, and 3) character-behavior (especially
        Jim's) was implausible.

                                1978

C87   Bryer, Jackson R. and Ruth M. Alvarez. "American Drama,
            1918-1940: A Survey of Research and Criticism." American
            Quarterly 30: 298-330.

        Thirty or so items, all in Raleigh's essay in Sixteen Modern
        American Authors.

C88   Carpenter, Frederic I. "Hughie: By Way of Obit." EON 2.2:
            1-3.

        Sees Hughie as a "parable of the creative imagination." Says
        Hughie is highly autobiographical in that Smith's struggle to
        reach his audience parallels O'Neill's.

C89   Egri, Péter. "O'Neill Productions in Hungary: A Chronological
            Record." EON 2.2: 14.

        Lists O'Neill productions and years.

C89a   Egri, Péter. "The Short Story in the Drama: Chekhov and
            O'Neill." Acta Litteraria Academiae Scientiarum
            Hungaricae 20: 3-28.

        Discusses at some length the connection between the short story
        and drama in Chekhov's and O'Neill's plays. Mentions how
        several O'Neill one-act plays developed out of short stories he
        had written or others he had read. Says O'Neill used "short
        story-like dramatic units" early in his career to help him
        structure multiple-act plays--i.e. Servitude. Discusses
        Misbegotten as a play with "unmistakable Chekhovian

atmosphere"--the Janus-like quality of the characters, the
lyricism of the play, the use of symbols, and the open-endedness
of the acts.

C90   Floyd, Virginia. "Eugene O'Neill: Citizen of the World, Man
           Without a Country." EON 2.1: 6-9.

Gives highlights of three papers delivered at the 1977 MLA
Convention: Tom Olsson's "O'Neill and the Royal Dramatic,"
Timo Tiusanen's "O'Neill's Significance: A Scandinavian and
European View," and Péter Egri's "An East-European View of
O'Neill: The Uses of the Short Story in O'Neill's and Chekhov's
Plays."

C91   Floyd, Virginia. "The Search for Self in The Hairy Ape: An
           Exercise in Futility?" EON 1.3: 4-7.

Contends that Yank's quest is for the reality and fullness of
himself. It is this quest that the modern world refuses to let
him (modern man) engage in.

C92   Fluckiger, Stephen L. "The Idea of Puritanism in the Plays of
           Eugene O'Neill." Renascence 30: 152-62.

Says that O'Neill in his plays suggests the puritan mentality
and attitudes partly through setting and partly through
rhetoric. In the latter case puritanism is sometimes treated
half humorously--though usually it is seen as repressive.
Comments on Diff'rent, Iceman, Electra, Dynamo, and Brown, but
especially on Horizon and Desire.

C93   Frenz, Horst. "Three European Productions of The Hairy Ape."
           EON 1.3: 10-12.

Looking back on the early European response to O'Neill's plays,
Frenz finds that the playwright received his first positive
reaction with Ape in London, Paris, and Berlin.

C94   Fuchs, E. "O'Neill's Poet: Touched by Ibsen." Educational
           Theatre Journal 30: 513-16.

Suggests that a re-thinking of Ibsen may have been responsible
for the change in O'Neill dramaturgy between Days and Iceman.
Sees Touch as a pivotal play.

C95   Goldman, Arnold. "The Culture of the Provincetown Players."
            Journal of American Studies 12: 291-310.

        Gives a history of the early days of the Provincetown Players.
        Says the group "preserved something of a progressive social
        vision, focused it, prompted it and passed it on as a legacy to
        later artists, and to the intellectual community, and to the
        public."

C96   Green, Charmian S. "Wolfe, O'Neill, and the Mask of Illusion."
            Papers on Language and Literature 14: 87-90.

        Says that in Wolfe's play Mannerhouse, as in O'Neill's
        expressionistic plays of the 1920s, characters are
        alienated--in Brown by masked faces and in Mannerhouse by a
        cynical expression. Also, in Look Homeward Angel, Eugene Gant's
        encounter with the ghosts of his emerging identity may pay
        homage to O'Neill, whom Wolfe admired. Proffers that Wolfe may
        have seen O'Neill's Mariner in which masks were used. Says the
        Mannerhouse (1925) and Brown (1926) bear striking similarities
        in their themes (paradox of illusion and reality) and in their
        use of the divided character. Look Homeward Angel, which also
        deals with the paradox of illusion and reality, may also reflect
        a debt to O'Neill.

C97   Hinden, Michael. "Ironic Use of Myth in The Hairy Ape." EON
            1.3: 2-4.

        Sees the myth of Dionysus as presented by Nietzsche as treated
        ironically by O'Neill in Ape. Says that the modern world, which
        is without a mythic center, prevents the ancient triumphant
        Dionysus.

C97a   Hsia, An Min. [O'Neill and the Tao]. Chung Wai Literary
            Monthly [Taiwan] Dec.: 104-09. See no. A171.

C98   Hughes, Ann D. "Biblical Allusions in The Hairy Ape." EON
            1.3: 7-9.

        Identifies the ship's great furnaces with those of Moloch, which
        were fed by human lives. Suggests that O'Neill is implying that
        the workers are sacrificed to industrialism. Mildred's
        references to a leopard's spots, her father as president of
        Nazareth Steel, and Dr. Caiaphas point to Yank's alienation from
        heaven.

299   Kellman, Alice J. "The Emperor Jones and The Hairy Ape: A
         Beginning and an End." EON 2.1: 9-10.

      Notes that whereas Jones brought the Provincetown Players into
      the limelight, Ape marked an end to their experimentation.

100   Knight, Michael. "Design for New Theater Picked in
         Provincetown." New York Times 20 Nov: C16.

      Discusses the choosing of architectural plans for a new (the
      fourth) Wharf Playhouse in Provincetown, MA.

101   Lawson, Steve. "José, Jason, and Gene." Horizon 21: 36-42.

      Attributes to O'Neill the position of "foremost American
      dramatist" in response to the collaboration of Jason Robards and
      Jose Quintero in Iceman (May '56), Journey (Fall, '56), and
      later in Hughie, and Misbegotten, and on the occasion for this
      article, the dproduction of Touch.

102   LeClaire, Anne. "Provincetown Awaits Rebirth of Playhouse."
         Boston Sunday Globe 12 Nov: A20.

      Discusses the incipient stages in the rebuilding of the
      Provincetown Playhouse, destroyed by arson in 1977. The first
      steps include the assembling of various architectural firms in
      Provincetown and the briefing of these representatives on the
      history of the area.

103   Lemanis, Mara. "Desire Under the Elms and Tragic Form: A Study
         of Misalliance." South Dakota Review 16.3: 46-55.

      Says that the characteristics of tragedy are found in Desire,
      but says the play is closer to disaster, as defined by Robert B.
      Heilman, than to tragedy. Conclusion reached by study of the
      dialogue and actions surrounding Abbie's murder of her child.
      Says Ephraim has tragic stature, but experiences no rebirth.
      Says that Abbie, on the other hand, experiences the rebirth but
      lacks awareness. Such a "hybrid" results in a "miscegenated
      tragedy."

104   Morrison, Kristin. "Conrad and O'Neill as Playwrights of the
         Sea." EON 2.1 18: 3-5.

      Posits that it is possible that O'Neill read Conrad's play One
      Day More. Points out similarities between it and O'Neill's Ile,

Caribbees, and Voyage. Conrad, article concludes, was not a
good playwright whereas O'Neill was.

C104a   Prasad, Hari Mohan. "The Symbolism of the Sea in Eugene
        O'Neill's Plays." Journal of the Karnatak University:
        Humanities 22: 108-13.

Says the sea is an ambivalent symbol in O'Neill's canon. In th
sea plays, it is a personification of the life force and a
"device for emotional pressure." The rhythm and beauty of the
sea is mentioned in Electra. In Horizon it is a motivating
force. The sea is a presence in Journey and Wilderness, and in
Anna it is life.

C105   Quinby, George H. "A Humanitarian Playwright." EON 2.2:
        8-11.

Article is the speech Quinby delivered in Feb. 1923 at Bowdoin
College. Says that in Jones, Anna, Ape we are taken to "such
heights of tragic emotion that we are made to sympathize with
the lowest strata of society." Applauds O'Neill's choice of
characters and emotionalism.

C106   Reilly, Kevin P. "Pitching the Mansion and Pumping the
        Morphine: Eugene O'Neill's Long Day's Journey into Night.
        Gypsy Scholar 5: 22-33.

A psychoanalysis of Mary Tyrone aimed at revealing the reason
for her addiction. Mary's drug-taking seems to be "an attempt
to escape the excrementalized bodily self of the present into
the vision of the spiritualized self of the past." She is one
of O'Neill's divided characters. She feels sullied by marriage
and her suicide attempt could be seen as an attempt to cleanse
the body. She is embarrassed by self, and she sees James's
coaxing her into marriage as a betrayal. Concludes that Mary
Tyrone's inability to come to terms with excremental self is t
cause of her addiction.

C107   Robinson, James A. "Christianity and All God's Chillun Got
        Wings." EON 2.1: 1-3.

Contradicting what other critics have said about the play,
Robinson asserts that the ending is not inconsistent with what
has come before. Says racism, madness, and Christianity are
closely connected in Act I. Says that Jim is ultimately duped
his own racism and religion into becoming a slave to a white
woman.

108   Scheick, William J. "Two Letters by Eugene O'Neill." <u>Resources</u>
           <u>for American Literary Study</u> 8: 73-80.

       Comments on and prints the text of two letters by O'Neill, now
       in the Humanities Research Center of the University of Texas at
       Austin, hitherto unknown by the Gelbs. One, to Lawrence
       Langner, dated 5 April 1927, talks of the Theatre Guild's
       upcoming production of <u>Marco</u> and anticipates its possibly
       producing <u>Interlude</u>. The other, to Philip Moeller, dated 19
       August 1933, discusses suitable people to play in <u>Wilderness</u> and
       notes that it is not a New England play.

109   Shaughnessy, Edward L. "Question and Answer in <u>Hughie</u>." <u>EON</u>
           2.2: 3-7.

       Sees <u>Hughie</u> as a play of the spiritually and psychologically
       broken, who never quite bridge the gap between them.
       Nonetheless, they are not left completely adrift. The Handshake
       and roll of dice are symbols of rapport.

110   Szilassy, Zoltán. "The Stanislavsky Heritage in the American
           Theatre." <u>Studies in English and American</u> [Budapest] 4:
           201-12.

       Touches very lightly on the perseverence of the Stanislavsky's
       influence in America. The influence was first felt with the
       American visit of the Moscow Art Theatre. Its impact on the
       American Laboratory Theatre, then the Group Theatre, and the
       Actors' Studio was manifest in the growing concern with the
       creative participation, in plays, of both actor and audience, in
       the concern with existential problems, and in the use of
       tragicomic characters. References very general and slight to
       <u>Iceman</u>, <u>Journey</u>, <u>Days</u>, and <u>Lazarus</u>.

111   Voelker, Paul D. "Eugene O'Neill's Aesthetic of the Drama."
           <u>Modern Drama</u> 21: 87-99.

       Says O'Neill's theories are expounded informally in interviews
       and letters, but they exist. Essay concerns itself with four
       areas of his aesthetic--realism and expressionsism, tragedy,
       production techniques, and the affective aspect of plays. Says
       also that O'Neill stressed the play as written work.

C112   Watson, James G. "The Theater in The Iceman Cometh: Some
           Modernist Implications." Arizona Quarterly 34: 230-38.

        Finds that Iceman is not about illusions but about theater.
        Says that Hickey almost kills theater, but when he assumes the
        role of a madman, he restores it.

C113   Welch, Dennis M. "Hickey as a Satanic Force in The Iceman
           Cometh." Arizona Quarterly 34: 219-29.

        Says that perhaps a case can be made for Hickey as an image of
        Milton's Lucifer. Hickey, after all, is a rebel against man's
        God--illusion.

C113a   Wolter, Jurgen. "O'Neill's 'Open Boat.'" Litteratur in
           Wissenschaftund Unterricht 11: 222-29.

        Points out parallels between Crane's "Open Boat" and O'Neill's
        early work especially "Thirst" and Fog."

                                    1979

C114   Adler, Thomas P. "Two Plays for Puritans." Tennessee William
           Newsletter 1.1: 5-7.

        Finds that "the numerous correspondences in plot, stage settin
        characters, language, imagery, use of biblical allusions and t'
        Oedipal motif, and even similar quasi-religious religious or
        philosophical attitudes all suggest that Tennessee Williams ha
        O'Neill's Desire at least unconsciously in mind when he wrote
        Kingdom of Earth (The Seven Descents of Myrtle)." Concludes,
        though, that Kingdom fails as a play while Desire succeeds.

C115   Barlow, Judith E. "Long Day's Journey into Night: From Early
           Notes to Finished Play." Modern Drama 22: 19-28.

        Says in early versions of Journey, the characters are bitter a
        selfish. Final version tones down some of the bitterness.

C116   Berlin, Normand. "Ghosts of the Past: O'Neill and Hamlet."
           Massachusetts Review 20: 312-23.

        Enumerates the many similarities between the mad scene in Ham'
        and scenes in Journey. Also cites Jamie's association of his
        mother with a whore, as similar to Hamlet's, and compares

Jamie's and Hamlet's death wish. Makes a case for the psychic
pressures on O'Neill exerted by an extensive knowledge of Hamlet
and for Jamie as the portrayal of O'Neill himself.

117   Billman, Carol. "Language as Theme in Eugene O'Neill's Hughie."
        Notes on Modern American Literature 3: Item 25.

Billman argues that O'Neill's sense of dialogue and use of
dialect in Hughie dramatize his theme that human beings can get
through to one another by means of the link of language, the
failure of which is the cause of violence in other one-acts such
as Albee's Zoo Story and Amiri Baraka's Dutchman.

118   Bowles, Patrick. "Another Biblical Parallel in Desire Under the
        Elms." EON 2.3: 10-12.

Likens Eben to Adonijah, who infuriated Solomon by asking for
Abishag's hand. Both stories tell of a young man in competition
with his master. Eben, like Adonijah, will presumably be
executed. Abbie is like Abishag, who was brought to warm King
David in his old age.

119   Bowles, Patrick. "The Hairy Ape as Existential Allegory." Eon
        3.1: 2-3.

Discusses Yank as representing "the human self which is prior to
either primitive or civilized consciousness." He is like the
Heideggerian man, who "can never belong since he is ever a human
becoming and never a human being." Concludes Yank is
"spreadeagled between ape and essence."

120   Brooks, Marshall. "New London: A Mental Traveller's Note."
        EON 3.2: 7-8.

Description and pictures of Monte Cristo Cottage.

121   Carpenter, Charles A. "Elusive Articles, Books, and Parts of
        Books about O'Neill, 1966-78: Addenda to Miller." EON
        2.3: 29-31.

A supplement to Miller's Eugene O'Neill and the American Critic.

C122   Cline, Francis X. "O'Neill's Words Echo and Play at Sea View
            Hospital." New York Times 12 June: B3.

        Describes a dress rehearsal of Misbegotten that took place at
        the Sea View Hospital, the municipal nursing home on Staten
        Island, on 6 June 1979.

C123   Cunningham, Frank R. "The Ancient Mariner and the Genesis of
            O'Neill's Romanticism." EON 3.1: 6-9.

        Points out that O'Neill's early adaptation of Coleridge's poem
        dramatizing the reconciliation of man with nature, revealed an
        interest which the playwright never lost.

C124   Curtis, Anthony. "London." Drama: The Quarterly Theatre
            Review 133: 46-47.

        Says of The Long Voyage Home (includes Voyage, Zone, and
        Caribbees) that it is good early O'Neill, enriched by incident
        from his own life and worked up with "a certainty of touch."

C125   Dee, James H. "Orestes and Electra in the Twentieth Century."
            Classical Bulletin 55.6: 81-87.

        Examines five 20th-century plays that use the Orestes-Electra
        myth: Hofmannsthal's Elektra, O'Neill's Electra, Giradoux's
        Electre, Sartre's Les Mouches, and Richardson's The Prodigal.
        All five plays exhibit the playwrights' "own programmatic
        concerns" at the expense of the issues raised in their sources.
        Though the characters in O'Neill's Mourning are "impressive as
        projections of the intense forces struggling inside O'Neill
        himself," "the love-hate relations among the characters . . .
        have exaggerately precise symmetry that borders on the comical"

C126   Fairservis, Walter. "Managing the Magic of Marco Millions."
            EON 2.3: 18-21.

        Explanation of how he staged his Aug. 1978 production of Marco
        at the Sharon Playhouse, in Connecticut. Essentially, he used
        the stage manager, minimized scenery, and pared down speeches
        make the production viable.

C127   Filipowicz-Findlay, Halina. "O'Neill's Plays in Poland." EON
             3.1: 9-11.

        Traces the history of O'Neill's plays on the Polish stage and
        says that although theatre historians in Poland have considered
        O'Neill one of the foremost playwrights, theatres have been very
        slow in introducing him to audiences. Investigates possible
        reasons for this and concludes that O'Neill's work is still
        terra incognita to Polish theatre-goers.

C128   Frazer, Winifred. "A Lost Poem by Eugene O'Neill." EON 3.1:
             4-6.

        Using internal and external evidence, Frazer concludes that "The
        American Sovereign," a poem published anonymously in Emma
        Goldman's Mother Earth, was written by O'Neill.

C129   Frazer, Winifred L. "Revolution in The Iceman Cometh." Modern
             Drama 22: 1-8.

        Shows that a poem called "Revolution" by the 19th- century
        German revolutionary and lyric poet Ferdinand Freiligrath is the
        source for two important lines from Iceman: "The days grow hot,
        O Babylon!/ 'Tis cool beneath thy willow trees!" Frazer says
        besides supporting the love-death bridegroom-iceman connotations
        of the play, the lines illustrate that revolution is one of the
        foolish ways men try to improve society.

129a   Frenz, Horst. "Eugene O'Neill and China." Tamkang Review 10:
             5-16.

        Discusses the influence of Chinese philosophy on O'Neill--his
        admiration of it and his conclusion that it is ultimately
        incompatible with aspirations of Western man--by alluding to
        several O'Neill plays. Then Frenz discusses O'Neill's influence
        on Chinese drama, particularly on playwrights Hung Sheng and
        Ts'ao Yu.

130   Gatta, John, Jr. "The American Subject: Moral History as
             Tragedy in the Plays of Eugene O'Neill." Essays in
             Literature 6: 227-39.

        Discusses specifically American origins of O'Neill's vision and
        the dependence of his writing upon a native literary tradition
        in Desire, Electra, Touch, and Mansions. Describes the struggle
        in many of O'Neill's characters between self-reliance and greed.

C130a   Hamilton, J.W. "Transitional Phenomena and the Early Writing o
        Eugene O'Neill." International Review of Psychoanalysis
        [London] Pt 1: 49-60.

C131   Hinden, Michael. "Desire Under the Elms: O'Neill and the
        American Romance." Forum 15: 44-51.

        Says that Desire is probably one of O'Neill's most significant
        works in relation to the American tradition. Relates it to
        works by Emerson, Hawthorne, Melville, and Whitman.

C132   Hinden, Michael. "'Splendid Twaddle': O'Neill and Richard
        Middleton." EON 2.3: 13-16.

        Contends that the poetry of Richard Middleton, which O'Neill
        knew and quoted, according to Agnes Boulton, may have affected
        the young O'Neill, possibly providing the name for Richard in
        Wilderness. Middleton, a suicide at 29, wrote moody, love-sick
        verse, which, for very good reasons, is quite forgotten today.

C133   Kakutani, Michiko. New York Times 15 Oct.: C15.

        Describes an evening at the Public Theater (14 Oct. 1979), in
        which O'Neill's birthday was celebrated by a public reading of
        Barbara Gelb's "O'Neill and Carlotta" written for the occasion
        The work was a dramatic collage of O'Neill's and Carlotta's ow
        words from letters, papers, Journey, Iceman, and Misbegotten.
        Recordings of Carlotta's voice were included. The readers wer
        Jason Robards, Colleen Dewhurst, Jose Quintero, Geraldine
        Fitzgerald, Philip Anglim, and Madeline Kahn. The director wa
        Robert Allan Ackerman, and the producer was Joseph Papp. (Mos
        of these are members of the Theater Committee for Eugene
        O'Neill.)

C134   Kennedy, Andrew K. "Natural, Mannered, and Parodic Dialogue."
        Yearbook of English Studies 9: 28-54

        Lengthy article only briefly mentions O'Neill, although it is
        often listed in O'Neill bibliographies.

C135   Lask, Thomas. "Publishing: Robards on the Touch of O'Neill."
        New York Times 1 June: C22.

        Part of a column on publishing news says that Robards, at the
        urging of Nan Talese, a vice president of Simon and Schuster,
        may do a book about the "place and influence of O'Neill on his
        life."

136   McDonald, David. "The Phenomenology of the Glance in Long Day's
          Journey into Night." Theatre Journal 31: 343-56.

       Says the essence of Journey is "watchers being watched." The
       three men watch Mary, and she watches them until she escapes
       their glances through drugs. Discusses the effect of seeing and
       being seen on the identity and outcome of each character in
       Journey.

137   McIlvaine, Robert. "Crane's Maggie: A Source for The Hairy
          Ape." EON 2.3:: 8-10.

       Fathoms the points of comparison between Crane's work and
       O'Neill's. Says the dialect Maggie and Jimmie use parallels
       Yank's as do York's and Jimmie's childhoods. Also, there is a
       hint of the hairy ape imagery in Maggie.

138   Moin-Ul-Islam. "O'Neill and the Expressionistic Techniques of
          Drama." Journal of Research: Humanities [U of the
          Punjab] 14: 59-69.

       An introductory-level treatment of O'Neill as experimental
       dramatist. Finds him Americanizing European notions and
       theatrical techniques, and thereby freeing the American theater
       from its earlier commercial and unimaginative chains.
       Exemplifies his point by reference to Jones, Ape, and Brown.

139   Myers, Andrew B. "Hysteria Night in the Sophomore Dormitory:
          Eugene O'Neill's Days Without End." Columbia Library
          Columns 28.2: 3-13.

       Touches on the reception by theater critics, the public, and
       O'Neill's publisher of Days. The production's and book's
       failure resulted "obviously because O'Neill had no clear line of
       thought." Quotes from correspondence between O'Neill and
       Bennett Cerf. Says that "it seems likely" there is unpublished
       material [more correspondence] in the Random House archives.

140   Packard, Frederick C., Jr. "Eugene O'Neill Dramatic Innovator."
          EON 3.2: 9-12.

       Reprint of an article first published in Chrysalis, now a
       defunct publication. Article discusses Eugene O'Neill's major
       contributions to theater technique by showing the innovations of
       his most acclaimed plays--masks in Brown, asides in Interlude,
       and range and scope in Electra.

C140a   Prasad, Hari Mohan.   "The Tragic Mode: A Study in Eugene
            O'Neill's Beyond the Horizon, The Emperor Jones, and The
            Hairy Ape."   Osmania Journal of English Studies [Hyderabad]
            15:   21-30.

        Tragedy for O'Neill lives in the failure of his central
        character to preserve his illusions in the face of the onslaught
        of reality.   "The tragic character awakens to the truth that he
        is human and learns through suffering that to be human is to be
        fully tragic.   Applied to Horizon, Jones, and Ape.

C141   Prasad. Hari M.   "Symbols of Fog and Home in the Plays of Eugene
            O'Neill."   Rajasthan Journal of English Studies 10:   1-9.

        Explores several possibilities of the symbolism of fog in
        O'Neill's plays: as indictor of the characters' inner natures
        (Fog, Journey), of death (Cardiff, Interlude, Electra,
        Fountain), or as cleansing agent (Anna).   Says the fog symbol
        achieves "greater complexity and a more universal sense" in
        Journey.   Also touches on the symbolism of home in Cardiff,
        Chillun, Interlude, Desire, Electra, Beyond, Touch, Misbegotten
        and Journey.   Concludes that in O'Neill's work "the whole
        history of man's disinheritance, which is the central message"
        of the plays is "wrought in this symbol."

C142   Robinson, James A.   "O'Neill and Albee."   West Virginia U
            Philological Papers, 25:   38-45.

        Finds many parallels between the theaters of O'Neill and
        Albee--concern with the American family, the dead child motif,
        urban alienation, Strindbergian sexual conflicts, symbolic or
        allegorical characters, thin treatment of the loss of the
        Christian God.   Some may result from having similar family and
        personal histories, some from the similarity of the 1920s to the
        1960s; but some, "the confessional monologue and a similar
        treatment of the illusion-reality theme, demonstrate an
        indeniable O'Neill influence on Albee's work."

C143   Robinson, James A.   "O'Neill's Symbolic Sounds."   Modern
            Language Studies 9:   36-45.

        Analyzes sound effects in Jones, Ape, Lazarus, and Dynamo in
        terms of function and symbolic meaning.

144   Robinson, Leroy. "John Harold Lawson on Eugene O'Neill, Man and
         Playwright." EON 3.2: 12-14.

     Robinson summarizes previously unpublished comments by Lawson on
     O'Neill and Dynamo, which bears a close resemblance to Lawson's
     earlier play Nirvana.

145   Sewall, Richard B. "Long Day's Journey into Night." Cross
         Currents 29: 446-56.

     Essay is a new chapter in the new edition of Sewall's The Vision
     of Tragedy. Talks about Journey as O'Neill's Lear, Job, and
     Karamozov. The tragedy is, however, not heroic or "great" (no
     curse or ancestral sin), but it contains a vision of the
     good--or at least what was missing in the family (unclear which
     family is meant--the O'Neill or the Tyrone family).

146   Shaughnessy, Edward L. "The Iceman Melteth." EON 3.2: 3-6.

     Suggests that in Iceman and Journey O'Neill tapped his creative
     powers by searching familial and cultural roots for inspiration.
     Doesn't suggest that O'Neill became Catholic again, but that he
     used Catholicism to his plays' advantage.

147   Van Laan, Thomas F. "Singing in the Wilderness: A Dark Vision
         of O'Neill's Only Mature Comedy." Modern Drama 22: 9-18.

     Says the play Ah, Wilderness! has undertones of criticism of the
     family life it seems to extol: satirizes the sentimental
     characters and their responses to the Fourth of July. Says to
     recognize that O'Neill's attitude differs from those of his
     characters is to recognize the richness of the play.

148   Voelker, Paul D. "The Uncertain Origins of Eugene O'Neill's
         Bound East for Cardiff." Studies in Bibliography: Papers
         of the Bibliographical Society of the University of
         Virginia 32: 273-81.

     First discusses the changes O'Neill made when he rewrote
     Children of the Sea into Cardiff. Says O'Neill softened coarse
     elements and heightened softer ones. Attempts to pinpoint the
     date of revision and theorizes that the date of composition
     O'Neill gave (1914) might be an autobiographical fiction. Says
     that 1915-16 is the more probable date and that O'Neill may have
     invented the earlier date so as to deny the influence of George
     Pierce Baker on his writing.

C149   Wertheim, Albert. "Gaspard the Miser in O'Neill's Long Day's
           Journey into Night." American Notes and Queries 18:
           39-42.

        Points out the many connotations of the reference to old Gaspar
        the miser in Journey. Says the allusions mocks Tyrone, not onl
        for his penuriousness, but also for playing melodrama.

C150   Wiles, Timothy J. "Tammanyite, Progressive, and Anarchist:
           Political Communities in The Iceman Cometh." CLIO: A
           Journal of Literature, History, and the Philosophy of
           History 9: 179-96.

        Rejects notion that Iceman is only a private tragedy or to be
        seen only in universal terms and examines it to find a middle
        ground of social and political concerns. Finds three areas of
        social and political concern: leftist radicalism,
        establishmentarianism and reform.

                                    1980

C151   Adler, Thomas P. "The Mirror as Stage Prop in Modern Drama."
           Comparative Drama 14: 355-73.

        Discusses four dramas--Pirandello's It is So! (If You Think So
        O'Neill's Touch; Camus' Caligula; Genet's The Balcony; and thr
        musicals--Man of La Mancha; Cabaret; and A Chorus Line--in ter
        of the mirror as prop. Says of Con Melody that when he first
        stands in front of the mirror, he tries to erase the "son of a
        thievin' shebeen keeper" but in his last appearance, he parodi
        his earlier performance as major.

C152   Barbera, Jack Vincent. "Pipe Dreams, Games and Delusions."
           Southern Review 13.2: 120-28.

        Concerned with the opposition between Transactional Analysis
        Alcoholics Anonymous as they relate to the compelling alcohol
        of John Barrymore. O'Neill's Iceman is used to illustrate th
        determinism of AA.

C153   Billington, Michael. "Why Are American Plays Suddenly Popula
           in Britain?" New York Times 23 Mar.: II 5.

        Maintains that the "collapse of the gentleman-code of English
        drama" has opened the way for more "uninhibited" self
        expression. Among American plays in Britain are Hughie, Voya
        and Iceman.

154   Brooks, Marshall. "Harry Kemp: Lest We Forget." EON 4.1-2:
           15-17.

       Reminder of the eccentric Kemp, who was, a footnote to O'Neill
       biography, playing the part of the poet in the 1916 Wharf
       Theatre production of Cardiff. Says Brooks, Kemp "knew, abused,
       or bored the right people."

155   Chioles, John. "Aeschylus and O'Neill: A Phenomenological
           View." Comparative Drama 14: 159-87.

       Discusses Electra as phenomenological in the sense that it
       places man at the center of the world. Also discusses O'Neill's
       concept of trilogy, use of masks, and use of chorus vis-a-vis
       Aeschylus' use of the same.

156   Clurman, Harold. "What was Broadway's All-Time Best Season?"
           New York Times 9 Mar. II 1, 9.

       Clurman considers what might have been Broadway's greatest
       season, even though he concedes this is highly speculative.
       Suggests that 1919-20 season, when Horizon played at the Morosco
       Theater, might be a contender, but says his favorite season was
       1924-25, when Desire appeared. Says the number of plays that
       season coupled with the stature of the actors determine his
       choice.

156a   Cooper, Gary. "Sharks." Theatre Crafts 14.3: 40+.

       About the special effects used in a University of Wisconsin
       experimental production of Thirst. The most challenging problem
       was creating the illusion of sharks moving on the stage floor.
       1 photograph.

157   Costley, Bill. "Black Bread vs. Strange Interlude: O'Neill
       Parodied." EON 4.3: 14.

       Calls attention to a parody/synopsis of Interlude by Eric
       Linklater, Scottish novelist and dramatist, in his book Juan in
       America (1931). Also mentions the Marx Brothers one-reeler
       "Strange Innertube."

158   Costley, Bill. "Spithead Revisited, 1979." EON 3.3: 5-6.

       Brief recounting of author's 1979 visit to Spithead [Bermuda] to
       former O'Neill residence.

C158a Egri, Péter. "A Touch of the Story-Teller: The Dramatic
        Function of the Short Story Model in Chekhov's Uncle Vany
        and O'Neill's A Touch of the Poet. Hungarian Studies in
        English 13: 93-113.

        Applies the theory expressed in his "The Short Story in the
        Drama" to Uncle Vanya and Touch. See no. C89. Finds that the
        dramatic function of the short story as it relates to the two
        plays is in turning them into tragi-comedies by bringing about
        concurrence of the high point of emotional tension, the turnin
        point of the plot and the "culminating point of the dramatic
        action: at the "penultimate structural unit (rather than at th
        end) of the play. . . ."

C158b Egri, Péter. "The Genetic and Generic Aspect of Stephen Crane
        The Red Badge of Courage." Acta Litteraria Academiae
        Scientiarum Hungaricae 22: 333-48.

        Explains why Crane's novel is not historical nor naturalistic
        fiction, nor an epic work. Only the last two pages mention
        O'Neill. Egri compares the charge led by Orin Mannon in Elect
        to that of Henry Fleming. Both react as if they were in a
        trance, both suffer head wounds, and both react with certain
        barbarism.

C158c Egri, Péter. "The Reinterpretation of the Chekhovian Mosiac
        Design in O'Neill's Long Day's Journey into Night." Act.
        Litteraria Academiae Scientiarum Hungaricae 22: 29-71.

        Lengthy discussion of Journey in terms of the use of short st
        patterns within the drama--"collision between material gain a
        spiritual loss; the conflict of illusion and reality; the
        constant oscillation of emotions between the poles of attract
        and repulsion, love and hate; and the confrontation of human
        aspirations and the workings of fate"--as they apply to the
        characters in Journey.

C159   Hinden, Michael. "Desire and Forgiveness: O'Neill's Diptych
        Comparative Drama 14: 240-50.

        Shows a change in the playwright's attitude and technique
        between early and late plays. Citing many similarities betwe
        Desire and Misbegotten, Hinden illustrates the autobiographic
        nature of both and the different attitude O'Neill had toward
        mother, father and Jamie when he wrote the later play.

160   Hinden, Michael. "The Emperor Jones: O'Neill, Nietzsche, and
          the American Past." EON 3.3: 2-4.

       Contends that Brutus Jones represents not specifically the black
       man but all Americans who have forgotten in their
       acquisitiveness the liberating principles upon which this
       country was founded. Thus, the protagonist enslaves his spirit
       and tragically brings about his own destruction.

61   Hinden, Michael. "The Transitional Nature of All God's Chillun
          Got Wings." EON 4.1-2: 3-5.

       Posits that Jim Harris may be thought the son of Brutus Jones,
       struggling at the center of society rather than on an island,
       torn between his desire for success in the white world and his
       allegiance to his ethnic past.

62   Jurich, Joseph. "Jack London, and The Hairy Ape." EON 3.3:
          6-8.

       Compares the disillusionment of Yank with that of the hero of
       Martin Eden, both of whom die without hope of finding love or
       success. Both protagonists are rejected by society and both are
       lower-class seamen. Both O'Neill and London were torn between
       concern for the masses and rugged individualism.

63   Kellar, Deborah. "Staging A Touch of the Poet." EON 4.1-2:
          10-12.

       Describes her experience directing Touch at Centralia College,
       in Washington. Budgetary constraints necessitated some
       improvisations, which she discusses in the article.

4   Leonard, Hugh. "Can a Playwright Truly Depict Himself?" New
          York Times 23 Nov.: II 5.

       Discusses the factualness of autobiography, especially
       autobiographical fictions. Journey is criticized, not as a
       play, but as dishonest. Interprets all characters in play, save
       Edmund, as betrayers, who finally are absolved by Edmund.
       Claims O'Neill couldn't accept responsibility for betrayals.

C165   Mayberry, Robert. "Sterile Wedding: The Comic Structure of
          O'Neill's Hughie." Massachusetts Studies in English 7:
          10-19.

       Shows Hughie in a comic tradition, having its roots in ancient
       ritual: comic in structure, because death is at the end denied
       when Erie finds a successor to the dead Hughie; in order,
       rebirth and continuance being finally celebrated; and in tone,
       in that there is final relief from tension. The wedding of the
       article's title is a reference to the final handshake between
       Hughie and Erie; thereafter, they have a friendship which
       suggests a kind of wedding. The pattern of Erie's behavior is
       one of courtship.

C166   Nolan, Patrick J. "The Emperor Jones: A Jungian View of the
          Origin of Fear in the Black Race." EON 4.1-2: 6-9.

       Sees Jones as a play about a black man undermined by the
       materialistic goals of the whites. The fear arising from the
       loss of his old God and the psychological destruction of the n
       brings about Jones's personal and racial downfall.

C167   Pecile, Jordan. "Where the Long Day's Journey Began: The
          O'Neill House Restoration." Hartford Current Magazine
          28 Dec.: 4-7.

       Brief account for the general reader of the connection between
       the O'Neill's and New London. The focus is on "Monte Cristo"
       illustrated.

C167a Perry, Thomas Amherst. "The Contribution of Petru Comarnescu
          Romanian-American Relationships." Southeastern Europe/
          l'Europe du Sud-Est. 7.1: 91-98.

       Describes scholar-critic Comarnescu's efforts to acquaint
       Romania with American literature and drama. Touches summaril
       on his special interest in O'Neill and translations of O'Neil
       plays.

C168   Prasad, Hari Mohan. "Nuances of Soliloquy in the Theatre of
          Eugene O'Neill." Commonwealth Quarterly 5.7: 48-59.

       Discusses O'Neill's use of soliloquy, monologues and thought
       asides in the plays (both early and late). Says these devic
       reveal character, and expose the plot. Emphasis is given to
       Interlude, Iceman, and Journey.

169   Robinson, James A. "Taoism and O'Neill's Marco Millions."
         Comparative Drama 14: 251-62.

       Reviews the extent to which Taoist thought is exemplified in
       Kukachin, Kublai, and especially in the advisor, Chu Yin.

170   Robinson, LeRoy. "John Howard Lawson's Souls: A Harbinger of
         Strange Interlude." EON 4.3: 12-13.

       Finds in Lawson's Souls (unpublished and unproduced) a curious
       anticipation of O'Neill's Interlude. In the development of Act
       II and the use of asides O'Neill may have been influenced by
       Lawson.

171   Rutenberg, Michael E. "Bob Smith Ain't So Dumb." EON 3.3:
         11-15.

       Explains the problems of making Yank a sympathetic character.

172   Sabinson, Harvey. "A Coronet for O'Neill." Theatregoers' Guide
         (advertising supplement to the New York Times) 7 Sept.:
         12, 14, 17.

       Recounts a meeting he had with Carlotta in August 1959 in order
       to get her permission for his client Lester Osterman to rename
       his theatre, the Coronet, after O'Neill. Taken from his book
       Darling, You Were Wonderful.

173   Schvey, Henry I. "'The Past is the Present, Isn't it?' Eugene
         O'Neill's Long Day's Journey into Night." Dutch Quarterly
         Review of Anglo-American Letters 10: 80-99.

       A general discussion of the play with reference to O'Neill
       biography. Sees the Tyrones as simultaneously jailers and
       prisoners.

174   Snyder, Phillip A. "A Wanderer's Tether: The Meaning of Home
         in O'Neill's Ah, Wilderness! and Long Day's Journey into
         Night." Encyclia: The Journal of the Utah Academy of
         Sciences, Arts, and Letters 57: 103-09.

       Discusses two of O'Neill's autobiographical plays in terms of
       the depiction of home in each. Says that although the
       atmosphere of the plays differ, in both plays home is where you
       can expect to find a certain amount of sympathy and
       understanding.

C175   Viswanathan, R. "The Ship Scene in The Emperor Jones." EON
          4.3: 3-5.

        Points out that the imaginary ship in Scene VI isn't a slave
        ship, but appears to be a Jungian symbol of Jones's regression
        to his roots. Author sees the sea setting as reflective of
        Jung's conception of the water as the archetypal symbol of the
        soul and the return to it as representative of the desire to be
        united with one's spiritual self, to "disinherit" one's "native
        tradition, one's lost cultural legacy."

C176   Vyzga, Bernard. "Designing O'Neill's The Hairy Ape." EON 3.
          15-16.

        Explains how he conveyed the central idea of the play--man's
        movement toward suicide--through set design in the summer 1979
        production at Dartmouth of O'Neill's play. Comments on his
        reliance upon monochromatic colors and steel.

C178   Wittenberg, Judith B. "Faulkner and Eugene O'Neill."
          Mississippi Quarterly 33: 327-41.

        Says Faulkner's personal and professional lives gave him access
        to the work of Eugene O'Neill. Also, Faulkner had a strong
        interest in drama and knew at least five O'Neill plays: Anna,
        Straw, Gold, Jones, and Diff'rent. Compares some of these plays
        to works by Faulkner. Perhaps even Interlude and Electra
        influenced, in the case of the former, The Sound and the Fury
        and, in the case of the latter, As I Lay Dying and Absalom,
        Absalom!

                                1981

C179   Apseloff, Stanford S. "Eugene O'Neill: An Early Letter."
          Resources for American Literary Study 1: 109-11.

        In the Department of Special Collections of the Kent State U
        Libraries is a letter from O'Neill to Edward Pierre Loving and
        his co-editor Frank Shay giving them permission to use any one
        of the sea plays or Dreamy Kid in their planned anthology. The
        letter indicates that O'Neill valued Caribbees most.

180   Badino, Margareth M. Scarton. "The Self Destructiveness of an
         Idealist: A Study of Mary Tyrone in Eugene O'Neill's Long
         Day's Journey into Night." Estudos Anglo-Americanos [Sao
         Paulo, Brazil] 5-6: 118-36.

       Explains Mary Tyrone's symbolic regression at the end of the
       play as a search "for lost innocence." Memories and illusions
       provide no comfort, however, and "she finishes as a loser when
       attempting to regain it [her innocence] by retreating to her
       past."

181   Ben-Zvi, Linda. "Exiles, The Great God Brown and the Specter of
         Nietzsche." Modern Drama 24: 251-69.

       Full form of a paper presented at the Eugene O'Neill-James Joyce
       Section of the James Joyce Symposium, Provincetown, MA, June
       1980. Points to the numerous similarities between the two and
       suggests that Joyce's play Exiles may have influenced O'Neill's
       Brown.

182   Blau, Eleanor. "News of the Theater." New York Times 11 Mar.:
         C19.

       Announces the removal of Geraldine Fitzgerald's Journey from the
       Theater at St. Peter's Church to Joseph Papp's Anspacher--to
       open there 18 Mar. 1981.

183   Blesch, Edwin J., Jr. "Lots of Desire, No Elms: A
         Consideration of Eugene O'Neill's Desire Under the Elms on
         Film." The Nassau Review: The Journal of Nassau Community
         College Devoted to Arts, Letters, and Sciences 4: 14-22.

       Examines the 1958 Paramount Film of Desire. Based both on the
       original play and on a screenscript begun by H. L. Davis and
       completed by Irwin Shaw, which in turn was based on a 13-page
       scenario done by O'Neill in 1928. O'Neill's scenario is widely
       divergent from the original play--a drama of lust and greed but
       one lacking the mythic dimension of Desire. Says film is inept
       in technical execution, interpretation of roles, casting, and
       artistic conception.

184   Butler, Robert. "Artifice and Art: Words in The Iceman Cometh
         and Hughie." EON 5.1: 3-6.

       Says verbal and moral disintegration in Iceman are reversed in
       Hughie. In Hughie, Butler says, O'Neill allows characters to
       overcome the silence and alienation by creating with words a

fictive world, which could be the source of useful illusions.
Says whereas Hickey's illusions about Evelyn are debilitating,
Erie's are creative.

C185   Butler, Ron. "O'Neill's New London Turns Back." Boston Heral
           America 22 Feb.: B10.

        Reports on restoration projects taking place in New England,
        including work on Monte Cristo Cottage.

C186   Dunning, Jennifer. "Quintero Takes on an Early O'Neill." New
           York Times 7 June: II 5, 28.

        Surveys the autobiographical character of Welded and the
        original critical reception. Interviews Quintero who cut no
        words and sought "to capture the sense of ritual in movement
        that is a little stylized, in almost the way of dance." Also
        talks about Quintero's relationship with his cast.

C186a   Egri, Péter. "European Origins and American Originality: The
           Case of Drama." Zeitschrift fur Anglistik und
           Amerikanistik 29: 197-206.

        See no. C187.

C187   Egri, Péter. "The Iceman Cometh: European Origins and Americ
           Originality." EON 5.3: 5-10; 6.1: 16-24; 6.2: 30-36.

        Three-part article shows parallels between The Wild Duck and
        Iceman and Iceman and Gorky's The Lower Depths. Also notes
        affinity of O'Neill's play to Synge's "The Well of the Saints"
        and Conrad's short story "Tomorrow," which later became a
        one-act play "One Day More." Concludes that Iceman draws fror
        works by Ibsen, Gorky, Synge, Chekhov, and Conrad.

C187a   Egri, Péter. "The Merger of the Dramatic and the Lyric in
           Chekhov's The Sea-Gull and O'Neill's Long Day's Journey"
           into Night." Annales, Universitatis Scientiarum
           Budapestinensis: Sectio Philologica Moderna 12: 65-86.

187b   Egri, Peter. "The Plight of War and the Predicament of
           Revolution: Eugene O'Neill's The Personal Equation." Acta
           Litteraria Academiae Scientiarum Hungaricae 23: 249-60.

        First part of the article is a plot synopsis of Equation. Then
        Egri appends some observations about the play--that it
        anticipates later plays (Voyage, Horizon, Chris Christopherson,
        The Ole Davil, Anna, Dynamo, Straw, Iceman, Electra) and that it
        is a play built on antitheses.

188   Ellis, Ted R., III. "The Materialization of Ghosts in Strange
           Interlude." American Notes and Queries 19: 110-14.

        Contends that the third act of the nine-act Strange Interlude
        was influenced by Ibsen's Ghosts.

189   Feldman, Robert. "The Longing for Death in O'Neill's Strange
           Interlude and Mourning Becomes Electra." Literature and
           Psychology 31.1: 39-48.

        Nethercot's articles have indicated that the extent of Freud's
        influence on O'Neill is debatable. Feldman disagrees with most
        critics who stress the Freudian Oedipal element in O'Neill's
        work. Says the Freudian death instinct, though, is apparent in
        the playwright's work: Caribbees, Horizon, Interlude, and
        Electra.

190   Frenz, Horst. "Marco Millions: O'Neill's Chinese Experience
           and Chinese Drama." Comparative Literature Studies 18:
           362-67.

        Lightly touches on O'Neill's Chinese associations and then
        briefly summarizes O'Neill's influence on the important Chinese
        dramatists Hung Sheng and Ts'ao Yu.

190a   Harris, Andrew B., Jr. "A Tangible Confrontation: Welded:"
           Theatre News 13-7: 9-10.

        The producer of Columbia U's production of Welded addresses the
        reasons why Quintero chose this play. Says that although
        critical reception to the play was unfavorable, the choice
        proved valuable as a learning experience for the students.
        Discusses too Quintero's vision of the play--that the
        relationship depicted was like Carlotta and O'Neill's but that
        Eleanor is modeled on Agnes Boulton.

C191   Jackson, Esther M. "Eugene O'Neill's More Stately Mansions:
          Studies in Dramatic Form at the University of
          Wisconsin-Madison." EON 5.2: 21-26.

       Sums up findings of a research seminar on dramatic form in More
       Stately Mansions, which was conducted by Jackson and John D.
       Ezell.

C192   Lawson, Carol. "Broadway." New York Times 27 Mar.: C2.

       Reports on an interview with Earl Hymen, the James Tyrone of
       Geraldine Fitzgerald's Journey. Hymen comments on the
       universality of the play.

C193   Lawson, Carol. "Broadway." New York Times 10 Apr.: C 2.

       Announces that Jose Quintero will lend himself to the Eugene
       O'Neill Festival at Columbia U to give three lectures and direc
       a summer production of Welded to open 10 June for a four-week
       run.

C194   Lawson, Carol. "Broadway Celebrates Eugene O'Neill's Birthday
          New York Times 20 Oct.: C9.

       Discusses the doings at the third annual celebration of Eugene
       O'Neill's birthday at Circle in the Square Theatre (Fri., 16
       Oct.). Quintero received the gold O'Neill birthday medal.

C195   Miller, Ronald R. "History as Image: Approaches to the Stagi
          of Eugene O'Neill's More Stately Mansions." EON 5.2:
          26-32.

       Discusses the stage reading production of the play at the U of
       Wisconsin, which was conducted by Esther M. Jackson and John D
       Ezell.

C196   Moleski, Joseph J. "Eugene O'Neill and the Cruelty of Theater
          Comparative Drama 15: 327-42.

       Moleski argues that in view of the philosophy of Jacques Derri
       and the dramatic theory of Antonin Artaud, O'Neill's work can
       "resituated" within the tradition of Western metaphysics as an
       example of the logocentric quest for presence: the
       self-sufficient presence of song as pure sound undiluted by
       meaning, the desire to forget past and future in fulfillment
       a living present, and the self-presence of the "self-possesse

individual. O'Neill's defense of the possibility of presence
and the present is both structural and thematic. It dictates
the construction of the plays as well as an alternation of
dualities in which the "musical" rhythm of alternation is itself
the "subject" of the work (hope and despair in Iceman), and it
is the basis for the notion that the present can be restored
even if only through the articulation of its loss (Interlude).
O'Neill's later work reflects "the obverse of the doctrine of
presence," the recognition of "fate," the immutable, inviolable
past as a time of origins (Journey).

97   Nolan, Patrick J. "Desire Under the Elms: Characters by Jung."
         EON 5.2: 5-10.

      Points to the Jungian influence on O'Neill's play and to
      examples of the influence--the polarities, the god of
      materialism versus the god of love. Unlike Jung, O'Neill offers
      no resolution.

98   Pace, Eric. "Preserving the Homes Where O'Neill Lived and
         Worked." New York Times 8 Feb.: D5, 18.

      Discusses the restorations of the family cottage in Connecticut
      and the taking over of Tao House by the National Park Service,
      as well as the plans for a new Provincetown Playhouse.
      Speculates as to why the renewed interest in O'Neill.

99   Petite, Joseph. "The Paradox of Power in More Stately
         Mansions." EON 5.3: 2-5.

      Studies the play by itself rather than trying to fit it into
      some preconceived notions about O'Neill's work.

)0   Pettegrove, J. P. "'Snuff'd Out by an Article': Anna Christie
         in Berlin." Maske und Kothurn: Internationale Beitrage
         zur Theaterwissenschaft 27: 335-45.

      Examines the impact on O'Neill scholars (especially Frenz, the
      Gelbs, and Sheaffer) of Rudolf Kommer's 1924 New York Times
      article on the reception of Anna in Germany. Shows that
      Kommer's slick writing concealed his ignorance of matters
      theatrical and his incompetence as a judge of English-German
      translations. Finds that the first German Anna was based on
      The Ole Davil.

C201   Phillips, David. "Eugene O'Neill's Fateful Maine Interlude."
        Down East 28 (Aug.): 84-87, 99-108.

        A detailed look at the summer (June-Oct. 1926) O'Neill spent a
        Belgrade Lakes in Maine. Reveals imminent family breakup,
        discusses his work on Strange Interlude, and calls the summer
        turning point in his personal and professional lives.

C202   Raphael, Jay E. "On Directing Long Day's Journey into Night."
        EON 5.1: 7-10.

        Says Journey is a fusion of techniques O'Neill used in earlier
        plays; Raphael plans to use mystical lighting and sparse sets
        when he directs the play at U of Virginia.

C203   Rich, Frank. "A Short Day's Journey to Eugene O'Neill's
        Childhood Home." New York Times 6 Aug.: C15.

        Author spends a July 1981 weekend visiting Monte Cristo Cottag
        in New London and the O'Neill Theatre Center in Waterford. Sa
        American theater past and present intersect because the
        Waterford home is the setting of Wilderness and Journey and t
        O'Neill Theatre Center gives opportunities to rising playwrig
        to see and hear their work done.

C204   Rollyson, Carl, Jr. "O'Neill's Mysticism: From His Historic
        Trilogy to Long Day's Journey into Night. Studies in
        Mystic Literature [Taiwan] 1: 218-36.

        Considers O'Neill's Fountain, Marco, Lazarus, discussing
        O'Neill's mysticism. Says these plays are not that successfu
        because they rely too heavily on spectacle and because they a
        plays which do not invite us to identify with the characters.
        Language is also abstract in these plays. But in Journey
        O'Neill relies on language rather than staging and effects to
        communicate the mystical experience and so Journey is "his be
        attempt to render the mystical experience in dramatic form."

C205   Tuck, Susan. "Electricity is God Now: D. H. Lawrence and
        O'Neill." EON 5.2: 10-15.

        Suggests that Lawrence's Women in Love, and particularly the
        chapter on "The Industrial Magnate," may have been an influer
        on Eugene O'Neill's Dynamo. Although there was no copy of t
        book in O'Neill's library, Carlotta had one. Both Reuben Li
        and Gerald Crich try to understand this godless world throug

the display of power found in electricity. Both feared their
fathers, and both scorned Christianity. Finally, both
substitute science for religion and are brought to the brink of
insanity.

206   Tuck, Susan. "House of Compson, House of Tyrone: Faulkner's
            Influence on O'Neill." EON 5.3: 10-16.

Says the Compsons and Tyrones are similar. The Compsons of The
Sound and the Fury and the Tyrones are both held together by a
common past of betrayal, not love. Both works have
quadripartite structures, and both focus on a family destroying
itself.

                                1982

207   Ben-Zvi, Linda. "Susan Glaspell and Eugene O'Neill." EON 6.2:
            21-29.

Suggests Glaspell is not just a footnote in O'Neill studies.
Says O'Neill respected her opinions--she was, after all, an
established writer when they met. Suggests her play The Verge
may have influenced O'Neill's Ape.

08   Bordewyk, Gordon, and Michael McGowan. "Another Source of
            Eugene O'Neill's The Emperor Jones." Notes on Modern
            American Literature 6: Item 2.

Argues that O'Neill found his model for Brutus Jones in Marcus
Garvey, whose Universal Negro Improvement Association had its
spectacular convention in Harlem during August 1920, while
O'Neill was in New York. Says that Garvey spoke before
20,000-25,000 people in Madison Square Garden and, dressed in a
dazzling uniform, took part in a parade several miles long.
Finds that Jones and Garvey had similar personalities.

09   Drucker, Trudy. "Sexuality as Destiny: The Shadow Lives of
            O'Neill's Women." EON 6.2: 7-10.

Comments on O'Neill's limited view of women, despite the fact
that he was exposed to some of the most avant-garde women of his
day.

C210   Dutta, Ujjal. "The Iceman Cometh: O"Neill's Theatre of Alien
        Vision." Journal of the Department of English [Calcutta]
        17.2: 72-78.

        Argues that Iceman, rather than being a tragedy, belongs to th
        Theatre of Alien Vision, a genre anticipating the work of
        Ionesco, Pinter, Beckett, and Albee in which the artist views
        "life as essentially fragmentary," speaks from a "background o
        nullity," denies "all possibilities of positive structure," an
        "attributes to death an autonomous significance."

C210a Egri, Péter. "'Belonging' Lost: Alienation and Dramatic Form
        in Eugene O'Neill's The Hairy Ape." Acta Litteraria
        Academiae Scientiarum Hungaricae 24.1: 157-90.

        Discusses Ape scene by scene as a play in which the protagonis
        moves from a state of illusion of belonging to the realization
        that he doesn't belong to a search for belonging. Discusses t
        effect that stage directions have on the drama and O'Neill's
        repetition of vowel and consonant sounds.

C211   Egri, Péter. "The Dramatic Role of the Fog/Foghorn Leitmotif
        Eugene O'Neill's Long Day's Journey into Night."
        Amerikastudien 27: 445-55.

        Discusses "the central conflict and leitmotif-technique" of
        Journey, which is alienation versus the desire for communion
        with others. Related are the tensions between materialism and
        spiritual loss, love and hate, illusion and reality, and human
        aspiration and fate. The characters' attitudes toward the fog
        and foghorn are "intimately connected with these forms of
        conflict."

C212   Gillespie, Michael. "Eugene O'Neill: The Theatrical Quest."
        Claudel Studies 9: 43-51.

        Discusses O'Neill's use of the mask in Brown, revealing the
        divided self, and Journey, where he used dialogue, not stage
        techniques, to achieve the same result.

C212a Goldhurst, William. "Misled by a Box: Variations on a Theme
        from Poe." Clues: A Journal of Detection 3.1: 31-37.

        Studies the use of the box--"a starting point for speculation
        about the unknown"--in Poe's "the Oblong Box," Arthur Conan

Doyle's "The Little Square Box," and O'Neill's In the Zone.
Notes that John Colt's murder of Samuel Adams, covered in the
newspapers in 1841, may have been Poe's source.

213   Hinden, Michael. "When Playwrights Talk to God: Peter Shaffer
          and the Legacy of O'Neill." Comparative Drama 16: 49-63.

Discusses Peter Shaffer as O'Neill's successor. Like O'Neill,
Shaffer experiments with thought-asides, masks, mime, the split
protagonist, spectacle, and theme.

214   Kakutani, Michiko. "Hospital Remembers Rebirth of O'Neill."
          New York Times 18 Oct.: C14.

On the occasion of Gaylord Sanitarium's 80th anniversary, some
comments on O'Neill's response to the place. The article
considers how Gaylord influenced his writing (Straw) and
furthered his career (he read Synge, Ibsen, Yeats, Lady Gregory,
Brieux, and Hauptmann while there).

15   Linney, Romulus. "About O'Neill." EON 6.3: 3-5.

Reflects upon his exposure to O'Neill when the author was an
undergraduate and when O'Neill's reputation was at an ebb.
Recalls also his response to the Frederic March-Florence
Eldridge-Jason Robards Journey.

16   Mandel, Betty. "Absence as Presence: The Second Sex in The
          Iceman Cometh." EON 6.2: 10-15.

Says revelations about women in Iceman reveal hatred. Women are
expected to betray men, and even Larry Slade must face the
reason he left the movement was disgust at Rosa's infidelity.

17   Manheim, Michael. "Dialogue Between Son and Mother in Chekhov's
          The Sea Gull and O'Neill's Long Day's Journey into Night."
          EON 6.1: 24-29.

Studies the similarities between the mother-son relationships in
the two plays. Rejection, addiction, and suicide are central to
both plays.

122

C218   Manheim, Michael. "O'Neill's Transcendence of Melodrama in A
        Touch of the Poet and A Moon for the Misbegotten."
        Comparative Drama 16: 238-50.

        Says early O'Neill plays were not melodramatic, but after the
        deaths of O'Neill's parents in 1920s, his plays waxed
        melodramatic. In the 1930s, O'Neill came to terms with his
        memories of them. Melodrama is treated humorously thereafter
        Touch and Misbegotten.

C219   Nelson, Doris. "O'Neill's Women." EON 6.2: 3-7.

        Women in O'Neill's plays, are defined by their biological role
        and by their relationship to men. Says that in O'Neill's play
        women search for the perfect husband and marriage, whereas men
        seek beyond the domestic realm. In women, men look for lovers
        or parents, not intellectual companions.

C220   Oku, Yasuko. "An Analysis of the Fourth Act of O'Neill's Long
        Day's Journey into Night: Mainly His Application of the
        Comic Perspective." Studies in English Literature 58:
        43-61.

        Says that Mary is the "symbol of tragic suffering" in the play
        and that O'Neill, in order to make Mary's suffering appear
        universal, drew four parallel images of suffering and reduced
        her comicality. Concludes that the Fourth Act takes us beyond
        despair to an affirmation of life.

C221   Perrin, Robert. "O'Neill's Use of Language in Where the Cross
        is Made." EON 6.3: 12-13.

        Analyzes the syntax of Nat's language and discovers that his
        syntax is normal when he is talking to those he doesn't fear.
        However, when threatened by his father and when he begins to
        lose control, his syntax is less mature and less consistent.

C222   Ratliff, Gerald L. "Fog: An O'Neill Theological Miscellany.
        EON 6.3: 5-20.

        Considers Fog in terms of the biblical parable "when the
        inevitability of suffering is grasped, and misery and despair
        are understood as part of the divine pattern of transfigurati
        the darker side of life must appear to us permeated by a rene
        belief in the immortality of the human soul."

222a   St. Pierre, Ronald. "'So Happy for a Time': O'Neill and the
        Idea of Belonging." Shoin Literary Review [Shoin
        University, Japan] 16: 53-79.

223   Sarlós, Robert K. "Nina Moise Directs Eugene O'Neill's The
        Rope." EON 6.3: 9-12.

        Sarlós reconstructs the Apr. 26, 1918, production of The Rope
        despite the fact that there are no pictures of it. Instead,
        Sarlós relies on Heywood Broun's review and 1963 conversations
        with Nina Moise and Charles Ellis.

224   Strickland, Edward. "Baudelaire's 'Portraits de maitresses' and
        O'Neill's The Iceman Cometh." Romance Notes 22: 291-94.

        Suggests the influence of Baudelaire's collection of prose poems
        Le Spleen de Paris (Paris, 1869) on O'Neill's Iceman. Draws
        parallels between the settings, climactic suicides, and the
        writers' questioning of the excruciating perfection of women.
        Although no complete translation of the work was available in
        O'Neill's time, Modern Library had published an abridged
        version, translated by Arthur Symons. O'Neill knew some of the
        poems; in fact he quotes from "Envirez-vous" in Journey.

225   Timár, Esther. "Possible Sources for Two O'Neill One-Acts."
        EON 6.3: 20-23.

        Asserts that Recklessness may be based on a novella in
        Boccaccio's Decameron and that In the Zone may be based on
        Arthur Conan Doyle's "That Little Square Box" or Edgar Allan
        Poe's "The Oblong Box."

226   Tuck, Susan. "O'Neill and Frank Wedekind." EON 6.1 and 6.2:
        29-35, 17-21.

        Describes similarities in the backgrounds of the two
        playwrights. Says O'Neill may have seen Wedekind's work in NYC.
        Points out the similarities between Frulings Erwachen or Erwaden
        and Ah, Wilderness! Part Two compares Erdgeist to Interlude in
        terms of character and common elements in scenes.

227   Watt, Stephen M. "The 'Formless Fear' of O'Neill's Emperor and
        Tennyson's King." EON 6.3: 14-15.

        Suggests that O'Neill may have gotten the phrase "formless fear"
        from Tennyson's "The Passing of Arthur" in Idylls of the King.

C228   Wertheim, Albert. "Eugene O'Neill's Days Without End and the
        Tradition of the Split Character in Modern American and
        British Drama." EON 6.3: 5-9.

        Notes the problem of drama's demonstrating a divided inner and
        outer self. Later O'Neill learned that character could be more
        effective than special effects. In Touch, Misbegotten, and
        Iceman he is more successful at demonstrating the split
        character than in his earlier plays. May have gotten the idea
        for Days from Alice Gerstenberg's play Overtones. Says Days is
        important because O'Neill puts his finger on a technique which
        is now being refined and successfully used.

C229   Young, William. "Mother and Daughter in Mourning Becomes
        Electra." EON 6.2: 15-17.

        Says since Vinnie is blind to her desire to be like her mother,
        she is more a pathetic than a tragic character. Christine, on
        the other hand, has more of a mind of her own and realizes she
        has wasted much of her time. She is more tragic.

                                1983

C230   Adler, Thomas P. "'The Mystery of Things': The Varieties of
        Religious Experience in Modern American Drama." Themes in
        Drama: An Annual Publication 5. Ed. James Redmond.
        Cambridge: Cambridge UP. 139-57.

        Says American plays with religious themes tend to be "less
        orthodox and tradition-bound" in their theology than English
        plays. O'Neill's contributions to the subject are Dynamo,
        Desire, and Days (all three reflecting "the remnants of puritan
        thought" and "the execrescences of conservative Irish
        Catholicism, characterized by an ardent devotion to Mary);
        Lazarus (in which the physical persists though "eternally
        transmuted," something spiritual abides); and Iceman (in which
        Hickey's killing of Evelyn represents his unwillingness to
        accept forgiveness--viewed in contrast with the resolution of
        Days as reflecting an ambivalence about the relationship with
        God.

C231   Ben-Zvi, Linda. "Eugene O'Neill and Film." EON 7.1: 3-10.

        Discusses the changes made when O'Neill's plays were adapted f
        film. Plays treated include: Anna, Wilderness, Ape, Breakfas
        Jones, Interlude, Journey, Iceman, and Electra.

232   Carpenter, Charles A. "American Drama: A Bibliographic Essay."
        American Studies International 21.5: 3-52.

        A general bibliographical essay on American dramatic literature.
        Concentrates on dramatic literature rather than performances,
        books rather than articles and books published after 1950.
        Pages 24-28 concern O'Neill. The importance of O'Neill to the
        larger work is indicated by the way the essay is divided:
        playwrights before O'Neill and playwrights after O'Neill.

233   Egri, Péter. "Beneath The Calms of Capricorn: O'Neill's
        Adoption and Naturalization of European Modes." EON 7.2:
        6-17.

        Studies the embryonic text of Calms for influences. Concludes
        that O'Neill's work was influenced by Shakespeare, Ibsen, the
        well-made melodrama, the well-made farce, Wildean comedy,
        Shavian comedy, Symbolist tragedy, the morality play, Chekhov,
        Strindberg, and Expressionistic and Absurdist drama.

234   Gannon, Barbara C. "Little Theater in America: 1890-1920."
        Bulletin of Bibliography 40: 189-92.

        A bibliography on the subject. Includes three categories:
        (1) Books published about or touching on, published between 1911
        and 1978; (2) periodicals and newspapers published between 1891
        and 1958; (3) dissertations published between 1937 and 1974. A
        total of 90 items, most of them contemporary with the movement.

235   Grimm, Reinhold. "A Note on O'Neill, Nietzsche and Naturalism:
        Long Day's Journey into Night in European Perspective."
        Modern Drama 26: 331-34.

        Sees Journey as reflecting the tightly knit structure of any
        classical Ibsen play ("say, Ghosts")--family drama,
        "naturalistic" setting and language, the three unities, even a
        similar symbolism. But the endings are different. The
        "naturalistic" touch of optimism, is missing from Journey (using
        optimism to mean, rather, realism). Here O'Neill dramatizes the
        tragic world-view of Nietzsche, as expressed by Edmund--in an
        imagery recognizable as coming from The Birth of Tragedy.

C236   Grimm, Reinhold. "The Hidden Heritage: Repercussions of
        Nietzsche in Modern Theater and its Theory." Nietzsche
        Studien: Internationales Jahrbuch für die
        Nietzsche-Forschung 12: 355-71

        Deals mainly with Nietzsche with only incidental references to
        his influence on O'Neill.

C237   Krafchick, Marcelline. "Film and Fiction in O'Neill's Hughie."
        Arizona Quarterly 39: 47-61.

        Argues that Hughie can be a successful play through the use of
        film and technological audio devices to handle those points of
        the stage directions that cannot be presented through normal
        staging. In the process she disagrees with Raleigh that Hughie
        is unperformable and disagrees too with Scheibler and Tiusanen
        who say approximately the same.

C238   Lai, Sheng-chuan. "Mysticism and Noh in O'Neill." Theatre
        Journal 35: 74-87.

        Discusses the influence on O'Neill of Mabel Collins' Light on
        the Path, which O'Neill read around 1915. Says the book
        misunderstands the Eastern philosophy it tries to present. Th
        misunderstanding appears in O'Neill's experimental plays, whic
        failed partly as a result. Says last plays reflect influence
        Noh drama, which O'Neill had known from 1920s. Says Journey,
        Iceman, Hughie, and Touch are similar to Noh drama in theme an
        form, though not in style.

C239   Murphy, Brenda. "O'Neill's Realism: A Structural Approach."
        EON 7.2: 3-6.

        Contends that from the realistic viewpoint O'Neill's career wa
        a development of two earlier impulses--the search for theatric
        ways to depict the deepest reality of his characters within
        dramatic forms he discovered and the search for a dramatic for
        that would give true shape to his realistic dramatic action.
        Says O'Neill only fulfilled these impulses in Iceman, Journey,
        Misbegotten, and Touch. Discusses Iceman in terms of structur
        realism.

239a   Norton, Elliot. "30 Years Later, a Look at Eugene O'Neill's
          Long Day's Journey into Night." Boston Sunday Globe 27
          Nov.: 85, 89.

       Contains 500-600 words on O'Neill's years with Carlotta: their
       spats, his/her warts, and the impact on his writing. Good
       journalism, for an uninformed audience.

240   Raleigh, John Henry. "Strindberg in Andrew Jackson's America:
          O'Neill's More Stately Mansions." CLIO: A Journal of
          Literature, History, and the Philosophy of History 13.1:
          1-15.

       Studies O'Neill's evolution as a historical dramatist from
       Electra to Touch to Mansions. Sees the relationships of the
       characters in Mansions as reflecting what was happening to
       America in the 1830s--the period of economic speculation. It
       was a time of monetary instability, predatoriness, a scrambling
       for control, and a shifting of power. The relationships in the
       play mirror the larger world.

241   Sheaffer, Louis. "Correcting Some Errors in the Annals of
          O'Neill." EON 7.3: 13-25.

       Corrects many misconceptions about O'Neill's life, many
       promulgated by O'Neill himself, other mistakes by other
       biographers. For the continuation see no. C261.

242   Sipple, William L. "From Stage to Screen: The Long Voyage Home
          and Long Day's Journey into Night." EON 7.1: 10-14.

       Says John Ford's The Long Voyage Home, adapted from four O'Neill
       one-acts, and Long Day's Journey into Night, directed by Sidney
       Lumet, successfully transfer O'Neill's stage dramas to screen.
       Discusses why films are successful by considering aural and
       visual images.

243   Smith, Madeline Catherine. "The Emperor Jones and Confession."
          The Bulletin West Virginia Association of College English
          Teachers. 8: 17-22.

       Says that "in The Emperor Jones, O'Neill, consciously or not,
       drew on Catholic ritual to resolve dramatic conflict and
       reconcile man to himself and man to God." As penitent, Brutus
       Jones admits his faults, regrets his sins, and accepts Penance.

C244   Wilkins, Frederick C. "Lawson and Cole Revisited." EON 7.2:
        23-27.

        Recaps the responses of Marxist critics to O'Neill's work
        shortly after his death. Lester Cole attacked O'Neill and was
        vituperative in his response to Lawson's analysis of O'Neill's
        work.

                                1984

C244a   Bermel, Albert. "The Liberation of Eugene O'Neill." American
        Theatre (July-Aug.) (1984): 4-9, 42.

        Comments on O'Neill's plays by José Quintero, Geraldine
        Fitzgerald, Colleen Dewhurst, James Earl Jones, Katherine
        Hepburn, George Ferencz, and Arvin Brown.

C245   Bloom, Steven F. "The Role of Drinking and Alcoholism in
        O'Neill's Late Plays." EON 8.1: 22-27.

        Studies O'Neill's use of alcohol in Iceman, Touch, Journey, and
        Misbegotten and concludes that though characters who imbibe are
        seeking transcendence, they find disappointment and emptiness.

C246   Bogard, Travis. "'My Yosephine': The Music from Anna
        Christie." EON 8.3: 12-13.

        Says no song of this title was copyrighted, but apparently
        O'Neill borrowed it from a bartender at the Hell Hole, who made
        it up. A letter from O'Neill to Agnes Boulton indicates as
        much.

C247   Brooks, Marshall. "Eugene O'Neill's Boston." EON 8.2: 19-2

        A walking tour of O'Neill's Boston, which points out places
        where O'Neill lived and places which he frequented when he liv
        in Boston as a student and toward the end of his life.

C248   Cardullo, Bert. "The Function of Simon Harford in A Touch of
        the Poet." EON 8.1: 27-28.

        Sees Simon Harford as a foil to Con Melody in Touch. Simon is
        symbol of truth, while Con is a symbol of deception. But in
        Mansions Simon ceases to be a symbol of truth.

249   Carpenter, Frederic I. "Strange Interlude--Strange Criticism."
         EON 8.3: 22-24.

      The receptions of recent London productions of Interlude and
      Journey, the first panned by critics and loved by audiences, the
      second applauded by critics but unsuccessful causes Carpenter to
      reflect on the standards critics use to judge the works.
      Concludes that Journey, which abides by the unities, is
      appreciated for that reason, whereas Interlude is more
      experimental. Inveighs against a narrowness of perception that
      finds only the Poetics' standards acceptable.

250   Egri, Péter. "O'Neill's Genres: Early Performance and Late
         Achievement." EON 8.2: 9-11.

      Considers how O'Neill integrated non-dramatic forms into his
      drama--the novel, the lyric, and the short story.

250a Finegan, John. "Big Mystery of Eugene O'Neill." Evening Herald
         [Dublin] 16 June: 15.

251   Frazer, Winifred. "O'Neill's Stately Mansions: A Visitor's
         Reminiscences." EON 8.3: 15-21.

      First recounts her aborted attempt to link O'Neill's residences
      with the work he produced. Later made a connection between
      Iceman and the farmhouse that Emma Goldman lived at in Ossining,
      NY. Goldman allowed Terry Carlin and Donald Vose to live there.
      Vose obtained the address of liberal Matthew Schmidt and
      betrayed it to the police. Like Rosa Parritt, Goldman felt
      betrayed.

252   Gilmore, Thomas B. "The Iceman Cometh and the Anatomy of
         Alcoholism." Comparative Drama 18: 335-47.

      Looks at Iceman in terms of the theories of Alcoholics Anonymous
      and Vernon Johnson. Sees Hickey's new-found sobriety and his
      reasoning about it as a travesty of AA. Says Harry Hope's
      patrons are sociopaths--"drunks without guilt"; Hickey and Slade
      are alcoholics--drunks who see their obsession as a violation of
      some right. Hickey, though controlling his drink, does so
      without self knowledge and so unbalances himself. Slade's
      problem is the conflict between his desire to be a thoughtless
      drunkard and his inability to reject the demands put on him by
      his conscience.

C253   Kalson, Albert E. "When Strangers Meet: A Response to Frederi
          I. Carpenter." EON 8.3: 24-26.

        Kalson defends his reviews of Interlude and Journey (London
        productions) against Carpenter's charge of elitism and of
        sticking too closely to the unities.

C254   Krafchick, Marcelline. "Hughie: Some Light on O'Neill's Moon.
          EON 8.3: 8-11.

        Sees Hughie's affinities to Misbegotten. Says that although
        Misbegotten, Hughie, Iceman, and Journey all try to salvage fro
        despair, in Iceman and Journey the efforts end in calamity and
        self-revelations are thwarted. However, both Josie and Erie an
        able to convert their pain into a life-creating force.

C255   Lauder, Robert E. "The Renegade Haunted by God: Eugene
          O'Neill's Dream of Forgiveness." Commonwealth 14 Dec.:
          690-92.

        A priest responds to the 1984 Broadway production of
        Misbegotten. Notes O'Neill's inability to "get the church out
        of" himself. Sees Misbegotten as an expression in Catholic
        symbols of O'Neill's belief in "the Force behind" and man's
        struggle "to make the Force express him . . . instead of
        being . . . an infinitesimal incident in its expression." Cal
        attention to the scene in which Leveau's lighting suggests the
        Pieta.

C256   McDermott, Dana S. "Robert Edmond Jones and Eugene O'Neill:
          Two American Visionaries." EON 8.1: 3-10.

        Reviews the artistic relationship between Robert Edmond Jones
        and Eugene O'Neill in productions of Desire, Iceman, and
        Electra.

257   Perrin, Robert. "Bringing O'Neill's Works to Life in the Drama
            Classroom." EON 8.3: 13-14.

        A plea for producing O'Neill's plays. They are filled with
        strong characters, who have strong emotions; filled with
        extended monologues and scenes between pairs of characters;
        filled with smaller self-contained units within the longer
        works; filled with experiments with language that provide range
        for actors.

258   Regenbaum, Shelly. "Wrestling with God: Old Testament Themes
            in Beyond the Horizon." EON 8.3: 2-8.

        An analysis of O'Neill's play in terms of the Jacob and Esau
        story. The Mayos are like the biblical brothers, but whereas
        the existence of God is never in doubt in the biblical story, it
        is in question in this O'Neill play.

259   Rutenberg, Michael E. "Eugene O'Neill, Fidei Defensor: An
            Eschatological Study of The Great God Brown." EON 8.2:
            12-16.

        Studies Brown as one of O'Neill's Catholic plays. Says the
        play's "subject matter is God, Christ, and the subsequent
        evolution of man's Catholic religiosity."

260   Shaughnessy, Edward P. "Eugene O'Neill: The Development of the
            Negro Portraiture." MELUS 11.2: 87-91.

        Considers O'Neill's plays which portray blacks (Dreamy,
        Caribbees, Jones, Chillun, and Iceman). Says that in O'Neill's
        short plays, blacks are often one-dimensional, while in the
        longer plays, they "are more complex, showing a great depth of
        emotional capability which is only suggested in the early
        plays." Says that O'Neill's sensitivity to blacks grew, even
        though he still relied on stereotypes in Iceman.

C261   Sheaffer, Louis. "Correcting Some Errors in the Annals of
        O'Neill (Part II)." EON 8.1: 16-21.

        As the title suggests, the article clarifies some misconception
        about O'Neill biography. Includes information on the sources o
        O'Neill's plays, on Jamie's romance with Pauline Frederick, on
        O'Neill's drinking, and on his plans for Journey. See no. C24

C262   Sheaffer, Louis. "Correcting some Errors in Annals of O'Neill.
        Comparative Drama 17.3: 201-32.

        Reprinted in two parts in EON 7 (Winter 1983): 13-24 and 8
        (Spring 1984): 16-21. See nos. C241 and C261.

C263   Voelker, Paul D. "An Agenda for O'Neill Studies." EON 8.1:
        11-15.

        Surveys recent achievements in O'Neill scholarship--the
        publication of documents and letters hitherto unavailable, wor
        by Tornqvist, Halfmann, and Tiusanen on O'Neill's staging--and
        considers directions for the future--publication of an
        authoritative complete works of O'Neill, more productions of
        O'Neill plays, and the restoration of Monte Cristo and Tao
        House.

C264   Voelker, Paul D. "Politics, but Literature: The Example of
        Eugene O'Neill's Apprenticeship." EON 8.2: 3-8.

        Considers the political/social elements in O'Neill's early pla
        (The Web, A Wife for a Life, Thirst, Recklessness, Cardiff,
        Bread and Butter, Abortion, The Personal Equation) and conclud
        that The Personal Equation reflects O'Neill's criticism of
        political activists--that they are self-seeking. Says O'Neill
        opted for changes within the individual as a way of bettering
        society.

C265   Wilkins, Frederick C. "Hughie--By Way of Intro." EON 8.3:
        27.

        Wilkins' note finds that Hughie is like Cardiff in that at "e
        play's central core is a nighttime duet for two men whose
        spiritual and emotional communion provides comfort and solace
        against the surrounding menaces of life and death."

C265a   Wilkins, Frederick C. "Publications by and about Eugene
            O'Neill, 1980-1983." EON 8.2: 22-28.

        Bibliography of O'Neill publications, 1980-83.

                                1985

C266   Adler, Thomas P. "A Cabin in the Woods, A Summerhouse in a
            Garden: Closure and Enclosure in O'Neill's More Stately
            Mansions." EON 9.2: 23-27.

        Argues that in Mansions "O'Neill achieves closure through
        multiple images of enclosure." Act II, for example, ends as
        Simon is encircled by his mother and his wife. The play ends as
        Sara locks herself in the cabin and Deborah entombs herself in
        the summerhouse. Suggests that Electra and Journey also achieve
        closure through enclosure.

267   Black, Stephen A. "Ella O'Neill's Addiction." EON 9.1:
            24-26.

        Theorizes that Ella O'Neill's addiction was due to her fear of
        pregnancy and attributes her cure at the age of 56 to the
        release from that fear.

268   Bloom, Steven F. "Drinking and Drunkenness in The Iceman
            Cometh: A Response to Mary McCarthy." EON 9.1: 3-11.

        Bloom refutes Mary McCarthy's criticism of Iceman (based on the
        Martin Beck Theatre's 1947 production) that the characters show
        "virtually no evidence in the performance of the effects that
        such an amount of drinking as occurs in the play would actually
        have on human beings." Bloom says that O'Neill was very aware
        of what hardened drunks were like and depicted them accurately
        in Iceman.

269   Bogard, Travis. "Eugene O'Neill in the West." EON 9.2:
            11-16.

        Discusses O'Neill's conception of California in plays O'Neill
        envisioned and those he realized. Concludes that "so far as the
        west itself was concerned, O'Neill made little use of it, other
        than as a poetic, thematic image. California writer though he
        was, he remained an easterner in thought and deed."

C270   Brown, Carolyn T. "Creative Imitation: Hung Shen's Cultural
          Translation of Eugene O'Neill's The Emperor Jones."
          Comparative Literature Studies 22: 147-55.

       Recognizing David Chen's and Márian Gálik's earlier studies of
       the influence of O'Neill on Hung Shen, this essay examines the
       cultural implications suggested by the similarities between and
       differences in Jones and Yama Chao. Sees Jones as the "master"
       of his destiny, reflecting the classic ideal of hero struggling
       with fate, while Yama Chao is the "victim" of his destiny--a
       view which reflects in a radical form, a traditional eastern
       attitude.

C271   Cardullo, Bert. "Parallelism and Divergence: The Case of She
          Stoops to Conquer and Long Day's Journey into Night." EON
          9.2: 31-34.

       Finds comparisons between the two plays: both have a maid
       Bridget, who is absent, lazy, and cantankerous; both Hardcastle
       and Tyrone are nostalgic and overly thrifty; and both plays use
       disguise.

C272   Egri, Péter. "Epic Retardation and Diversion: Hemingway,
          Strindberg, and O'Neill." Zeitschrift fur Anglistik und
          Amerikanistik 33.4: 324-30.

       A recasting of Egri's "The Origins and Originality of American
       Culture: The Case of Drama" and "The Epic Tradition of the
       European Drama and the Birth of American Tragedy." Discusses
       retarding motifs in drama--factors which "hold up the pace" of
       the action. Egri distinguishes between retarding motifs and
       retrogressive ones, which "divert the action from its goal."
       Finds examples of retrogressive motifs in Hemingway's A Farewell
       to Arms and For Whom the Bell Tolls. Epic retardation is found
       in Sillitoe's "The Loneliness of The Long Distance Runner" and
       Strindberg's The Dance of Death. But he concentrates on
       O'Neill's Interlude, discussing a number of examples of "epic
       retardation." Concludes that the "novelistic building up and
       relinquishing of motive" help us to understand character.
       Suggests that O'Neill's own youth provided ample opportunity t
       witness how ambitions are thwarted. Finds in that Interlude t
       epic and dramatic fuse.

C273   Einenkel, Robert. "Long Day's Journey toward Separation: The
          Mary-Edmund Struggle." EON 9.1: 14-23.

       Says Edmund, at the start of the play, is the only family memb
       who can believe in Mary's redemption from addiction. He may

dying--his redemption looks to her redemption. Therefore, he
must separate himself from the immortal son that she sees him
as. The article discusses four scenes between mother and son.
Einenkel says Edmund's dropping of Mary's hand in their last
scene together symbolizes his releasing her forever.

274 Fleming, Robert E. "O'Neill's The Hairy Ape as a source for
        Native Son." College Language Association Journal 28.4:
        434-43.

     Contends that Ape influenced Richard Wright "in his creation of
     Bigger Thomas and Mary Dalton, in his attacks on religion and
     leftist political movements, and perhaps even in certain
     surrealistic elements in the setting of Native Son."

275 Gallup, Donald. "The Eugene O'Neill Collection at Yale." EON
        9.2: 3-11.

     Gallup's article indicates the extent of the holdings at Yale
     and explains the circumstances of their acquisition. Carlotta
     O'Neill's interest in gifts to Yale and her relationship with
     Gallup are explained in detail. He also explains Carlotta's
     decision to give publication rights to Yale of Journey.

276 Garvey, Sheila Hickey. "Recreating a Myth: The Iceman Cometh
        in Washington, 1985." EON 9.3: 17-23.

     Considers Quintero's 1985 production of The Iceman Cometh.
     Article provides background and makes observations about this
     production vis-a-vis the 1956 production.

277 Gelb, Barbara. "O'Neill's Iceman Sprang from the Ashes of His
        Youth." New York Times 29 Sept.: II 1, 4.

     Discusses the play in light of the Quintero-Robards revival.
     Notes that the play is highly autobiographical--that O'Neill is
     reminiscing about his days at Jimmy-the-Priest's. Suggests that
     Willie Oban is partly O'Neill. Recaps others' observations
     about the play.

278 Hawley, William. "The Iceman Cometh and the Critics--1946,
        1956, 1973." EON 9.3: 5-9.

     Discusses three American productions, focusing on the role of
     Hickey. Says the 1946 production had a strong ensemble, but a

weak Hickey; 1973 production had a strong Hickey, but a weak
ensemble; and the 1956 production was strong in both.

C279   Jenckes, Norma. "O'Neill's Use of Irish-Yankee Stereotypes in *A*
       Touch of the Poet." EON 9.2: 34-38.

       Discusses Irish stereotypes of early American theater and song.
       Says that in Touch O'Neill "redrew the stereotypes to suggest
       not merely their inadequacy but also their culpability, as part
       of a propaganda of assimilation, in generating false
       consciousness and raising false hopes of ultimate equality and
       acceptance."

C280   Manheim, Michael. "Eugene O'Neill: America's National
       Playwright." EON 9.2: 17-23.

       Tries to define a national playwright by showing what he is
       not--an apologist or a regionalist. His voice should be a broad
       cross-section of the population, and he must be well known.
       Says O'Neill's reputation as a national playwright rests on the
       plays at the end of his career. The characters' dialect in
       these plays, is recognizably American, as is their temperament.

C281   McQueen, Joan. "O'Neill as Seth in Mourning Becomes Electra."
       EON 9.3: 32-34.

       Contends that Seth is modeled after the playwright himself.
       Both speak of the sea, are privy to family secrets.

C282   Pond, Gloria Dribble. "A Family Disease." EON 9.1:   12-14.

       Discusses alcoholism as a family disease in Journey. Says the
       Tyrones reinforce one another's addictions and "use morphine,
       whoring, and greed as opiates analogous to alcohol."

C282   Roberts, Nancy L. "The Cottage with a Glimpse of Eugene
       O'Neill." Boston Sunday Globe 5 May: 25-26.

       Eighteen hundred words on Monte Cristo Cottage ("Hours: Monday
       through Thursday, 1-4 p.m. and by appointment") and the O'Neill
       connection. For the general reader.

283   Selmon, Malcolm. "Past, Present, and Future Converged: The
          Place of More Stately Mansions in Eugene O'Neill's Canon."
          Modern Drama 28: 553-62.

       Sees Mansions as a "watershed" play in O'Neill's canon in that
       even in its imcomplete form, its themes, character types,
       techniques repeat those seen in earlier plays or anticipate
       those of later plays, thus helping to clarify the continuity of
       that career--and especially in its "growing concern for the
       immediate past . . . in O'Neill's drama."

284   Sheaffer, Louis. "O'Neill's First Wife Defamed." EON 9.1:
          26-29.

       Corrects some of Bennett Cerf's stories about O'Neill's drinking
       (including the story of O'Neill's marrying his first wife
       following a night of drinking). Takes Donald Hall to task as
       editor of The Oxford Book of American Literary Anecdotes for
       reprinting the myth.

285   Vena, Gary. "Chipping at the Iceman: The Text and the 1946
          Theatre Guild Production." EON 9.3: 11-17.

       Considers the changes in dialogue made in the 1946 Theatre Guild
       production. Says the length of the play necessitated some
       cutting; some cuts were made to suit the physical attributes of
       the actors. Notes that most of the changes in dialogue were
       made in Hickey's lines.

286   Waterstradt, Jean Anne. "Another View of Ephraim Cabot: A
          Footnote to Desire Under the Elms." EON 9.2: 27-31.

       Sees Ephraim not as hard and unyielding but rather as "the most
       creative, the most fulfilled member of the Cabot family." Says
       that the stones with which Ephraim is identified are suggestive
       of his unity and strength. Concludes that he has experienced
       "something eternal."

287   White, George C. "Directing O'Neill in China." EON 9.1:
          29-36.

       White explains the problems he encountered directing Anna
       Christie in Beijing and comments on the adaptations made in that
       1984 production.

C288   Williams, Gary Jay. "Turned Down in Provincetown: O'Neill's
            Debut Re-examined." Theatre Journal 37.2: 155-66.

        Citing letters written by Hutchins Hapgood and Harry Kemp,
        Williams questions Susan Glaspell's recounting of O'Neill's
        arrival at Provincetown. Says that the evidence suggests that
        O'Neill's arrival was June, not July, 1916 and wonders why, if
        O'Neill's promise were recognized by George Cram Cook and
        Glaspell, no play of his appeared on the first billing (July
        13). Theorizes that Glaspell may have exaggerated O'Neill's
        reception to gain for her husband a sound place in the history
        of O'Neill's career. Also discusses the changes by O'Neill in
        reworking Children of the Sea into Cardiff--changes that may
        have resulted from his seeing Children in production.

FOREIGN LANGUAGE PUBLICATIONS

1973

1   Camilucci, Marcello. "Il dramma dell' Interiorita: Strano
    interludio." Studium [Italy] 69: 201-09.

2   Cortina, José Ramón. Ensayos sobre el teatro moderno. Madrid:
    Editorial Gredos.

    A portion (pp. 93-99) of chapter two is headed "O'Neill y The
    Iceman Cometh."

3   Dinu, Mihai. "Continuité et changement dans la stratégie des
    personnages dramatiques." Cahiers de Linguistique Théorique
    et Appliquée 10: 5-26.

    Solomon Marcus' idea for investigating dramatic works with methods
    developed from distributional linguistics is applied to fourteen
    plays including Journey.

    Drimba, Ovidiu. "Eugene O'Neill." Teatrul de la origine si pînă
    azi. [The Theater from the Origin to Date] Bucharest:
    Albatros. 345-8.

    Frenz, Horst, and Mary Gaither. "Amerikanische Dramatiker auf den
    Bühnen und vor der Theaterkritik der Bundesrepublik."
    Nordamerikanische Literatur in deutschen.Sprachaum seit 1945.
    Beiträge zu ihrer Rezeption. Eds. Horst Frenz and
    Hans-Joachim Lang. Munich: Winkler. 79-102.

    Frenz, Horst, and John Hess. "Die nordamerikanische Literatur in
    der Deutschen Demokratischen Republik." Nordamerikanische
    Literature im deutschen Sprachraum seit 1945. Beiträge zu
    ihrer Rezeption. Eds. Horst Frenz and Hans-Joachim Lang.
    Munich: Winkler. 171-99.

a   Fridshteĭn, Ĭu. "Lorens Oliv'e v p'ese O'Nila." Teatr [Russia]
    10: 127-28.

    Observations about the National Theatre (London) production of
    Journey.

    Gierow, Karl Ragnar. "Lång dags färd var fel pjäs." Svenska
    Dagbladet [Stockholm] 1 Apr.

140

D8   Koike, Misako. "O'Neill Kenkyu - Genjo to Kadai." Eigo Seinen
      [Tokyo] 119: 548-50.

D9   Kŏnya, Judit. "Utazás az éjszakába." Kalandozás a dramaturgia
      világában. Ed. Géza Hegedüs and Judit Kŏnya. Budapest:
      Gondolat. 240-52.

      Concerns Journey.

D9a   Mednikova, E. [Preface to and commentary on a trans. of Journey
      Three American Plays. Moscow: n.p.

D10   Paduano, Guido. "Manierismo e struttura psicologica
      nell'esperienza greca di Eugene O'Neill." Annali della
      Scuola Normale Superiore di Pisa. Classe di lettere e
      filosofia 3.2: 761-816.

D11   Sirakov, Martin. "Teatărăt na bunta i tragičnija svjat na Judzi
      O'Nijl" [The Theatre of rebellion and tragic world of Eugen
      O'Neill]. Godisnik na VITIZ 'Kr Sarafov' 13: 217-36.

D11a Voĭtkevich, N. "Dolgoe puteshestvie v noch'." Teatr [Russia]:
      66-69.

      Observations about a performance of Journey.

                                  1974

D12   Bécsy, Tamás. Utazás az éjszakába. A drámamodellek és a mai
      dráma. Budapest: Akadémiai. 294-300.

D13   Brantsaeter, Per L. "Eugene O'Neill - Hans skuespil og hans
      virkelighet." Samtiden: Tidsskrift for Politikk, Littera
      og Samfunnssporsmal 83: 166-72.

D14   Haas, Rudolf. "Eugene O'Neill: The Iceman." Das Amerikanisch
      Drama. Ed. Paul Goetsch. Düsseldorf: Bagel. 86-105.

5   Halfmann, Ulrich. "Eugene O'Neill: Beyond the Horizon." Das
       Amerikanische Drama. Ed. Paul Goetsch. Düsseldorf: Bagel.
       27-49.

6   Hoffmann, Gerhard. "Eugene O'Neill: Mourning Becomes Electra."
       Das Amerikanische Drama. Ed. Paul Goetsch. Düsseldorf:
       Bagel. 50-87.

7   Jordt, Heinrich. "Sucht und Charakter." Jahrbuch der Wittheit zu
       Bremen 18: 169-88.

7a Markov, P.A. O Teatre. 4 vols. Moscow: Iskusstvo 1974-1977.
       1: 490-91; 2: 98-100, 132, 295-6; 3: 191-92, 212, 334-35,
       357-59.

8   Pardo Gutiérrez, Nieves. "La Tragedía en el teatro norteamericano
       actual: O'Neill, Miller y Albee." Diss. U of Madrid.

                                1975

    Bérubé, Renald. "Eugene O'Neill." Liberté [Montreal, Quebec] 99:
       42-65.

a   Fateeva, S.P. "Pozdnee tvorchestvo Íudzhina O'Nila."
       Issledovaniía po romanskoĭ i germanskoĭ filologii. Kiev:
       n.p. 47-51.

    On the later works of O'Neill.

    Filipowicz-Findlay, Halina. Eugene O'Neill. Warsaw: Wiedza
       Powszechna.

a   Gelb, Barbara. "Dzheĭson Robards, Íudzhin O'Nil." Amerika
       [Russia] 19 (Jan.): 33-37.

    Translation of an article by Barbara Gelb on Jason Robards.

D21   Hensel, Georg. "Eines langen Tages Reise in die Nacht."
      Frankfurter Allgemeine Zeitung 29 Apr.

      Review of Journey directed by Rudolf Noelte, a production in
      German that opened 27 April 1975 at the Deutsches Schauspielhaus
      in Hamburg.

D22   Hoffmann, Gerhard. "Auffassungsweisen und Gestaltungskategorien
      der wirklichkeit im Drama: zum tragischen, komischen,
      satirischen, und Grotesken bei O'Neill." Amerikanisches
      Drama und Theater im 20. Jahrhundert. Eds. Alfred Weber a
      Siegfried Nevweiler. Göttingen: Vandenhoeck and Ruprecht.
      60-123.

D23   Kaes, Anton. "Charakterisierung bei O'Neill und Kaiser."
      Expressionismus in Amerika: Rezeption und Innovation.
      Tübingen: Niemeyer. 102-07.

D24   Kaes, Anton. "Expressionismus und der frühe O'Neill."
      Expressionismus in Amerika: Rezeption und Innovation.
      Tubingen: Niemeyer. 74-87.

D24a Malikov, V. "Trilogiia O'Nila." O'Nil Iu. Traur--uchast'
      Elektry. Moscow: n.p. 214-229.

      Commentary on a Alekseev's translation of Electra.

D25   Meged, Matti. "Shlosha Mishorim: Machaze Ehad (al Ish ha-kera
      Ba le-O'Neill)." Bama 64-65: 25-42.

D26   Michaelis, Rolf. "Hamburg: Noelte inszeniert O'Neill." rev.
      Eines langen Tages Reise in die Nacht. Theater heute, 16.
      6-8.

D27   Mounier, Catherine. "Le Marchand de glâce est passé d' Eugene
      O'Neill et la Mise-en-scène de Gabrial Garran au Théâtre d
      la Commune d' Aubervilliers." Les Voies de la Création
      théâtrale. Eds. Denis Bablet and Jean Jacquot. Paris:
      CNRS. 65-105.

      Excerpted and translated into English in Frenz and Tuck's Euge
      O'Neill: Voices from Abroad. See nos. A167 and A185.

28   Scheller, Bernhard. "O'Neill und die Rezeption
      Spätbürgerlichkritischer Dramatik." Zeitschrift für
      Anglistik und Amerikanistik 23: 314-21.

28a   Treĭmanis, G. "Poesiĭa sotsial'nogo i psikhologicheskogo
      obobshcheniĭa." Golos Rigi [Riga] 25 Aug.

28b   Tsimbal, I.S. "Tragediĭa otchuzhdeniĭa." Nauka o teatre.
      Leningrad: n.p. 260-76.

      On a production of Desire.

29   Vianu, Lidia. "O'Neill." Secolul XX [Romania] 168-69:
      140-51.

30   Wiese, Eberhard von. "Orationen für Maria Wimmer und Ouadflieg."
      Review. Eines langen Tages Reise in die Nacht. Hamburger
      Abendblatt 28 Apr.

                                  1976

1   Alagna, Giulia. "L' Aside in Strange Interlude." Blue Guitar 2:
      219-31.

2   Dalgard, Olav. Teatret i det 20. hundreoåret. Oslo: Det Norske
      Samlaget.

      An expanded edition of an earlier work that includes a brief
      introduction to O'Neill.

3   Döblin, Alfred. "Eugene O'Neill." Ein Kerl Muss eine Meinung
      haben. Berichte und Kritiken 1921-1924. Olten, Freiburg im
      Breisgau: Walter Verlag. 214-16.

      Künstler, Gustav. "Vom Wesenskern des dramatischen Kunstwerks als
      Vision der Menschheitskatastrophe--Beispiele von: O'Neill,
      Christopher Fry, Cocteau, Brecht, Lorca, Eliot, Georg
      Kaiser." Interpretationen: De Aussage dramatischer und
      lyrischer Werke. Vienna: Schroll. 88-113.

      Essays by the late Gustav Künstler, several, including the above,
      previously unpublished: Iceman, Mourning.

D35   Mennemeier, Franz Norbert. "Eugene O'Neill." Das moderne Drama
      des Auslandes. Interpretationen. Düsseldorf: Bagel.
      43-65.

D36   Müller, Henning. "Theater im Zeichen des kalten Krieges.
      Untersuchungen zur Theater-und Kulturpoliti in den
      Westsektoren Berlins 1945-1953." Diss. U of Berlin [West].

D36a Mylov, V. "Esli by ne O'Nil. . . ." Tiumen. pravda [Russia]
     17 July.

     On the Omsk production of Desire.

D37   Pašteka, Július. "Aspekty moderného tragična: metamorfózy
      tragédie v západnej dramatike." Estetické paralely umenia:
      štúdie o divadle, dramatike a filme. Bratislava: Veda.
      201-45.

      See pages 201-45 (especially 201-03, 205-07). Indexed.
      References to Anna, Jones, Dynamo, Lazarus, Electra, and Brown.

D38   Pašteka, Július. "Podoby a problémy moderného herectva: Tvár a
      maska v divadle i vo filme." Estetické paralely umenia:
      štúdie o divadle, dramatike a filme. Bratislava: Veda.
      51-74.

      See especially pages 66-71; also throughout the book. Indexed.

D39   Rühle, Günther. Theater in unserer Zeit. Frankfort a m Main:
      Suhrkamp.

D39a Shelmaru, T. "Dolgii den' yxodit v noch' Iu. O'Nila: (Teatr ir
     Sturdzy-Bulandry)." Rumyn. Lit. [Russia] 3: 129-31.

     Observations about the San Francisco touring company's producti
     in Russia of Desire.

D39b Smirnov, B. A. Teatr S.SH.A. XX veka: ucheb. posobie. Leningr
     gos. in--t teatra, muzyki i Kinematografii. 43-58.

     On O'Neill and the development of realism in the American theat

39c Tsimbal, I. S. "Ot O'Nila--k sovremennoĭ amerikanskoĭ drame: Preemstvennost' problematiki." <u>Sotsial'naĭa tema v sovremennom zarubezhnom teatre i kino.</u> Leningrad: n.p. 103-20.

40 Vodă-Căpusan, Maria. "Mască si destin la Eugene O'Neill." <u>Teatru şi Mit.</u> Cluj: Dacia. 96-111.

40a Zmudzka, E. "Przyjazie na pewno." <u>Teatr</u> [Warsaw] 24: 8-9.

1977

40b Buzduganov N. "Interesni proĭavi na mladite." <u>Teatur</u> [Sofia] 3: 34-35.

Concerns a production of <u>Desire</u> in the "Dramaticheskom teatre," Sofia.

1 Castro, Ginette. "Les Femmes dans le théâtre d'O'Neill: essai d'interprétation féministe." <u>Annales</u> [Center of Research on English-speaking America of the U of Bordeaux/ Talence]: 131-158.

2 Comarnescu, Petru. "Introducere la <u>Straniul interludiu</u> (1939)." <u>Scrieri despre Teatru.</u> Ed. Mircea Filip. Iaşi [Romania]: Junimea. 97-148.

Reprint of an essay first published in 1939.

3 Conradie, P.J. "<u>Mourning Becomes Electra</u> en O'Neill se Griekse droom." <u>Standpunte</u> [Capetown] 127: 17-36.

3a Gorshkova, V. "Krakh illiĭuziĭ. <u>Teatr. zhizn'</u> [Russia]: 14-15.

4 Grabes, Herbert. "Das amerikanische Drama nach O'Neill." <u>Die Amerikanische Literatur der Gegenwart: Aspekte und Tendenzen.</u> Ed. Hans Bungert. Stuttgart: Reclam. 28-48.

Surveys from the 40s to the 60s, from Broadway to off-off. O'Neill, Miller and Williams are dealt with under the rubric of "The psychological drama and its extension in the 1950s."

D45   Haas, Rudolf. "Das moderne Drama in Amerika als amerikanisches
      Drama." Die Amerikanische Literatur der Gegenwart: Aspekte
      und Tendenzen. Ed. Hans Bungert. Stuttgart: Reclam.
      112-21.

D46   Haas, Rudolf. Theorie und Praxis der Interpretation:
      Modellanalysen englischer und amerikanischer Texte.
      Grundlagen der Anglistik und Amerikanistik 5. Berlin:
      Schmidt. 193-211.

D46a Koreneva, M. "Zhizn' i tvorchestvo Iudzhina O'Nila v otsenke
      kritikov i biografov, 1970-e gody: Obzor." Sovrem.
      Khudozh. lit. za rubezhom. [Russia] 2: 107-13.

D46b Kostov, K. "NameReniia i vǔzmozhnosti." Teatǔr [Sofia] 4:
      18-20.

      Concerns a production of Desire in Bulgaria.

D46c Libman, V. A. Amerikanskaia literatura v russkikh perevodakhi
      kritike. Moscow: Nauka. 186-88.

D47   Link, Franz H. Dramaturgie der Zeit. Freiburg: Rombach.

D47a Liubimova, E. Iudzhin O'Nil i Dzhordzh Krem Kuk--opyt
      tvorcheskogo sodruzhestva: (Iz istorii teatra
      "Provinstaun"). Problemy Zarubezhnogo teatra i
      teatrovedeniia. Moscow: n.p. 62-77.

D48   Martin, Gerald. "Eine verspätete, aber gegluckte
      Zuckmayer-Premiere: zur deutschen Erstauffuhrung des
      Kranichtanz." Blatter der Carl-Zuckmayer-Gesellschaft 3:
      20-26.

D49   Müller, Kurt. "Die Benandlung der Rassen- und Klassen problema
      in den expressionistischen Stücken O'Neills." Konventione
      und Tendenzen der Gesellschaftskritik in expressionistisch
      amerikanischen Drama der zwanziger Jahre. Studien zur
      Anglistik und Amerikanistik. Frankfurt: Lang. 97-127.

49a Obraztsova, A. G. Sovremennaîà angliiskaîà stsena. Moscow:
     Nauka. 167-69.

50   Olsson, Tom J.A. O'Neill och Dramaten [with a summary in
     English]. Stockholm: Akademilitteratur.

     Recounts the Royal Dramatic Theater's staging of O'Neill's plays
     from 1923 on, but devotes most space to the Journey, Touch,
     Hughie, and Mansions productions. Includes correspondence between
     Carlotta O'Neill and Karl Ragnar Gierow. Sources include the
     RDT's archives.

50a Pinaev, S. M. "Na dne M. Gor'kogo i Rznoschik l'da griâdet
     Iu O'Nila: k voprosu o problematike i ideinom svoeobrazii
     p'es." Vopr. gor'kovedeniîà: (P'esa Nadne). Gorki
     [Russia]: n.p. 59-71.

50b Pinaev, S. M. "O nekotorykh osobennostîàkh dramaturgicheskoî
     tekniki Iudzhina O'Nila: (Semantika sveta i osveshcheniîà)."
     Iazyk i stil'. Volgargrad [Russia]: n.p. 100-09.

0c   Stefanov, O. "Dva spektakliîà." Teatŭr [Sofia] 2: 30-32.

     Refers to a production of Desire in Bulgaria.

1   Tiusanen, Timo. Linjoja: tutkielmia kirjallisuudesta ja
     teaterista. Helsinki: Otava.

1a   Wawrzyniak, E. K. "Rozgrzebywanie prezeszlości." Teatr [Warsaw]
     22: 1-7.

     Concerns a Polish production of Journey.

                                  1978

     Ahrends, Günter. Traumwelt und Wirklichkeit im Spätwerk Eugene
     O'Neills. Heidelberg: Winter.

     Bauzyte, Galina. "Eschilas ir Judzino o'Nylo dramaturgija."
     Literatura: Lietuvos TSR Aukstuju Mokyklu Mokslo Darbai,
     [Vilnius, Lithuanian S.S.R., U.S.S.R.] 20. 3: 36-39.

D53a Dneprova, I. "Problema nravstvennogo dualizma chelovecheskoĭ
      prirody v pozdneĭ dramaturgii Ĭudzhina O'Nila i eë
      sootnoshenie s khudozhestvennym metodom pistelĭa."
      Nekotoyre filologicheskie aspekty amerikannstiki. Moscow:
      n.p. 289-309.

D53b Dumitrescu, C. "Fire de Poet. de Eugene O'Neill." Teatrul
      [Bucharest] 11: 31-32.

      Concerns a Romanian production of Touch.

D54 Egri, Péter. "Csehov és O'Neill (Eugene O'Neill: Utazás az
      éjszakába)." Filológiai Közlöny 24: 231-35.

D54a Istoriĭa zarubezhnoĭ literatury posle Oktĭabr'skoi revoliĭutsii.
      Moscow: Izd-vo MGU [Moscow State University]. 292-298.

D55 Juhl, Peter. "Eugene O'Neills The Hairy Ape: Bemerkungen zu Si
      und Struktur des Dramas." Theater und Drama in Amerika:
      Aspekte und Interpretationen. Eds. Edgar Lohner and Rudolf
      Haas. Berlin: Schmidt. 235-53.

D56 Knežević, Debora Julii. "Eugene O'Neill na prazskem jevisti
      [Eugene O'Neill in the Prague Theater]". Unpublished Thesi
      Charles U [Prague].

D56a Literatura S.SH.A. XX veka: Opyt tipologicheskogo issledovaniĭa
      Moscow: Nauka. 22-27.

D57 Lohner, Edgar, and Rudolf Haas, eds. Theater und Drama in
      Amerika: Aspekte und Interpretationen. Berlin: Schmidt.
      9-41.

D58 Melchinger, Siegfried. "Die Yankee-Elektra. "O'Neill und
      Aischylos - vergleichende Bemerkungen." Theater und Drama
      Amerika: Aspekte und Interpretationen. Eds. Edgar Lohner
      and Rudolf Haas. Berlin: Schmidt. 254-62.

D58a Monova, D. "Tŭrseniĭata na kolektivo." Teatŭr [Sofia] 7: 33-

      Concerns a production of Desire in the city of Vratsa, Bulgaria

9   Nascimento, Abdias do. "Teatro negro del Brasil: una experiencia
      socio-racial." Popular Theater for Social Change in Latin
      America: Essays in Spanish and English. Ed. Gerardo
      Luzuriaga. Los Angeles: UCLA Latin American Center.
      251-69.

      Reprint of an article published in Conjunto: [Revista de] teatro
      Latinoamericano [Havana] 9 (1971): 14-28.

9a Pinaev, S. M. "K voprosu o nekotorykh osobennostiakh
      khudozhestvennoĭ struktury dram Ĭu. O'Nila i T. Uil'iamsa."
      Voprosy romanticheskogo metoda i stilĭa. Kalinin [Russia]:
      n.p. 145-52.

      On O'Neill and Tennessee Williams.

9b Pinaev, S.M. "O dramaturgicheskoĭ tekhnike Ĭu. O'Nila i T.
      Uil'iamsa." Literaturnye sviazi i problema vzaimoponimaniĭa.
      Gorki [Russia]: n.p. 30-48.

)   Romm, Anna S. Amerikanskaya dramaturgiya pervoi poloviny xx veka.
      Leningrad: Iskusstvo.

a   Scheller, B. "Lass doch Sara lachen." Theater der Zeit [Berlin]
      5: 29-30.

      Concerns a production of Touch in Rostock, Germany.

      Sittler, Loring. "The Emperor Jones - ein Individuationspross im
        Sinne C. G. Jungs?" Amerikstudien 23. 1: 118-30.

      Stuby, Anna Maria. "Tragödie und PrivateigentusM zu Desire Under
        the Elms von Eugene O'Neill." Gulliver: deutsch-englische
        Jahrubücher 3. Berlin: Argument. 78-96.

      Thies, Henning. Namen im Kontext von Dramen: Studien zur
        Funktion von Personennamen im englischen, amerikanischen und
        deutschen Drama. Frankfurt: Lang.

      Tsimbal, I.S. "Rannie 'Morskie' miniatĭury Ĭudzhina O'Nila
        Parokhod Glenkern: Iz nablĭudenniĭ nad stilem pisatelĭa."
        Analiz stilĭa zarubeshnoĭ khudozhestvennoĭ i nauchnoĭ
        literatury. Leningrad: n.p. I: 97-105.

150

D63b Bach, Gerhard. Susan Glaspell und die Provincetown Players: di
Anfänge des Modernen amerikanischen Dramas und Theaters.
Frankfurt am Main: Lang.

D63c Bakošová-Hlavenková, Z. "Film a divadlo." Bratislava 21: 24.

Concerns the Prague production of Voyage.

D63d Bruna, O. "Theater, das von sich reden macht." Theater der Ze
[Berlin] 8: 34-38.

D64 Lagerroth, Ulla-Britta. "Ny nordisk forskning om drama och
teater." Samlaren 100: 200-15.

D64a Lev, Sverdlin. Stat'i. Vospominaniîa. Eds. N. A. Velekhova a
A. G. Obraztsova. Moscow: Iskusstvo. 117-19, 160.

D65 Medvedeva, N.P. O zhanrovom svoeohrazii p'esy Iu. O'Nila
'Strannaîa interliûdiîa' [The originality of genre of
O'Neill's play Interlude]. Sbornik nauchnykh Trudov
Sverdlovskogo pedagogicheskogo instituta [Russia] 319:
88-94.

D66 Milfull, John. "Die Stummen Gewalten: über die Sprachlosigke:
der Sprachbegabten: 'stumme Stücke' von Beckett, Handke
Müller." Handke: Ansätze--Analysen--Anmerkungen. Ed.
Manfred Jürgensen. Bern: Francke. 165-71.

D67 Reiss, Walter. "Die Weltliterarische Leistrunge Maksim Gor'ki
bei der Schaffung einer Dramenpopöe: M. Gorkijs . . . i
drugie-Zyklus im Vergleich zu M. Krlezas Glembajevi und
O'Neills Mourning Becomes Electra." Wissenschaftliche
Zeitschrift der Humboldt-Universität zu Berlin:
Gesellschafts-und Sprachwissenschaftliche Reiche 28:
347-51.

D67a Spasova, E. "Na Kamerna Stsena." Teatŭr [Sofia] 4: 26-28.

Concerns a production of Misbegotten in the city of Gabrovo,
Bulgaria.

67b Tsimbal, I. S. "Negritîanskaîa tema v dramaturgii O'Nila: (Imperator Dzhons)." Problemy realizma v zarubezhnom teatral'nom iskusstve. Leningrad: n.p. 11-21.

1980

8 Ćosic, Ileana. "Judžin O'Nil: Velikan svoje epohe." Scena [Yugoslavia] 16. 1-2: 147-67.

9 Filip, Traian. "Relatii editoriale cu România." Manuscriptum: Revista Trimestriala Editata de Muzeul Literaturii Romane [Romania] 11: 166-68.

0 Lange, Wigand. Theater in Deutschland nach 1945: zur Theaterpolitik der amerikanischen Besatzungsbehorden. Frankfurt am Main: Lang.

Scattered references to O'Neill, especially pages 363-68, 446-56, and 459-61.

Oswald, Josef. The Discordant, Broken, Faithless Rhythm of Our Time:" Eine Analyse der späten Dramen Eugene O'Neills. Neue studien zur Anglistik und Amerikanistik 21. Frankfurt am Main. Lang.

Suyama, Shizuo. "Eugene O'Neill Iceman Kitaru: Moo Hitori no Sisyphe to Kankyaku no Shisei." Bungaku to America: Ohashi Kenzaburo Kyoju Kinen Ronbunshu. 3 vols. Tokyo: Nanundo. 3: 297-312.

Törnqvist, Egil. "De Bewerking von de realiteit: Het Historie - Drama." Scenaríum 4: 9-20.

Includes examples from Ibsen, Strindberg, Brecht, and O'Neill.

1982

Abe, Hiroshe. "Eugene O'Neill." America Bungaku no Ji Kotenkai 20-seiki no America Bungaku II. Ed. Toshihiko Ogata. Kyoto: Yamaguchi. 205-39.

D74a Fridshteĭn, Ŭriĭ Germanovich, ed. and comp. Ŭdzhin O'Nil:
       bibliograficheskiĭ ukazatel'. Moscow: Kniga.

    Introduction. Primary and secondary bibliographies, including
    translations. International in scope. Immensely useful for
    non-English language material.

D75 Plett, Heinrich F., and Renate Plett. "New York: Variationen
       über das Thema Metropolis im amerikanischen Drama der
       Zwanziger Jahre." Zeitschrift für Literaturwissenschaft un
       Linguistik 12: 103-33.

D76 Schäfer, Jürgen. Geschichte des Amerikanischen Dramas.
       Stuttgart: Kohlhammer.

D77 Seidel, Margot. "Goethes Faust und O'Neill." Archiv für das
       Studium der Neueren Sprachen und Literaturen 219: 2:
       365-72.

D77a Thébaud, M. "Delivrez-nous d'O'Neill." Le Figaro 23 Nov.: 2℃

                              1983

D78 Furukawa, Hiroyuki. "Chihei no Kanata." Eibungaku to no Deai.
       Ed. Naomi Matsuura. Kyoto: Showado. 185-205.

D79 Ichinose, Kazuo. "Sengo no Eugene O'Neill." Sengo Amerika Eng
       no Tenkai. Eds. Kuniaki Svenaga and Koji Ishizuka. Tokyo
       Bun'eido. 155-80.

D80 Pitavy-Souques, Danièle. "L'Intruse: Stratégie du désir dans
       Desire Under the Elms et A Streetcar Named Desire." Coup
       Théâtre [Publication du Centre de Recherches sur les Arts
       Dramatiques Anglo-Saxons Contemporains] 3: 17-27.

D81 Seidel, Margot. Bibel und Christentum im dramatischen Werk Eug
       O'Neills. Studien zur englischen und amerikanischen
       Literatur 3. Frankfurt am Main: Lang.

1984

82 Hoffman, Gerhard. "Eugene O'Neill: Realismus, Expressionismus,
        Mystizismus." Das Amerikanische Drama. Ed. Gerhard
        Hoffman. Bern: Francke. 76-120.

83 Seidel, Margot. Aberglaube Bei O'Neill. Frankfurt am Main:
        Lang.

ENGLISH LANGUAGE PRODUCTIONS AND REVIEWS

E1   Ah, Wilderness!

          Long Wharf Theater
          New Haven, CT

          Opened 20 Dec. 1974

          Then Circle-in-the-Square Theater
          NYC
          Opened 18 Sept. 1975 for 77 performances

          Dir. Arvin Brown
          Settings - Steven Rubin
          Costumes - Bill Walker
          Lights - James Gallagher/Ronald Wallace
          Art Dir. - Theodore Mann

          Tommy Miller - Kevin Ellicott/Glenn Zachar
          Mildred Miller - Christine Whitmore
          Arthur Miller - Paul Rudd
          Essie Miller - Geraldine Fitzgerald
          Nat Miller - William Swetland
          Richard Miller - Richard Backus
          Lily Miller - Teresa Wright
          Sid Davis - John Braden
          David McComber - Emery Battis/John Drischell
          Nora - Linda Hunt
          Wint Selby - Sean G. Griffin
          Belle - Susanne Lederer
          Bartender - Stephen Mendillo
          Salesman - Don Gantry
          Muriel McComber - Susan Sharkey/Swoozie Kurtz

                Barnes, Clive. "Theater: A Magical Ah, Wilderness!"
                    New York Times 23 Dec. 1974: 32.

                Is enthusiastic about this production in all areas.
                Stresses the nostalgia and fantasy, which, should be
                seen reflected against Journey, whereupon Wilderness
                becomes "a delicate, even sweet, but troubled fantasy."

                Barnes, Clive. The Theater/"O'Neill's Only Comedy."
                    New York Times 19 Sept. 1975: II 5; NYTCR 1975:
                    212.

                The play is a "nostalgic threnody," the production
                "enchanting." Direction tries to "underplay the
                American aspects of the play." Solid acting. A little
                bit of Life with Father.

>   Beaufort, John. Theatre Reviews. <u>Christian Science</u>
                 <u>Monitor</u> 26 Sept. 1975; <u>NYTCR</u> 1975:   212-13.

               The production is a "glowing" revival of a "warm,
               sun-dappled play."

>   Clurman, Harold. Theatre. <u>Nation</u> 4 Oct. 1975:
                 317-18.

               Finds the production skillfully directed by Arvin
               Brown. Especially liked Geraldine Fitzgerald as Mrs.
               Miller and Teresa Wright as Aunt Lily. Faulted the
               production for being too contemporary and Richard Backu
               for playing Richard for laughs.

>   Davis, Curt. Review. <u>Encore</u> 3 Nov. 1975:   35-6.

>   Gill, Brendan. "Paradise Enow." <u>New Yorker</u> 29 Sept.
                 1975:   100.

               The production was "exceptionally attractive:"
               director Brown cut little and Richard Backus played hi
               role with "exemplary tact."

>   Gottfried, Martin. Theater/"Ah, Wilderness!--A Magic
                 Spell." <u>New York Post</u> 19 Sept. 1975; <u>NYTCR</u> 1975
                 211.

               Comments on the light and dark sides of O'Neill and
               says of this production that it is "shamelessly
               sentimental and entirely charming." Compares O'Neill
               Norman Rockwell.

>   Hughes, Catharine. "<u>Ah, Wilderness!</u> (Oh, O'Neill?)."
                 <u>America</u> 1 Nov. 1975:   283-84.

               Sees the play as a pleasant celebration of a
               charming past but criticizes the characters as
               one-dimensional. Also finds the play verbose and
               basically dull, but sees it as a positive print of the
               negative we see later in <u>Journey</u>.

Kauffmann, Stanley. "Stanley Kauffmann on Theatre."
New Republic 11 Oct. 1975: 22-23.

Criticizes "O'Neill's ode to middle-class
respectability . . . whose emptiness he so fiercely
exposed elsewhere." The casting is generally bad with
the exception of William Swetland.

Kerr, Walter. "A Long Day's 'Wilderness.'" New York
Times 28 Sept. 1975: II 5.

Notes that the original production (1933) charmed
by its novelty and by its star, George M. Cohan. Says
nowadays the play must be seen against the knowledge of
Journey, and therefore, our response to it is to what
isn't in the play. The play itself is bland, but the
production is generally solid except that it lacks
"variation or progression" and Uncle Sid is badly cast.

Kissel, Howard. The Theatre. Women's Wear Daily
19 Sept. 1975; NYTCR 1975: 210.

Thinks the play "one of the most solid, durable and
satisfying of O'Neill's works and one of the treasures
of the American theater." Says that like other O'Neill
works this one is dominated by the image of woman as
whore or mother. The production was "splendid" and
the cast "superb."

Mallet, Gina. "Sweet Dreams." Time 6 Jan. 1975: 93.

Thinks the play should have been cut, but commends
Brown's staging, calling the production a "meticulous
revival."

Novick, Julius. Review. Village Voice 29 Sept. 1975:
105.

O'Connor, John J. Review. New York Times 13 Oct.
1976: 86.

Observes that the easy tendency of the play to
become cloying and sentimental is avoided by this
production's realistic treatment of the characters--who
can be "taken seriously." The only directional error
was in using the "soft focus" cliche.

> Pacheco, Patrick. Review. <u>After Dark</u> Nov. 1975: 30, 80, 82.

The production was "relaxed," the ensemble "brilliant," and the play "enchanting theater."

> Rich, Alan. "Long Day's Joy Ride." <u>New York</u> 6 Oct. 1975: 68-69.

The play has "miscalculations, some of them crucial, but the spirit of Eugene O'Neill's only comedy does fitfully show through." O'Neill's writing is gracious, unlike so much of his "waterlogged prose," but except for Brown's cuts, would be too long. Brown's direction is generally sympathetic to O'Neill except in the dinner scene which is played for laughs. Finds the actors good to excellent, though Richard is badly cast.

> Watt, Douglas. "This Wilderness Paradise Enow." <u>Daily News</u> 19 Sept. 1975; <u>NYTCR</u> 1975: 210.

Finds this comedy "our richest comedy" and approves of the production.

> Wilson, Edwin. The Theater. "The Past as it Perhaps Never Was." <u>Wall Street Journal</u> 19 Sept. 1975; NYTCR: 213.

Says that after writing this play O'Neill used more humor and returned to realism.

E2   Ah, Wilderness!

Summer 1975 on tour

Barbara Bel Geddes
Richard Kiley
Donna Pescow

E3   Ah, Wilderness!

Waynesburg College
Waynesburg, PA

21 Oct. 1975

Dir. Rev. Gilbert V. Hartke

E4   Ah, Wilderness! -- alternating with Journey, see no. E148.

Milwaukee Repertory Theater Co.
Milwaukee, WI

18 Nov. 1977 to 18 Jan. 1978.

Dir. Irene Lewis

Design - R.A. Graham

Richard Miller/Edmund - Anthony Heald
Essie Miller/Mary - Regina Davis
Nat Miller/Tyrone - Robert Burr
Uncle Sid/Jamie - Ronald Frazer

Kalson, Albert E. "Review of Ah, Wilderness! and Long
Day's Journey into Night." Educational Theatre
Journal 30 Oct. 1978: 422-24.

Notes that the productions were performed in tandem
with the same actors and setting. Says this doubling
allows the audience to see into the dark corners of
Wilderness and adds depth to Journey.

Noth, Dominique Paul. Review. New York Theatre Review
Jan. 1978: 34.

5   Ah, Wilderness!

Playmakers Repertory Co.
Chapel Hill, NC

Closed 2 Apr. 1978

Dir. Tom Haas

5   Ah, Wilderness!

Heights Players
Brooklyn Heights, NY

8 - 23 Sept. 1978

Dir. Roy Clary

E7   Ah, Wilderness!

          American Conservatory Theatre
          San Francisco, CA

          Opened 31 Oct. 1978, Toured Hawaii--12 - 25 June 1979
                                Played Tokyo--30 June - 9 July 1979

          Dir. Allen Fletcher

E8   Ah, Wilderness!

          Arena Stage
          Washington, D.C.

          1 Dec. 1978 - 7 Jan. 1979

          Dir. Edward Cornell

E9   Ah, Wilderness!

          Whole Theatre Company
          Montclair, NJ

          4 May - 3 June 1979

          Dir. Ron Van Lieu

E10 Ah, Wilderness!

          The Young Company of Ontario
          George Ignatieff Theatre
          Toronto, ONT

          11 - 21 July 1979

          Dir. Graham Harley

E11 Ah, Wilderness!

          Boston University Stage Troupe
          Hayden Hall
          Boston U
          Boston, MA

          26 Oct. - 3 Nov. 1979

12   Ah, Wilderness!

          Apple Corps
          NYC

          8 Nov. - 1 Dec. 1979

          Dir. Will Maitland Weiss

13   Ah, Wilderness!

          Dunster House
          Harvard U
          Cambridge, MA

          6 - 15 Mar. 1980

14   Ah, Wilderness!

          The Wisdom Bridge Theatre
          Chicago, IL

          19 Mar. - 20 Apr. 1980

          Dir. R. Falls

5   Ah, Wilderness!

          American Theatre Company
          Tulsa, OK

          21 Mar. - 5 Apr. 1980

          Dir. James E. Runyan

6   Ah, Wilderness!

          American Conservatory Theatre
          San Francisco, CA

          8 Apr. 1980 - 30 May 1980

          Dir. A. Fletcher

E17   Ah, Wilderness!

                Assumption College
                Worcester, MA

                20 - 22 Apr. 1980

                Dir. Donald H. Letendre

E18   Ah, Wilderness!

                Ringling Museums Court Playhouse
                Asolo State Theater
                Sarasota, FL

                Closed 1 May 1980

                Dir. John Reich

E19   Ah, Wilderness!

                Barter Theater
                Abingdon, VA

                18 June - 29 Aug. 1980 in repertory

                Dir. Jeff Meredith

E20   Ah, Wilderness!

                Polka Dot Playhouse
                Bridgeport, CT

                4 - 26 July 1980

E21   Ah, Wilderness!

                Penn State U Resident Theater
                Pavilion Theater
                University Park, PA

                17 July - 3 Aug. 1980

22 Ah, Wilderness!

        Hangar Theater
        Cass Park
        Ithaca, NY

        5 - 16 Aug. 1980

23 Ah, Wilderness!

        Seattle Repertory Theatre
        Seattle, WA

        31 Dec. 1980 - 25 Jan. 1981

        Dir. Daniel Sullivan

4 Ah, Wilderness!

        Boars Head Theater
        Lansing Center for the Arts
        Lansing, MI

        12 Feb. - 1 Mar. 1981

5 Ah, Wilderness!

        Studio Arena Theatre
        Buffalo, NY

        13 Feb. - 14 Mar. 1981

        Dir. Geoffrey Sherman

5 Ah, Wilderness!

        Indiana Repertory Theatre
        Indianapolis, IN

        24 Apr. - 16 May 1981

        Dir. David Rotenberg

E27   Ah, Wilderness!

          Lakewood Theater Company
          Skowhegan, ME

          Summer 1981

E28   Ah, Wilderness!

          South Coast Repertory
          Costa Mesa, CA

          Closed 18 Oct. 1981

          Dir. Martin Benson

>   Hansen, Eugene K. Review. EON 6.1 (1982): 45-48.

E29   Ah, Wilderness!

          Marymount Manhattan Theater
          NY

          11 - 14 Nov. 1981

          Dir. Michael Jameson

E30   Ah, Wilderness!

          New York U Department of Undergraduate Drama
          NYC

          31 Mar. - 3 Apr. 1982

          Dir. Penelope Hirsch

E31   Ah, Wilderness!

          Trinity Theatre Ltd.
          Trinity Lutheran Church
          NYC

          7 - 31 Oct. 1982 in repertory

          Dir. Dale Kaufman

E32   Ah, Wilderness!

        GeVa Theatre
        Rochester, NY

        26 Mar. - 17 Apr. 1983

E33   Ah, Wilderness!

        The Roundabout Theater Company
        The Haft Theater
        NYC

        14 June - 24 July 1983

        Dir. John Stix
        Setting - Kenneth Foy
        Costume - Gene K. Lakin
        Light - Ron Wallace
        Music - Philip Campanella

        Nat Miller - Philip Bosco
        Essie Miller - Dody Goodman
        Arthur - John Dukakis
        Richard - Scott Burkholder
        Mildred - Kelly Wolf
        Tommy - Mark Scott Newman
        Sid Davis - Robert Nichols
        Lily Miller - Laurinda Barrett
        David McComber - Joseph Leon
        Muriel McComber - Liane Langland
        Wint Selby & Bartender - Robert Curtis-Brown
        Belle - Jean Hackett
        Nora - Bernadette Quigley
        Salesman - Scott Gordon Miller

                Bennetts, Leslie. Comments on Dody Goodman as Essie
                    Miller. New York Times 8 July 1983: C3.

                Says that as Essie Miller, Goodman, despite the
                importance of Richard and even Nat, draws the audience's
                "warmest response."

                Rich, Frank. Review. New York Times 29 June 1983:
                    C21.

                Notes that our way of seeing Wilderness has changed
                since the appearance of Journey: says now we look

for the shadows to peak--and sometimes they do.
Though the play is "flimsily constructed . . . O'Neill
was masterly at tucking the sorrows in slyly. . . ."

>   Simon, John. Review. New York 18 July 1983: 62-63.

The direction by John Stix was mediocre, the acting
essentially the same, but then again so is the play.
The play's humor is forced.

E34 Ah, Wilderness!

      The Players
      Castleton State College Fine Arts Center
      Castleton, VT

      30 Nov. - 3 Dec. 1983

E35 Ah, Wilderness!

      Angus Bowmer Theatre Festival
      Ashland, OR

      11 Sept. - 30 Oct. 1983

      Dir. Jerry Turner

E36 Ah, Wilderness!

      McCarter Theatre Company Fine Arts Center
      Princeton, N.J.

      Jan. 18 - Feb. 5, 1984

      Dir. Margaret Booker

E37 Ah, Wilderness!

      Alumnae Theatre
      Toronto, ONT

      22 Mar. - 7 Apr. 1984

338   Ah, Wilderness!

          Community Theater Company of East Hampton, NY
          East Hampton, NY

          Opened 4 May 1984

339   Ah, Wilderness!

          Body Politic Theatre
          Chicago, IL

          13 Sept. - 21 Oct. 1984

          Dir. James O'Reilly

40   Ah, Wilderness! -- in repertory with Journey, no. E175.

          San Diego Repertory Theatre
          San Diego, CA

          4 Oct. - 18 Nov. 1984

          Dir. Douglas Jacobs
          Design Dan Dryden

          Sid - Ric Barr
          Lily - Barbara Murray
          Essie - Jo Ann Reeves
          Mildred - Amy Herzberg
          Richard - Thom Murray
          Tommy - Jonathan Grantham
          Nat - William Anton
          Arthur Selby - Wayne Tibbetts
          Wint Selby - Wayne Tibbetts

41   Ah, Wilderness!

          Kennedy Theatre
          U of Hawaii, Honolulu

          18 Apr. - 3 May 1985

          Dir. Glenn Cannon

          Richard - Daniel Kelin
          Essie & Nat - Meg Roach and Dean Turner
          Lily Miller - Sylvia Hormann-Alper
          Sid Davis - Wayne Kischer

E42   Ah, Wilderness!

          Hartford Stage Company
          Hartford, CT

          28 May - 30 June 1985

          Dir. Mary B. Robinson

E43   All God's Chillun Got Wings

          Circle in the Square Theater
          NYC

          Opened 20 March 1975 for 53 performances

          Dir. George C. Scott
          Setting - Ming Cho Lee
          Costumes - Patricia Zipprodt
          Lighting - Thomas Skelton/Ronald Wallace
          Art Dir. - Theodore Mann

          Children - Ginny Binder/Beatrice Dunmore/Helen Jennings,
                     Kathy Rich/Derrell Edwards

          Mickey, as a child - Jimmy Balo
          Joe, as a child - Robert Lee Grant
          Jim, as a child - Carl Thomas
          Shorty, as a child - Tommy Gilchrist
          Ella, as a child - Susan Jayne
          Shorty - Ken Jennings
          Joe - Tim Pelt
          Mickey - Tom Sminkey
          Jim Harris - Robert Christian
          Ella Downey - Trish Van Devere
          Vino - Chuck Patterson
          Mrs. Harris - Minnie Gentry
          Hattie Harris - Vickie Thomas
          Street People - Alice Nagel/Ted Snowden/Arthur French/
                          Verona Barnes/Robert Earl Jones/
                          Garcie Carroll
          Harmonica player - Craig Wasson
          Singers - Chuck Patterson/Craig Wasson

>   Barnes, Clive. "All God's Chillun at Circle in the
                 Square." New York Times 21 Mar. 1975: 30;
                 NYTCR 1975: 290-91.

The play is dated in its handling of racial themes.
O'Neill's lines are like "dead rocks." The production's
emphasis on the elements of melodrama, of violence was
"heavy-handed." Trish Van Devere was not "at home" as
Ella; Robert Christian as Jim performed exquisitely.
The settings were "flawless."

Beaufort, John. "All God's Chillun." Christian Science
     Monitor 3 Apr. 1975; NYTCR 1975: 292.

The play with its "stumbling compassion and
inevitably dated attitudes" should be read rather than
staged. Direction was "heavy-handed."

Carmody, Deidre. "Seeing God's Chillun for What It Is."
     New York Times 17 Feb. 1975: 28.

These comments anticipate the production (to be
previewed 28 Feb.). Contrasts the contemporary view of
the play as concerned with fundamental human emotions
(an encoded treatment of the playwright's parents'
relationship) with the 1924 popular view of the play as
advocating interracial marriage.

Clurman, Harold. Theatre. Nation 12 Apr. 1975:
     442-43.

Although Chillun is not one of O'Neill's best plays, it
is not without merit. Compares James and Ella Tyrone's
relationship to Ella and Jim Harris' and Con and Nora
Melody's to Jim and Ella's. Says of the present
production that Robert Christian as Jim gives "one of
the most memorable performances of the season." Also
thought Trish Van Devere as Ella good, but found Scott's
direction difficult to judge.

Gill, Brendan. The Theatre. New Yorker 31 Mar. 1975:
     47-48.

Says that the roles are "thankless" and that the
actors have not given "exceptional life" to them. Sees
Jim and Ella are caricatures of O'Neill's father and
mother.

Gottfried, Martin. Theater/"Oh, Mr. Scott!" New York
     Post 21 Mar. 1975; NYTCR 1975: 291.

The play's handling of racial themes is dated. The
production is badly cast, badly directed, badly staged

> Kalem, T. E. "Haunted House." Time 31 Mar. 1975: 6

Suspects that Chillun has been revived for its
topicality and that we are expected to respond to a pl
which does not elicit a deep response. Calls O'Neill'
prose "dead-battery," and thinks that neither Robert
Christian nor Trish Van Devere projects the torment th
the roles necessitate.

> Kerr, Walter. "O'Neill's Uneasy Study in Black and
>   White." New York Times 30 Mar. 1975: II 1.

Finds Chillun "ambivalent about its theme" and "a
skeletal piece." Scott makes a "bold attempt" at
directing the play--creating a "quasi-poetic
dream-state." This is successful in the first half bu
not in the second. The evening is "evocative"
nonetheless.

> Probst, Leonard. NBC Radio. 20 Mar. 1975; NYTCR
>   1975: 293.

A "chilling, powerful drama, strongly directed and
acted, and fully absorbing."

> Sanders, Kevin. WABC-TV 7 20 Mar. 1975; NYTCR 1975:
>   293.

O'Neill's "worst" play, dated and "unactable."
Imaginative direction.

> Sharp, Christopher. The Theatre/"All God's Chillun G
>   Wings." Women's Wear Daily 24 Mar. 1975; NYTCR
>   1975: 292.

Stresses less "the racial issues than the emotions
that reduce the races to a common denominator." The
director "turned what could have been a brilliant
evening into only a decent one." The emphasis is on
pathos as out of Aeschylus. Trish Van Devere is
"excellent," Robert Christian "over-directed."

Simon, John. Review. <u>New York</u> 7 Apr. 1975: 78, 80.

The revival of the play is a "major disaster" and
the play itself a "clinker." The problems are not the
topic (miscegenation) but "the psychological
inconsistencies and improbabilities," "rickety
stagecraft" and "leaden language." Scott's direction is
no help.

Watt, Douglas. "O'Neill Rarity in Weak Revival." <u>Daily</u>
     <u>News</u> 21 Mar. 1975; <u>NYTCR</u> 1975: 290.

The play is "unsuccessful." The performance lacks
"tension and rhythm." The play is "as crude in outline
and clumsy in speech" as is O'Neill's worst. The
setting was good but the acting was not.

Wilson, Edwin. The Theatre/"<u>All God's Chillun Got</u>
     <u>Wings</u>." <u>Wall Street Journal</u>. 29 Mar. 1975:
     <u>NYTCR</u> 1975: 292.

A play marked by "faulty construction and
theatrical extravagance." In this production melodrama
was given too much opportunity to control things.

+ <u>All God's Chillun Got Wings</u>

     Horace Mann Theater
     Columbia U
     NYC

     21 - 23 Oct. 1982

     Dir. Virlana Tkacz

<u>Anna Christie</u>

     Soho Repertory (off off Broadway)

     30 Jan. 1976

E46   Anna Christie

                    Imperial Theatre
                    NYC

                    Opened 14 Apr. 1977 for 124 performances

                    Presented by Alexander H. Cohen by arrangement with Gabriel
                    Katzka and Edward L. Schuman

                    Dir. José Quintero
                    Decor and Lighting - Ben Edwards
                    Costumes - Jane Greenwood

                    Johnny-the-Priest - Richard Hamilton
                    Longshoremen - Edwin McDonough/Vic Polizos
                    Larry - Ken Harrison
                    Postman - Jack Davidson
                    Chris Christopherson - Robert Donley
                    Marthy Owen - Mary McCarty
                    Anna Christie - Liv Ullmann
                    Sailors - Vic Polizos/Ken Harrison
                    Johnson - Jack Davidson
                    Mat Burke - John Lithgow

>   Barnes, Clive. Theater/Liv Ullman's Anna Christie."
                         New York Times 15 Apr. 1977: III 3; NYTCR 197
                         278.

                    "A clumsy play" that can be made to work since
                    O'Neill provided "scarecrows" that can be clothed by
                    actors of invention. Says Ullmann was "born for Anna
                    Christie."

>   Beaufort, John. Theater Reviews/"A Powerful O'Neill
                         Broadway." Christian Science Monitor 20 Apr. 19
                         NYTCR 1977: 279.

                    Superlatives.

>   Clurman, Harold. Theatre. Nation 30 Apr. 1977:
                         538-39.

                    Concludes that the plot is banal as are most of the
                    characters. Although Liv Ullmann looks the part, she
                    quintessentially not Anna. Support actors Robert Dor⬛
                    and John Lithgow are good and Quintero's direction

intelligent, but the production as a whole "does not
speak to the inner voice."

Gill, Brendan. "Mal de Mer." New Yorker 25 Apr. 1977:
    92.

The play is "coarsely conceived, coarsely constructed,
coarsely composed." This production makes one feel
"battered not purged." Faults Ullmann for "failing to
command the stage," Donley for his near indecipherable
accent, and John Lithgow for being "at a loss" in the
impossible role of Mat.

Gottfried, Martin. Theater/"What's a Nice Girl Like Liv
    Doing in a Play Like This?" New York Post 15 Apr.
    1977; NYTCR 1977: 281.

The play is bad; the direction is "corny," the design is
inept; and the supporting cast doesn't support. The
only excuse for the play is Liv Ullmann and for her only
praise.

Kalem, T. E. "Liv in Limbo." Time 25 Apr. 1977: 84;
    NYTCR 1977: 282.

The play is "a cheap, cosmetic come-on of a drama."
Rates the production a failed effort--largely because
almost everthing is wrong with the play. Approves of
Liv Ullmann's performance.

Kauffmann, Stanley. "Stanley Kauffmann on Theatre."
    New Republic 7 May 1977: 22-23.

"Anna is an example of early 20th-century American
naivete about realism." But it has elements that
anticipate O'Neill's maturity. Of this production the
direction was unimpressive as was the acting, with the
exception of Robert Donley.

Kerr, Walter. "There's More to Anna Christie than this
    Production Knows." New York Times 24 Apr. 1977:
    II 5.

Liv Ullmann is talented, but miscast. She doesn't look
like any of the things she tells us she is--defeated,
tired, cynical. Robert Donley's performance is "all

one color and all one key." John Lithgow as Mat Burke
is a "real howler."

> Kissel, Howard. The Theater/"Anna Christie." Women's
    Wear Daily 15 Apr. 1977; NYTCR 1977: 279-80.

Insists that O'Neill's plays have to be seen not read.
The 1922 Anna has much that is "quaint and dated," but
"the metaphor of the sea gives the play a poetry" that
lifts it above its stilted dialogue and "soap operatic
plot." Superlatives for the production.

> Kroll, Jack. "Liv's Anna." Newsweek 25 Apr. 1977:
    89.

Unenthusiastic about Donley's Chris but thought
Lithgow and Ullmann were excellent. Says of the play
that it is a "heavy, hooting scow of a play."

> Mayer, David. Review. Plays and Players 27.3 (197
    30-31.

This production proves that while on paper O'Neill
has many faults--tin ear, leaden philosophizing, clum
asides and soliloquizing--still on the stage his play
have "a crude vitality and disturbing turbulence."

> Probst, Leonard. NBC Radio. 14 Apr. 1977; NYTCR 197
    282.

The play is "rambling, awkward, early O'Neill," but i
is made "memorable" by Liv Ullmann.

> Rich, Alan. Review. New York 12 May 1977: 68-69.

Says that Anna stands at a turning point in O'Neill's
work between the "dark, terse personal melodramas," t
sea plays, and experimental plays of the 1920's. Fi
the plot and language deficient, but the current
production better than the play.

> Rogoff, Gordon. "The Mere Human Props of Eugene
    O'Neill." Saturday Review 28 May 1977: 38-39

Approves of the casting--especially Liv Ullmann--but
says the play itself is clumsy, the action forced an

the characters stereotypes. Thinks the play came at a
good point in O'Neill's career. With the country
looking for a serious playwright, how could someone
"grumbling about fate and hammering away at destiny
miss?"

Watt, Douglas. "To See Liv is to Luv Her." Daily News
    15 Apr. 1977; NYTCR 1977: 278-79.

As in all O'Neill "there is an awesome power at work
beneath the surface of this somewhat old-fashioned
melodramatic triangle." The production is "something to
see, and its star . . . [Liv Ullmann] someone to take
home."

Wilson, Edwin. The Theater/"Anna Christie." Wall
    Street Journal 19 Apr. 1977; NYTCR 1977: 282.

The play is old-fashioned and awkward, but it has
some of the strength O'Neill is capable of and some of
his themes which we find in later plays. Liv is
"well-directed" and "ably supported." She is a "joy to
behold."

7   Anna Christie

        Royal Shakespeare Company at The Other Place
        Stratford-upon-Avon

        Opened 18 Sept. 1979

        Also May - Sept. 1980

        Dir. Jonathan Lynn
        Design - Saul Radomsky
        Light - Leo Leibovici

        Johnny the Priest - Ian East
        Larry - Ian McNeice
        Chris Christopherson - Fulton MacKay
        Marthy Owen - Lila Kaye
        Anne Christopherson - Susan Tracy
        Mat Burke - Gareth Thomas

E48   Anna Christie

New England Repertory Theatre
Worcester, MA

23 Oct. - 15 Nov. 1981

Dir. John Knowles

E49   Anna Christie

St. Nicholas Theater Company
Chicago, IL

18 Nov. - 20 Dec. 1981

Dir. Cynthia Sherman

E50   Anna Christie

American Folk Theater
The Richard Allen Center for Culture and Art
NYC

5 - 24 Apr. 1983

Dir. Bob Sickinger

E51   Anna Christie

Your Theatre
New Bedford, MA

19 - 29 Sept. 1984

Dir. Cynthia J. Messier

Anna Christie - Linda Sue McCallester
Chris - Edward J. Maguire
Mat - Gregory F. Leonard

52   Anna Christie

           Seventh Sign Theatre Company
           Good Shepherd-Faith Presbyterian Church
           NYC

           Closed 18 May 1985

           Dir. Anthony Osnato

53   Before Breakfast

           Chichester Festival
           England

           July 1978

           Dir. Sylvia Miles

--   Before Breakfast -- see [Three Lost Plays of Eugene O'Neill],
      no. E243.

           Nameless Theater
           125 W. 22nd St.
           NYC

           Closed 19 Nov. 1978

           Dir. Michael Alexander

4   Before Breakfast

           American Theatre Arts Conservatory
           Los Angeles, CA

           Fall 1981

           Dir. Barry Bartle

               Hansen, Eugene K.   Review.   EON 6.1 (1982):   45-48.

E55   Before Breakfast

        No Smoking Playhouse
        NYC

        Closed 15 Dec. 1985

        Dir. Francisco Rivela

E56   Beyond the Horizon

        The McCarter Theater Company Fine Arts Center
        Princeton, NJ

        10 Oct. 1974

        Producing Dir. Michael Kahn
        Setting - Robert U. Taylor
        Lighting - David F. Segal

        Robert Mayo - Richard Backus
        Andrew Mayo - Edward J. Moore
        James Mayo - Hugh Reilly
        Ruth Atkins - Marta Tucci
        Kate Mayo - Laurinda Barrett
        Capt. Dick Scott - Paul Larson
        Mrs. Atkins - Camila Ashland
        Mary - Sharon Chazin
        Ben - Michael Houlihan
        Dr. Fawcett - Daniel Saltzer

>   Barnes, Clive. Beyond the Horizon. New York Times 12
                    Oct. 1974: 18:1.

               Says O'Neill "stammers out miracles" and this is one c
               them. The play is simple on the surface but contains
               themes which recurred in O'Neill for the next 30 year:

257 Beyond the Horizon

        78th Street Theater Lab
        NYC

        Closed 18 Nov. 1979

        Dir. Christian Renaud

258 Beyond the Horizon

        Theatre Exchange
        NYC

        26 Mar. - 12 Apr. 1981

        Dir. Charles Clubb

259 Beyond the Horizon

        ATA Theatre
        NYC

        Closed 25 Apr. 1981

        Dir. James Jennings

260 Beyond the Horizon

        Queens College Little Theatre
        Flushing, NY

        18 - 20 Mar. 1982

261 Beyond the Horizon

        Source Theatre Company
        Washington, DC

        8 Nov. - 7 Dec. 1985

--- Bound East for Cardiff -- see The Sea Plays of Eugene O'Neill,
     no. E237.

--- Bound East for Cardiff -- see The Long Voyage Home, no. E183.

E62 Bound East for Cardiff

          Tufts Arena Theater
          Medford, MA

          Spring 1981

          Dir. Sean Skilling

--- Bound East for Cardiff -- see Six Plays of the Sea, no. E240.

--- Bound East for Cardiff -- see Sea Plays at Monte Cristo, no. E23

E63 Chris Christopherson

          The Goodman Theatre
          Chicago, IL

          1982 Season

E64 Desire Under the Elms

          ACSTA
          The Village Church (off off Broadway)
          NYC

          9 Mar. 1974 till the 2nd week in April.

          Dir. Sonia Moore

          Ephraim Cabot - Philip G. Bennett
          Eben Cabot - Bill Baker
          Abbie Cabot - Cathy Brady

>   Thompson, Howard. "Ibsen and O'Neill." New York Time
                    12 Apr. 1974: 18.

               Applauds the ACSTA ensemble "whose artful, unified
               sensibility continues to give one of the steadiest
               theater glows in town."

5   <u>Desire Under the Elms</u>

       Queensboro Community College

       Opened 14 Mar. 1974 for seven performances.

6   <u>Desire Under the Elms</u>

       Academy Festival Theatre
       Lake Forest, IL

       Dir. Vinnette Carroll

       Cicely Tyson

       June, 1974

           Zimmerman, Paul D. Review. <u>Newsweek</u> 24 June 1974:
              76-77.

       Calls the production with its mostly black cast an
       "interesting experiment," one, however, which was not
       entirely successful.

7   <u>Desire Under the Elms</u>

       Jean Cocteau Repertory (off off Broadway)

       11 Oct. 1975

8   <u>Desire Under the Elms</u>

       ACSTA
       The Village Church (off off Broadway)
       NYC

       9 Jan. 1976

E69   Desire Under the Elms

         San Francisco American Conservatory Theater
         Academy Theater
         Playing in Moscow [Soviet Union]

         Opened 27 May 1976

         Art Dir. William Ball

>   Anon. Report on ACT in Russia. New York Times
              8 June 1976: 28.

         ACT's production of Desire (Lyubov pod Viasami) in
         Russia is getting full-house reception. Russian
         translation comes through earphones at each seat.
         During the three-week tour, the company will also
         perform in Riga and Leningrad.

>   Powers, Dennis. "The Russians said Hello to Dolly
              Levi." New York Times 5 Sept. 1976: II 5 and 24

         Comments on the reception given the ACT in Russia.
         Notes that its two productions--one was Desire--were
         excerpted for Soviet TV.

E70   Desire Under the Elms

         The Asolo Theatre
         Ringling Art Museum
         Sarasota, FL

         1977 Season

         Dir. Richard Fallon

>   Frazer, Winifred. Review. EON 1.3 (1978): 17-18.

E71   Desire Under the Elms

         Gainesville Little Theatre
         Gainesville, FL

         5 - 15 Apr. 1978

         Dir. Craig Hartley

>   Frazer, Winifred. Review. EON 2.2 (1978): 16.

72 Desire Under the Elms

        Royall Tyler Theatre
        U of Vermont
        Burlington, VT

        18 - 21 Oct. 1978

73 Desire Under the Elms

        Playwrights Horizons
        Queens, NYC

        13 Oct. - 4 Nov. 1979

        Dir. Irene Lewis

74 Desire Under the Elms

        Dartmouth Players
        Warner Bentley Theater
        Hopkins Center
        Hanover, NH

        26 Feb. - 1 Mar. 1980

        Dir. Robert Berlinger

            Wilkins, Frederick. Review. EON 4.1-2 (1980): 25-26.

75 Desire Under the Elms

        Guthrie Theater
        Minneapolis, MN

        23 Aug. 1980 - 22 Nov. 1980

        Dir. George Keathley

            Voelker, Paul D. "Lust Under Some Elms: Desire at the
                Guthrie." EON 4.3 (1980): 9-12.

E76   Desire Under the Elms

      American Stanislavsky Theater (off off Broadway)

      NYC

      1982

E77   Desire Under the Elms

      Tacoma Actors Guild
      Tacoma, WA

      4 - 27 Feb. 1982

      Dir. William Becvar

E78   Desire Under the Elms

      V. A. Smith Chapel Theatre
      656 Sixth Avenue
      NYC

      Opened 12 Feb. 1982

      Dir. Sonia Moore

E79   Desire Under the Elms (off off Broadway)

      Urban Arts Theatre

      30 Apr. - 23 May 1982

      Dir. Vinnette Carroll with songs by Micki Grant

E80   Desire Under the Elms

      Pennsylvania Stage Company
      Allentown, PA

      16 Feb. - 13 Mar. 1983

      Dir. Gregory S. Hurst

81   Desire Under the Elms

       Indianapolis Repertory Theatre
       Indianapolis, IN

       15 Mar. - 10 Apr. 1983

       Dir. Tom Haas

           Tuck, Susan. Review. EON 7.1 (1983): 15-19.

32   Desire Under the Elms

       Bay Players
       Duxbury, MA

       11 - 19 Nov. 1983

       Dir. Maggie McGovern

33   Desire Under the Elms

       Roundabout Theatre Company (Stage One)
       NYC

       20 Mar. - 3 June 1984

       Dir. Terry Schreiber
       Scenic Designer - Michael Sharp

       Abbie - Kathy Whitton Baker
       Ephraim - Lee Richardson
       Eben - Lenny Von Dohlen
       Simeon - Tom Spiller
       Peter - Patrick Meyers

4   Desire Under the Elms

       East-West Fusion Theatre
       Center for Far East-West Studies
       Sharon, CT

       Opened mid-June 1984

       Dir. Balwant Gargi

E85   Desire Under the Elms

            Rand Theater
            U of Massachusetts
            Amherst, MA

            11 - 20 Oct. 1984

            Dir. Edward Golden

            Abbie - Danielle DiVecchio
            Eben - John Campbell Finnegan
            Ephraim - Harry Mahnken

>   Wilkins, Frederick C. Review. EON 8.3 (1984): 31-33.

E86   Desire Under the Elms

            Hartford Stage Company
            Hartford, CT

            19 Apr. - 19 May 1985

            Dir. Mary K. Robinson

E87   Desire Under the Elms

            Horse Cave Theatre
            Horse Cave, KY

            5 July - 25 Aug. 1985 (in repertory)

            Dir. Warren Hammack

E88   The Dreamy Kid

            Di Pinto Di Blu (off off Broadway)
            NYC

            1975 - 76 Season

89   Dynamo

        The Impossible Ragtime Theater (off off Broadway)
        NYC

        29 Oct. 1976

        Dir. George Ferencz
        Setting - Bill Stabile
        Lighting - John Gisondi

        Minister Hutchins Light - Frank Hamilton
        Amelia Light - Helen Breed
        Reuben Light - Ray Wise
        Mae Fife - Rosemary Foley
        Ramsey Fife - David Tress
        Ada Fife - Shelley Wyant

              Gussow, Mel. Dynamo. New York Times 12 Nov. 1976:
                 C22:1.

              The play is "overwrought, the dialogue thunderstruck"
              yet the work "survives as a play of ideas." This
              production "makes Dynamo throb with renewed energy."

90   The Emperor Jones

        Perry Street Theater
        NYC

        Opened by 22 Sept. 1977

        Dir. Donald J. Schulte/Vasek Simek
        Ritual Dance Choreography - Randy Thomas
        Afro-Cuban Score - Eric Diamond

        Brutus Jones - Rodney Hudson
        Smithers - Philip Karnell

              Baker, Rob. Review. After Dark Nov. 1977: 94.

              The acting by Rodney Hudson and Philip Karnell was
              "exemplary."

>   Gussow, Mel. Off Off Broadway. New York Times 23 Sept
                  1977: C5.

             Endorses the production and play. Says recent politica
             events and personalities [Idi Amin] make the play even
             more meaningful. Commends the performances of Rodney
             Hudson and Philip Karnell.

>   Hill, Holly. Review. New York Theatre Review.
             Nov. 1977: 94.

>   Wilkins, Frederick C. Review. EON 1.3 (1978): 18-19.

E91 The Emperor Jones

        Seven Ages and on tour
        NYC

        1977

E92 The Emperor Jones

        Masque and Gown of Bowdoin College
        Brunswick, ME

        Feb. 1979

        Dir. Peter Honchaurk

E93 The Emperor Jones

        American Theatre Experiment
        Fordham U Theatre
        NYC

        10 - 22 Sept. 1979

        Brutus Jones - Stephen D. Agins

E94 The Emperor Jones

        Fusion Project
        28th St. Theater

        4 - 16 Oct. 1982

295   The Emperor Jones

            American Music Theater Festival
            Philadelphia, PA

            23 June – 15 July 1984

            Dir. Donald McKayle
            Music by Coleridge Taylor Perkinson

296   The Emperor Jones

            SUNY – Purchase
            Purchase, NY

            18 – 22 and 25 – 29 July 1984

            Dir. and choreographer – Donald McKayle

            Brutus Jones – James Earl Jones

297   The First Man

            Stage Left, Inc.
            2nd Avenue and 14th St.
            New Vic Theatre
            NYC

            10 – 28 Oct. 1984

            Dir. Ray Hubener

                Vena, Gary. Review. EON 8.3 (1984): 28-29.

E98   The Great God Brown

                 The Phoenix Repertory Company
                 149 W. 45th Street
                 The Lyceum Theater
                 NYC

                 Opened 10 Dec. 1972 for 19 performances

                 Dir. Harold Prince
                 Scenery - Boris Aronson
                 Costumes & Masks - Carolyn Parker
                 Lighting - Tharon Musser

                 William Brown - John Glover
                 Mrs. Brown - Bonnie Gallup
                 Mr. Brown - Paul Hecht
                 Dion Anthony - John McMartin
                 Mrs. Anthony - Charlotte Moore
                 Mr. Anthony - James Greene
                 Margaret - Katherine Helmond
                 Cybel - Marilyn Sokol
                 Older Son - Robert Phelps
                 Younger Son - Thomas A. Stewart
                 Older Draftsman - Bill Moor
                 Younger Draftsman - Clyde Burton
                 Committee - David Dukes, Peter Friedman and Ellen Tovatt
                 Policeman - Curt Karabalis

                 [listed because of reviews published in 1973.]

>   Clurman, Harold. Theatre. Nation. 1 Jan. 1973:
                              28-29.

                         Says that, "though a rather confusing play," it has a
                         certain staying power. It's about "personal torment"
                         that, however, "acquires an extension in social
                         meaning." The fault with this production is that
                         "Brown's centrality in the play has not been realized.
                         The characters lack dimension or depth so that the the
                         and conflict have been trivialized. Still, O'Neill's
                         voice is not entirely lost.

99   The Great God Brown

        Germinal Theatre
        Denver, CO

        Fall 1977

        Dir. E. Baierlein

            MacKay, Brenda.   Review.   New York Theatre Review
                 Dec. 1977: 32.

100 The Great God Brown

        Laurie Theatre
        Brandeis University
        Waltham, MA

        11 - 15 Apr. 1984

        Dir. David Wheeler

        Billy Brown - Christopher Scheithe
        Margaret - Gayle Keller
        Billy's Mask - Bump Heeter
        Dion's Mask - Norm Silver

101 The Great God Brown

        Department of Theatre
        SUNY - Albany

        20 - 23 Nov. 1985

        Dir. Jarka Burian

E102 The Hairy Ape -- played with Ile, no. E135 and Voyage, no. E181.

      Morgan's Bar
      134 Reade Street
      NYC

      Jan. 1976

>   Gussow, Mel. Review of three plays by O'Neill. New
            York Times 14 Jan. 1976: 17:4.

            Ile is played during lunch. Voyage is played with the
            bar at Morgan's used as the central prop. The plays ar
            introduced by sea chanties.

E103 The Hairy Ape

      Impossible Ragtime Theater (off off Broadway)
      NYC

      10 Jan. 1976

      Art Dirs. Ted Story and George Ferencz

      Dir. George Ferencz
      Environment - Ron Daley and George Ferencz
      Lighting - John Gisondi

      Parasite - Pattie Baker
      Jail Guard - Louis Braunstein
      Paddy - Richard Carballo
      Political Prisoner - Spencer Cohen
      Mildred's Aunt - Cynthia Crane
      Secretary I.W.W. - Greg Fabian
      Parasite - Margaret Flanagan
      Second Engineer - Jonathan Foster
      Lang - Jonathan Frakes
      Cop - Drew Keil
      Mildred Douglas - Annette Kurek
      Parasite - Karen L. Pontius
      Parasite - Kristen Richards
      Yank - Ray Wise
      Fourth Engineer - Stephen Zuckerman

>   Rich, Alan. Review. New York 15 Mar. 1976: 75.

            Finds the play is a bad one. Asks what the point
            is--"Rich is bad and poor is good? An ignorant brute

a happy brute?" Says, though, that the Impossible
Ragtime Theater under the direction of George Ferencz
produced O'Neill "agreeably" and "intelligently.

104 The Hairy Ape

Hanover College Theatre of Indiana
at Tao House
Danville, CA

July 1976

Staged by Tom G. Evans

Yank - Jim Baird

Wilkins, Frederick C. Review. EON 1.3 (1978): 19-20.

105 The Hairy Ape

Hopkins Center
Dartmouth College
Hanover, NH

8 - 29 Aug. 1979

Dir. Michael Rutenberg

Wilkins, Frederick C. Review. EON 3.3 (1980): 9-10.

06 The Hairy Ape

Studio Theatre Production
Washington Square--New York U
NYC

16 - 26 June 1982

Dirs. Rob Mulholland and Harold Easton

Wilkins, Frederick C. Review. EON 6.1 (1982): 47-49.

E107 <u>The Hairy Ape</u>

        725 Broadway Theatre
        NYC

        27 Oct. - 5 Nov. 1983

E108 <u>The Hairy Ape</u>

        Strider Theater, Runnels Union
        Colby College
        Waterville, ME

        7 - 9 Feb. 1985

        Dir. Susan Perry

E109 <u>The Hairy Ape</u>

        Wilma Theatre
        Philadelphia, PA

        12 Mar. - 21 Apr. 1985

        Dir. Blanka Zizka

E110 <u>Hughie</u>

        Lolly's Theater Club (off off Broadway)
        NYC

        9 Aug. 1973

E111 <u>Hughie</u>

        American Theatre Company (off off Broadway)
        NYC

        9 Nov. 1973

112 Hughie

        Chicago-At-The-First, Chicago Center
        Chicago, IL

        Opened in April 1974

        Then the John Golden Theatre
        NYC

        Opened 11 Feb. 1975

        Dir. Martin Fried
        Setting - James E. Maronek
        Lighting - Bengt Nygren

        Presented - Jay Julien/Sidney Eden

        Night Clerk - Peter Maloney
        "Erie" Smith - Ben Gazzara

            Anon. New York 3 Mar. 1975: 64-65.

            Thinks of Hughie as an unfinished work. Says if Robards
            couldn't do much with it, what can Ben Gazzara expect to
            do.

            Barnes, Clive. "Stage O'Neill's Hughie." New York
                Times 9 Apr. 1974: 35.

            Reviews one of the Chicago performances. The play
            is among O'Neill's "finest achievements" Gazzara "is
            absolutely right for Erie Smith."

            Barnes, Clive. "O'Neill's Hughie and David Milton's
                Duet." New York Times 12 Feb. 1975: 48;
                NYTCR 1975: 355.

            "Brief but perfect . . . celebrating in lean, even brisk
            language, the spirit of man's hopeful failure."
            Enthusiastic over the production in all respects (seems
            not to sense that the night clerk is anything but a pair
            of ears).

> Beaufort, John. Theater/"Gazzara Duo." Christian
Science Monitor 21 Feb. 1975; NYTCR 1975: 355

Discusses the themes of loneliness and lost illusions.
Gazzara "exposes the hollowness behind the braggadocio
The night clerk is his audience.

> Clurman, Harold. Theatre. Nation 15 Mar. 1975:
314-15.

Hughie is "one of O'Neill's most admirable small-scale
accomplishments." Comments that Ben Gazzara is
"successful in playing it [the role of Erie] for
laughs."

> Gill, Brendan. The Theatre. New Yorker 24 Feb. 1975
95.

Says that without the background film and sound track
miss the important "bitter humor" that the hotel clerk
own fantasies are just "as vivid as Smith's and even
more pitiful."

> Gottfried, Martin. Theater/"Gazzara Revives O'Neill."
New York Post 12 Feb. 1975; NYTCR 1975: 354.

The play is "second-rate," rambles, but ends touching
Erie is a "slight variation on Hickey."

> Hughes, Catharine. "Revival of (some of) the Fittest.
America 22 Mar. 1975: 219-20.

Finds the play in quality "distinctly second drawer"
Hughie a "one-dimensional" character.

> Kerr, Walter. "Looking into O'Neill's Mirror in
Hughie." New York Times 23 Feb. 1975: II 1.

Hughie is really a mirror--"a pair of credulous eyes."
Erie creates a new Hughie out of the Nightclerk.
Supportive of the production.

> Morrow, Lance. "The Uses of Illusion." Time 22 Apr
1974; NYTCR 1974: 356.

Reviews one of the Chicago performances. Ben Gazzara
plays Erie Smith superbly."

> Probst, Leonard. NBC-Radio. 11 Feb. 1975; <u>NYTCR</u> 1975:
>   357.

Gazzara lacks "the depth to penetrate <u>Hughie</u>." is
"leaden and monotonous."

> Sanders, Kevin. WABC-TV 11 Feb. 1975; <u>NYTCR</u> 1975:
>   357.

"A very good example of very bad O'Neill." Erie is
"another one of O'Neill's relentlessly boring drunks,
who tells his "desolately dull story." The play is a
"long, rambling harangue," "has no context to give it
resonance, no layers to give it depth." "Gazzara tries
his best" but . . .

> Thompson, Howard. "O'Neill's <u>Hughie</u> is Star Gazzara."
>   <u>New York Times</u> 18 Aug. 1974: 40.

An announcement (erroneous) that <u>Hughie</u> is scheduled to
open at the Booth Theater, NYC, 15 Oct., starring Ben
Gazzara, in his first stage appearance in NYC since
1963, when he played in the Actors Studio revival of
<u>Interlude</u>. Gazzara, interviewed by phone, finds Erie
Smith, despite his losing streak, "a prince of a man,
brave in the face of defeat, and the play, unlike a lot
of O'Neill, does end on a note of hope."

Watts, Douglas. "Gazzara Shines in Slim Twin Bill."
    <u>Daily News</u> 12 Feb. 1975; <u>NYTCR</u> 1975: 354.

The play is sometimes funny but "hardly seems worth the
effort." The night clerk is a "sounding board" for
Erie, who is "a character in search of a play."

113 <u>Hughie</u>

No Smoking Playhouse
354 45th St.
NYC

Dec. 1978

Dir. Frank Girardeau

E114 <u>Hughie</u>

>   Old Creamery Theatre Company
        Garrison, IA

        7 - 8 Dec. 1979

E115 <u>Hughie</u>

        Hudson Guild Theatre (off off Broadway)
        441 W. 26th St.
        NYC

        14 Jan. - 5 Feb. 1980

        Dir. David Kerry Heefner

E116 <u>Hughie</u>

        National Theatre
        Cottesloe
        London

        22 Jan. - Apr. 1980

        Dir. Bill Bryden
        Design - Hayden Griffen
        Lights - Andy Phillips

        Erie Smith - Stacy Keach
        Night Clerk - Howard Goorney

>   Gow, Gordon. Review of <u>Hughie</u>. <u>Plays and Players</u>. 2
                    (1980): 22-23.

                Speaks well of the play and of the production. Keach
                "gripping" as Erie Smith. Observes that Charles Hughe
                goes "off into imaginative flights of his own," but he
                doesn't say how the audience could know.

>   Taylor, John Russell. "London." <u>Drama: The Quarterl</u>
                    <u>Theatre Review</u> 136 (1980): 37-48.

                Finds Stacey Keach a "formidable actor" who needs
                "something more substantial . . . to stretch his
                powers." The play is "not very complex" but "quite
                clever."

E117 <u>Hughie</u>

> Studio Theatre Production
> Washington Square, NYU
> NYC
>
> 27 - 30 Jan. 1980
>
> Dir. Rob Mulholland

118 <u>Hughie</u>

> Black Swan Theatre
> Oregon Shakespearean Festival
> Ashland, OR
>
> July - Sept. 1980

119 <u>Hughie</u>

> Great Lakes Shakespeare Festival
> Lakewood Civic Auditorium
> Cleveland, OH
>
> 7, 9 - 10, 15, 20 Aug. and 4, 7 Sept. 1980

120 <u>Hughie</u>

> Hyde Park Festival Theater
> Hyde Park, NY
>
> 17 - 21 June 1981
>
> Later The White Barn Theater
> Westport, CT
>
> 16 - 18 Oct. 1981
>
> Erie Smith - Jason Robards
> Night Clerk - Jack Dodson

E120 <u>Hughie</u> -- double-billed with <u>The Stranger</u>

      South Street Theater
      424 W. 42nd St. (off off Broadway)
      NYC

      4 Nov. - 6 Dec. 1981

      Dir. Gino Giglio
      Setting - Bob Phillips
      Lighting - Malcolm Sturchio
      Sound - Amy Steindler

      Erie Smith - Michael Fischetti
      Night Clerk - Frank Geraci

>   Gussow, Mel. <u>New York Times</u> 1 Jan. 1982: 15.

          Finds Michael Fischetti's Erie Smith particularly
          effective. Nightclerk Frank Geraci is good as well.
          Giglio's direction is "resourceful."

E122 <u>Hughie</u> -- double-billed with <u>Carribees</u>, no. E229.

      Studio Theatre Productions
      Washington Square, NYU
      NYC

      26 - 30 Jan. 1982

      Dir. Rob Mulholland and Harold Easton

E123 <u>Hughie</u>

      American Repertory Theatre
      Cambridge, MA

      7 Apr. - 6 May 1983

      Dir. Bill Foeller

>   Connolly, Thomas F. Review. <u>EON</u> 8.1 (1983): 20-21.

124 Hughie

> One Act Theatre Company
> San Francisco, CA
>
> 23 Mar. - 5 May 1984
>
> Dir. Tom McDermott

125 Hughie

> Provincetown Playhouse
> Provincetown, MA
>
> 20 - 21 Sept. 1984
>
> Dir. John MacDonald
>
> Erie Smith - Stephen Joyce
> Night Clerk - Robert Zukerman

26 The Iceman Cometh

> Circle in the Square - Joseph E. Levine Theatre
>
> Preview 9 Dec. 1973
> Opened 13 Dec. 1973 for 85 performances
>
> Dir. Theodore Mann
> Set - Clarke Ducham
> Lighting - Jules Fisher
>
> Rocky - Joseph Ragora
> Larry - Michael Higgins
> Hugo - David Margulies
> Willie - Walter McGinn
> Harry - Stefan Gierasch
> Joe - Arthur French
> Don - Stephen McHattie
> Cecil - Jack Gwillim
> Piet - George Ebeling
> James Cameron - Tom Aldredge
> Pat - Rex Everhart
> Ed - Patrick Hines
> Margie - Marcia Savella
> Pearl - Jennie O'Hara
> Cora - Lois Smith
> Chuck - Pierrino Mascarino
> Hickey - James Earl Jones

Moran - Gene Fanning
Lieb - Ronald Siebert

> Anon. Review. New York 31 Dec. - 7 Jan. 1974: 84.

Says that the set and costumes are "fine," the lighting
"good." The blocking "works," but the cast is
indifferent in ability, inadequate in interpretation,
and undistinguished (except for James Earl Jones, who a
Hickey, is "impossible").

> Barnes, Clive. Iceman. New York Times 14 Dec. 1973:
    54.

Theodore Mann's direction is "careful, reverent but
lacks something in immediacy." James Earl Jones as
Hickey "was all right but all wrong": Jones seemed as
if he were "selling insurance rather than dreams."
Liked Michael Higgins as Larry, as well as Jack Gwilli
as the Captain and Tom Aldredge as the newspaperman.

> Clurman, Harold. Theatre. Nation 5 Jan. 1974: 29-3

Says it is the ambiguity of Iceman that holds the
viewer's attention, but this cast has faults.

> Gill, Brendan. "Stars in your Eyes." New Yorker
    24 Dec. 1973: 56.

The current production risks odious comparison with th
1956 Circle production and the American Film Theatre
version.

> Gottfried, Martin. The Theatre/"The Iceman Cometh."
    Women's Wear Daily 14 Dec. 1973; NYTCR 1973:
    149-50.

The play is technically a "mess," and too long for it
needs. Finds the production badly directed and Jones
inadequate as Hickey.

> Holder, Geoffrey. Review. NBC-TV 13 Dec. 1973; NYTC
    1973: 151.

The play is "great . . . where everyone suffers . . .
and you suffer with them." Jones is "brilliant and
inspired." Higgins is "haunting and penetrating."

Kalem, T. E. "Agon of the Sad Cafe." Time 24 Dec.
     1973: 57.

The actors, with the exception of Jones, are like
puppets, while Jones's performance is "disconcertingly
and divisively strong."

Kerr, Walter. "The Iceman is Absent Too Much." New
     York Times 23 Dec. 1973: II 3.

Is enthusiastic about Jones's Hickey, but finds that
there are vast portions of the play which must simply be
"endured," especially the segments without Jones. The
play should however be seen.

Kroll, Jack. Theater. Newsweek 31 Dec. 1973; NYTCR
     1973: 150.

A play one either loves or doesn't. Kroll loves it, but
Jones is ineffective as Hickey.

Simon, John. "Theatre Chronicle." Hudson Review 27
     (1974): 82-90.

Director Mann either chose poor actors or miscast good
ones. Jones as Hickey is implausible.

Watt, Douglas. "O'Neill's Iceman: A Spellbinder."
     Daily News 14 Dec. 1973; NYTCR 1973: 148.

"Enthralling play," "absorbing revival," a
"spellbinder."

Watts, Richard. Theater/"O'Neill's Defense of
     Illusions." New York Post 14 Dec. 1973;
     NYTCR 1973: 148.

Ranks this play as "only slightly beneath those other
masterpieces, Journey and Mourning." Jones is not up to
his standard.

Wilson, Edwin. The Theater/"Harry Hope's Hopeless Bar."
     Wall Street Journal 21 Dec. 1973; NYTCR 1973:
     149.

Mostly kudos for Jones.

E127 The Iceman Cometh

Aldwych Theatre
Royal Shakespeare Company
London

18 June 1976

Dir. Howard Davies
Designed - Chris Dyer
Lighting - David Hersey

Harry Hope - Norman Rodway
Ed Mosher - Harry Towb
Pat McGloin - Raymond Marlowe
Rocky - Bob Hoskins
Chuck - David Daker
Piet Wetjoen - Hal Galili
Cecil Lewis - Richard Simpson
Jimmy Tomorrow - John Warner
Joe Mott - Cy Grant
Larry Slade - Patrick Stewart
Hugo Kalmar - Patrick Godfrey
Willie Oban - Gary Bond
Don Parritt - Kenneth Cranham
Pearl - Patti Love
Margie - Paola Dionisotti
Cora - Lynda Marchal
Hickey - Alan Tilvern
Moran - Larry Hoodekoff
Lieb - Karl Held

>   Gussow, Mel. "Stage View." New York Times 18 July
                 1976: II 5:1.

            Says London reviews were enthusiastic but anyone who
            seen Robards' Hickey will be dissatisfied. Alan Tilv
            "falls far short of emcompassing" Hickey's character.
            The others in the cast are not effective.

>   Lambert, J. W. Review. Drama: The Quarterly Theatr
                 Review 122 (1976): 51-53.

            Finds this version of the play well done but not well
            enough to dispel irritation with O'Neill's
            repetitiveness. Tilvern as Hickey, "the most despera
            of hollow men," "looked strangely like a rough-diamor
            Nixon."

Mairowitz, David Zane. "The Iceman Cometh." Plays and
    Players 23 (1976): 17.

The play is a "masterpiece despite great structural
flaws and a second-rate 'philosophy.'" But the
production is timid, doing nothing to overcome the
flaws, and so the play "lumbers and wallows."

Wardle, Irving. Review. Times 21 June 1976: 13d.

Sees Iceman as O'Neill's transition play, standing
between two phases of O'Neill's dramatic career, the
early, secretly autobiographical plays, like Dynamo,
Brown, and after O'Neill "came out into the open," with
Journey. Notes that the theme, "that mankind in general
are kept going by their dreams," is Ibsen's, in The Wild
Duck, but O'Neill blurs the theme's universality by
placing it in the "context of alcoholic futility." The
production is "altogether a rich extension" to the Royal
Shakespeare Company repertory.

28 The Iceman Cometh

Loretto-Hilton Repertory Theatre
St. Louis, MO

13 Oct. - 11 Nov. 1978

Dir. Davey Marlin-Jones

9 The Iceman Cometh

National Theater
Cottesloe
London

Opened March 1980

Dir. Bill Bryden
Design - Hayden Griffin
Music - John Tams

Hickey - Jack Shepherd/Robert Stephens
Rocky - John Satthouse
Larry - Niall Toibin
Hugo - Tony Haygarth
Willie - James Grant
Harry - JG Devlin

Joe Mutt - Oscar James
Don Parrit - Kevin McNally
Cicil Lewis - Frederick Treves
Piet Wetjoen - Jeffrey G. Chiswick
Cameron - Gawn Grainger
McGloin - Brian Glover
Margie - Edna Dore
Pearl - Ann Lynn
Ed Mosher - Derek Newark
Cora - Morag Hood
Morello - Brian Protheroe
Moran - John Tams
Lieb - Elliott Cooper & Anthony Falkingham

>   Hayman, Ronald. "Summary of Hayman's review of Iceman
                Plays and Players 27.6 (1980): 23.

            Generally unenthusiastic. The production was awkwardl
            conceived and Hickey badly cast. The handling of the
            large number of people on stage was inept.

>   Taylor, H. Hobson, Jr. Review. Drama: The
                Quarterly Theatre Review 136 (1980): 35-36.

            Says that the production refreshes, strengthens, and
            fills one with the "high tragic significance of life."
            Acknowledges that O'Neill's phrases are "lame,"
            "pretentious," and "repetitive," but says the play ra
            with Othello and the Agamemnon. Says Hickey's scene
            the last supper with Hickey "a destructive Christ
            rendering through an equivocal gospel sordid misery i
            a yet more miserable sordidness."

E130 The Iceman Cometh

            New Theater (Hasty Pudding Playhouse)
            Holyoke St.
            Cambridge, MA

            10 - 27 Apr. 1980

            Dir. Larry McCarthy

131 The Iceman Cometh

        Trinity Square Repertory Company
        Providence, RI

        30 Jan - 29 Feb. 1981

        Dir. Philip Minor

            Wilkins, Frederick C. Review. EON 5.1 (1981): 15-17.

132 The Iceman Cometh

        Sea View Playwrights' Theatre
        Staten Island

        29 Sept. - 2 Oct. 1983

33 The Iceman Cometh

        American National Theater
        Eisenhower Theater, Kennedy Center
        Washington, DC

        31 July - 14 Sept. 1985

        Then the Lunt-Fontanne Theatre, Broadway
        NYC

        21 - 29 Sept. 1985

        Dir. José Quintero
        Scenery - Ben Edwards
        Costumes - Jane Greenwood
        Prod. - Lewis Allen, James Nederlander, Stephen Orchard,
            Ben Edwards

        Hickey - Jason Robards
        Larry Slade - Donald Moffat
        Harry Hope - Barnard Hughes
        Rocky - John Pankow
        Joe Mott - Roger Robinson
        Chuck - Harris Laskawy
        Margie - Natalie Nogulich
        Don Parrett - Paul McCrane
        Gen. Wetjuen - Frederick Neumann
        Cora - Caroline Aaron
        Willie Oban - John Christopher Jones

Hugo Kalmar - Leonard Cimini
Pat McGloin - Pat McNamara
Ed Mosher - Allen Swift
Cecil Lewis - Bill Moor
Pearl - Kristine Nielsen
Jimmy Tomorrow - James Green

> Brown, Joe. "The Iceman Cometh Again." Washington Po
Weekend 16 Aug. 1985: 7.

Salutes the cast as "excellent." Says that Robards'
30-minute monologue is a "tour de force" and that Ben
Edwards' set suggests a "patina of neglect." The play
itself, is as "monumental (and slow-going) as a
glacier."

> Henry, William A. III. "Recreating a Stage Legend."
Time 14 Oct. 1985: 75.

Says the Quintero-Robards revival of Iceman, 28 years
after the 1956 Quintero-Robards Iceman, is a "triumph,
thanks to a "superb cast."

> Wilkins, Frederick C. "Family Reunion at the Bottom c
the Sea." EON 9.3 (1985): 23-28.

E134 Ile

The Quaigh
Quaigh Theater,
808 Lexington Avenue (at 62d Street).

Jan. 1976

Dir. Mary Tierney

With William Hickey, Peter Hadreas, Brian Dennehy, James D
Marse, Evelyn Seubert, Jere Allen, Ralf Nemec.

E135 Ile -- played with Voyage, no. E181, and Ape, no. E102 (q.v. fc
review).

Morgan's Bar
134 Reade Street
NYC

Jan. 1976

E136 Ile -- played with The Long Voyage Home, no. E182.

        Source at the ASTA
        507 8th St. SE
        Washington, DC

        Aug. 1978

        Dir. Camille David

--- Ile -- Six Plays of the Sea, no. E240.

--- Ile -- see Sea Plays at Monte Cristo, no. E237.

--- In the Zone -- see The Sea Plays of Eugene O'Neill, no. E238.

--- In the Zone -- see The Long Voyage Home, no. E183.

E137 In the Zone -- played with Voyage, no. E184.

        Spectrum
        277 Park Avenue South

        Spring 1979 in repertory

        Dir. Norman Morrow

E138 In the Zone

        Ensemble Company
        New Haven, CT

        23 - 26 July 1980

--- In the Zone -- see Six Plays of the Sea, no. E240.

--- In the Zone -- see Sea Plays at Monte Cristo, no. E237.

E139 Long Day's Journey into Night

        National Theatre Company
        London

        21 Dec. 1971 - 8 Jan. 1973. (122 performances in rep.)

        Tyrone - Laurence Olivier
        Mary - Constance Cummings
        Jamie - Dennis Quilley
        Edmund - Ronald Pickup

>   Clarke, Gerald. Viewpoints. _Time_. 12 Mar. 1973:
              67-68.

           Touches on the background of "America's greatest play.
           Olivier and Constance Cummings both handle well the
           contrarities of the characters they play. Quilley and
           Pickup are adequate.

>   Gautier, J. J. Review. _Le Figaro_ 14 Sept. 1973: 21.

E140 Long Day's Journey into Night (off off Broadway)

        Actors Studio
        NYC

        10 Dec. 1973 for nine performances

E141 Long Day's Journey into Night (off off Broadway)

        Hudson Guild Theater
        NYC

        Dec. 1974

E142 Long Day's Journey into Night

        Thorndike Theatre
        London

        Winter 1974

        Frank Grimes, Trevor Bannister as the brothers Tyrone

143 Long Day's Journey into Night

> Kennedy Center
> Washington, DC
>
> Then Brooklyn Academy of Music
> NYC
>
> 28 Jan. - 8 Feb. 1976
>
> Dir. Jason Robards
> Decor - Ben Edwards
> Costumes - Jane Greenwood
> Lighting - Ken Billington
>
> James Tyrone - Jason Robards
> Mary Cavan Tyrone - Zoe Caldwell
> James Tyrone Jr. - Kevin Conway
> Edmund Tyrone - Michael Moriarty
> Cathleen - Lindsay Crouse

>> Barnes, Clive. "Long Day's Journey into Greatness."
>> New York Times 29 Jan. 1976: 26; NYTCR 1976:
>> 343.

>> Robards as Tyrone is "unable to reach the pain of the
>> play." The play dawdles under his direction but can
>> survive even bad handling.

>> Feingold, Michael. "Robards Returns to O'Neill's
>> Journey." New York Times 25 Jan. 1976: II 5.

>> Says that Journey is the "greatest American play,"
>> partly because it is "the least pleasant." Mixed
>> response to the Robards-directed production. Says Zoe
>> Caldwell is the best, Robards is competent as Tyrone,
>> but sons Kevin Conway (Jamie) and Michael Moriarty are
>> lacking.

>> Gottfried, Martin. "An Endless Night in Brooklyn." New
>> York Post 29 Jan. 1976; NYTCR 1976: 346.

>> Thinks the play overrated, the plotting blurry.
>> Characterization was "heavy except for Zoe Caldwell's
>> Mary. . . ."

> Gussow, Mel. Review. New York Times 22 Dec. 1975:
      44:1.

Writes on Jason Robards as actor in and director of
Journey. Robards previously saw the Jamie-Tyrone-Mary
trinity as the core of the play. Now he sees the core
as Edmund.

> Kissel, Howard. The Theatre/"Long Day's Journey into
      Night." Women's Wear Daily 29 Jan. 1976; NYTCR
      1976: 345.

American tragedy hinges on the lack of resolution, on
the back of any "new wisdom and therefore of the need
accept pain." Journey "begins with false hopes and en
with bitter wisdom." This production is "soundly pace
and sensitively acted." "Solid, honest, and deeply
responsive to the extraordinary riches of the play."

> Kroll, Jack. "The Haunted Tyrones." Newsweek 9 Feb,
      1976: 52-53.

The production, which was originally staged for the
Kennedy Center, is "absolute reality". Says play
entitles O'Neill to "sit in the shade with Sophocles."

> Oliver, Edith. "Journey into Brooklyn." New Yorker
      9 Feb. 1976: 78.

Although she doesn't find Journey a masterpiece, she
compliments this production of the play, which she say
Mary dominates.

> Probst, Leonard. NBC-Radio. 29 Jan. 1976.

The play is great, although this is not the finest
production. Nonetheless, it is a "memorable" one.
"Slow to start." Direction is "soft and bland."

> Sterrit, David. "Dramatic Star Also Makes Directing
      Debut." Christian Science Monitor 5 Feb. 1976
      NYTCR 1976: 344.

A "gloomy" play, "difficult to bring off." This
production is slack in pace, but Mary looms large.

Tucker, Carl. "O'Neill Explores the Wilderness of
    Despair." Village Voice 9 Feb. 1976: 99.

Journey is boring, obvious, uneventful, goes nowhere,
and has a creed of hopelessness, but though an unlikely
masterpiece, it is still one.

Watt, Douglas. "A Divided Homefront." Daily News 29
    Jan. 1976; NYTCR 1976: 344.

The play towers, the cast is "stellar" but doesn't quite
gel. Zoe Caldwell's Mary is thoughtfully portrayed to
emphasize the "spitefulness underlying her sad
addiction."

Wertheim, Albert. Review. Educational Theatre Journal
    28 (1976): 122-24.

Says the production turns the play into a character
study of Mary and considers her effect on others.
Script cuts eliminate the Catholicism and the references
to the Virgin Mary and the convent days. The
Characters' main concern is in curing her. Says such
"slanting . . . need not . . . necessarily do the
original disservice."

+4 Long Day's Journey into Night

Creative Arts Center
West Virginia University
Morgantown, WV

April 1976

Dir. John Whitmore

E144 <u>Long Day's Journey into Night</u>

> Ahmanson Theater
> Los Angeles, CA
>
> Feb. 1977
>
> Dir. Robert Fryer
>
> Tyrone — Charlton Heston
> Mary — Debora Kerr
> Tyrone sons — Andrew Prine, George Burke

>

> Flatley, Guy. "At the Movies." <u>New York Times</u> 11 Feb
> 1977: III 9.
>
> Makes reference to the Ahmanson Theater production. Sa
> the role of Tyrone is "histrionically taxing, minimal
> lucrative."

>

> Murray, William. "A Long Day's Journey to the Bar."
> <u>New West</u> 14 Mar. 1977: 19-20.
>
> Calls the cutting of <u>Journey</u> "artistic rape." Says
> O'Neill was not a slick writer and required time to
> develop the ideas. Says Charlton Heston had "gall" t
> attempt the role of James Tyrone, played by such emin
> actors as Sir Laurence Olivier and Frederic March. S
> Andrew Pine and Robert Burke but "dimly impersonate"
> Tyrone boys.

E146 <u>Long Day's Journey into Night</u>

> Shubert Theatre
> Boston, MA
>
> 3 - 15 May 1977
>
> Dir. Michael Kahn
>
> Tyrone — Jose Ferrer
> Mary — Kate Reid

147 Long Day's Journey into Night

        Provincetown Playhouse on the Wharf
        Goswold St.
        Provincetown, MA

        Summer 1977

148 Long Day's Journey into Night -- alternating with Wilderness,
    no. E4 (q.v. for reviews).

        Milwaukee Repertory Theatre Company
        Milwaukee, WI

        4 Nov. 1977 - 22 Jan. 1978

        Dir. Irene Lewis
        Design - R.A. Graham

        Richard Miller/Edmund - Anthony Heald
        Essie Miller/Mary - Regina Davis
        Nat Miller/Tyrone - Robert Burr
        Uncle Sid/Jamie - Ronald Frazer

149 Long Day's Journey into Night

        Academy Theatre
        Atlanta, GA

        23 Mar. - 21 Apr. 1978; on tour 7 Sept. - 1 Oct. 1978

        Dir. F. Wittow

150 Long Day's Journey into Night

        George St. Playhouse
        New Brunswick, NJ

        24 Nov. - 16 Dec. 1978

E151 Long Day's Journey into Night

>American Stanislavski Theatre
Greenwich Mews Theatre
141 W. 13th St.
NYC

1 Dec. 1978 - 21 May 1979

Dir. Sonia Moore

E152 Long Day's Journey into Night

>Playmakers Repertory Company
Chapel Hill, NC

In rep. 1978-79 Season

E153 Long Day's Journey into Night

>Cohoes Music Hall
Cohoes, NY

27 Jan. - 8 Feb. 1979

Dir. L. Ambrosio

E154 Long Day's Journey into Night

>Haymarket Theatre
Leicester, England

7 - 24 Feb. 1979

E155 Long Day's Journey into Night

>Asolo State Theater
Sarasota, FL

6 Apr. - 12 July 1979

Dir. Bradford Wallace

156 Long Day's Journey into Night

       Queens College Summer Theatre
       Flushing, NY

       9 - 11 Aug. 1979

157 Long Day's Journey into Night

       The Nassau Repertory
       The Adelphi Calderone Theater

       22, 23, 29 Feb. and 1, 7, 8, 14, 15 Mar. 1980

       Dir. Clinton J. Atkinson
       Setting - Kenneth Hollamon

       Mary - Catherine Byers
       Tyrone - Patrick Beatey
       Jamie - Brian Evers
       Edmund - Mark Arnott
       Cathleen - Nancy Elizabeth Kammer

           Klein, Alvin. "Theater in Review." New York Times
               2 Mar. 1980: XXI 4-5.

           The staging is "fragmented," and the production lacks a
           "sense of momentum." There is "no tragic fiber." A
           disservice to O'Neill.

158 Long Day's Journey into Night

       Avon Theatre, Stratford Festival
       Stratford, ONT

       In rep. 4 Oct. - 8 Nov. 1980

       Dir. Robin Phillips
       Setting - Susan Benson
       Lighting - Michael J. Whitefield

       Tyrone - William Hutt
       Mary - Jessica Tandy
       Edmund - Brent Carver
       Jamie - Graeme Campbell

           Czarnecki, Mark. "The Reign of Dissension." Macleans
               20 Oct. 1980: 69.

Journey is "more sauna than play," endured because
"overexposure to truth is considered good for the soul.
Refers to the "loving twist of the knife," the "hate-
prompted hug,: the clear exposition of all passions.
Phillips' production is "not great theatre" but good.
Hutt's Tyrone is "a masterful portrait," Carver's
Edmund is "suitably tender and poetic," but Jessica
Tandy overemphasizes Mary's frailty and Campbell is
miscast--his Jamie too robust.

>   Wilkins, Frederick C. Review. EON (1980): 25-27.

E159 Long Day's Journey into Night

        The Virginia Players
        Culbreth Theatre, U of Virginia
        Charlottesville, VA

        5 - 13 Dec. 1980

        Dir. Jay E. Raphael

E160 Long Day's Journey into Night

        Apple Corps Theatre Company
        NYC

        8 Jan. - 1 Feb. 1981

        Dir. David O. Glazer

E160 Long Day's Journey into Night

        The Richard Allen Center for Culture & Art
        The Common Theater, St. Peter's Church
        Then the Public/Anspacher Theatre (Presented by Joseph Papp

        NYC

        18 Mar. 1981 for 87 performances

        Dir. Geraldine Fitzgerald
        Set - Paul Scheffler
        Light - John Matthiessen

Tyrone - Earle Hyman
Jamie - Al Freeman, Jr.
Mary - Gloria Foster
Edmund - Peter Francis-James
Cathleen - Samantha McKoy

>

Barnes, Clive. "Long Day's Journey into Night." New
York Post 4 Mar. 1981; NYTCR 1981: 270-71.

Sees the long day as the "watershed" in the Tyrones'
family life.

•

Brooks, Marshall. Review. EON 5.1 (1981): 10-12.

•

Gussow, Mel. Theater/"Black Cast Stages O'Neill." New
York Times 3 Mar. 1981; NYTCR 1981: 271-72.

The production presents not a "black" but a "non-ethnic"
version of Journey. All play their roles well by
stressing relationships rather than atmosphere, and
prove that blacks can use the play as well as Irish
whites.

Kroll, Jack. "Passionate Journey." Newsweek 20 Apr.
1981: 104.

Says this all-black production works. Sees the play as
"both epic and tragic . . . an emotional Iliad . . .
that produces the great tragic entity of the modern
world--waste, pure human waste."

Sharp, Christopher. The Theatre/"Long Day's Journey
into Night." Women's Wear Daily. 3 Mar. 1981;
NYTCR 1981: 272.

Motivation is badly established in the first act but
good thereafter. Jamie's charm can only show when he is
drunk.

>   Sterrit, David. Theater/"Splendid Black Version of
           O'Neill Drama." <u>Christian Science Monitor</u> 23 Apr
           1981; <u>NYTCR</u> 1981: 272-73.

        A "drama" for all seasons--that rises above color. "Al
        the performers are splendid" but especially "the
        consistently touching" Mary.

>   Watt, Douglas. "<u>Long Day's Journey into Night</u>." Daily
           <u>News</u> 3 Mar. 1981; <u>NYTCR</u> 1981: 271.

        The Mary is "exquisite," the Jamie "superb," the Edmund
        "enormously appealing," the Tyrone "likable but dull."
        Though the director has not been able "to pull all the
        strands together," the production (staged in two halves
        with cuts) shows "the remarkable."

E162 <u>Long Day's Journey into Night</u>

        Floorboards Theatre Company
        Edinburgh

        The Edinburgh Festival Fringe

        Fall 1981

        Dir. Kate Harwood

>   Berkowitz, Gerald M. Review. <u>EON</u> 6.3 (1982): 27-28.

E163 <u>Long Day's Journey into Night</u>

        S. J. Experimental Theatre
        Yale School of Drama
        New Haven, CT

        30 Oct. - 7 Nov. 1981

        Dir. J. Michael Sparough

164 Long Day's Journey into Night

>   Richmond Shepard Theater Studios
    Hollywood, CA

    Late Spring 1982

>   Hanson, Eugene K.   Review.   EON 6.3 (1982):   28-29.

165 Long Day's Journey into Night

    Nucleo Eclettico
    Boston, MA

    Closed 3 Apr. 1982

    Dir. Marco Zarattini

        Brooks, Marshall.   Review.   EON 6.1 (1982):   42-43.

166 Long Day's Journey into Night

    Denison U Theatre
    Denison U
    Granville, OH

    12 - 20 Nov. 1982

    Dir. William Brasmer

167 Long Day's Journey into Night

    The Richard Allen Center for Culture & Art
    NYC

    2 performances on 18 Nov. 1982

    Dir. Geraldine Fitzgerald

E168 Long Day's Journey into Night

      North Carolina Shakespeare Festival
      High Point, NC

      27 July - 31 Aug. 1983

      Dir. Malcolm Morrison

>   Lister, Joedy. Review. EON 7.3 (1983): 26-27.

E169 Long Day's Journey into Night

      Arts Theatre
      London

      5 Apr. 1984

      Dir. Ludovica Villar-Hauser

      Mary - Darlene Johnson
      Jamie - Michael Deacon
      Tyrone - Trevor Martin
      Edmund - Sean Mathias

E170 Long Day's Journey into Night

      Warehouse Repertory
      Source Theater
      Washington, DC

      Closed 15 Apr. 1984

      Dir. Dorothy Neumann

2171 Long Day's Journey into Night

        Court Theatre
        U of Chicago

        12 Apr. – 13 May 1984

        Dir. Nicholas Rudall

        Tyrone – Tony Mockus
        James – Scott Jaeck
        Mary – Peg Small
        Edmund – Joseph Guzaldo

2172 Long Day's Journey into Night

        Intiman Theatre
        Seattle, WA

        8 June – 7 July 1984

        Dir. Margaret Booker

173 Long Day's Journey into Night

        Gateway Playhouse
        Wareham, MA

        22 June – 14 July 1984

        Dir. George W. Hayden

        Tyrone – Niels Miller
        Mary – Dorothy Taylor
        Edmund – Richard Giles
        Jamie – Roger Kelly

174 Long Day's Journey into Night

        Byrdcliffe Theater
        Woodstock, NY

        10 – 15 July 1984

E175 <u>Long Day's Journey into Night</u> -- in repertory with <u>Wilderness</u>,
     no. E40.

          San Diego Repertory Theatre
          San Diego, CA

          6 Sept. - 1 Nov. 1984

          Dir. Sam Woodhouse
          Design - Dan Dryden

          Mary - Jo Ann Reeves
          Tyrone - Mitchell Edmonds
          Jamie - Tavis Ross
          Edmund - Thom Murray
          Cathleen - Darla Cash

E176 <u>Long Day's Journey into Night</u>

          Abbey Theatre
          Dublin, Ireland

          Opened 14 Feb. 1985

          Dir. Patrick Laffan
          Design - Alfo O'Reilly

          Mary Tyrone - Siobhan McKenna

E177 <u>Long Day's Journey into Night</u>

          Marian Theatre
          Pacific Conservatory of the Performing Arts
          Santa Maria, CA

          Closed 17 Feb. 1985

          Dir. Bernard Kates

          Mary - Dorothy James
          Edmund - Robert Elliot
          James - Vincent Dowling

178 <u>Long Day's Journey into Night</u>

        Royal Exchange Theatre
        Manchester, England

        Opened 14 Mar. 1985

        Dir. Braham Murray

        Mary - Dilys Hamlett
        Jamie - Jonathan Hackett
        Edmund - Michael Mueller

179 <u>Long Day's Journey into Night</u>

        Long Wharf Theatre
        New Haven, CT

        1 Mar. - 14 Apr. 1985

        Dir. Arvin Brown

        Mary - Geraldine Fitzgerald

180 <u>Long Day's Journey into Night</u>

        New Day Repertory Company
        Vassar Institute Theater
        New Paltz, NY

        21 - 24 Aug. 1985

81 <u>The Long Voyage Home</u>--played with <u>Ile</u>, no. E135, and <u>Ape</u>, no. E102
   (q.v. for review).

        Morgan's Bar
        134 Reade Street
        NYC

        Jan. 1976

        Dir. Alex Sokoloff
        Musical Dir. Dan Emerich

        With - J.R. Horne, John Michaiski, Judith Gero, Robert
        Boardman, Ryan Kelley, Peter Jolly, Dan Emerich, Melissa
        Sutherland, Mary Shortkroff, Michael Zuckerman

The Long Voyage Home -- see The Sea Plays of Eugene O'Neill,
no. E238.

E182 The Long Voyage Home -- played with Ile, no. E136.

Source at the ASTA
507 8th St. SE
Washington, DC

Aug. 1978

Dir. Bart Whiteman

E183 The Long Voyage Home (Comprising under that title Caribbees,
Cardiff, Zone, Voyage)

National Theatre Company
Cottesloe Theatre
London

20 Feb. 1979 - 17 Mar. 1979. Revived Jan. 1980, see no. 18

Dir. Bill Bryden
Design - Hayden Griffen
Lighting - Andy Phillips
Music - John Tams
Sound - Ric Green

Driscoll - Niall Toibin
Yank - Dave King
Cocky - Bill Owen
Smitty - Jack Shepherd
Olson - Mark McManus
Scotty - James Grant
Big Frank, & Fat Joe - Brian Glover
Davis - Trevor Ray
Paul - John Tams
Captain and Donkeyman - Howard Goorney
1st Mate & a Sailor - Peter Armitage
Jack and Nick - Gawn Grainger
Ivan - Frederick Warder
Bella - Nadia Cottouse
Violet - Marsha Miller
Pearl - Shirley Allan
Freda - Edna Dore
Edna - June Watson

Elsom, John. "All at Sea." Listener 101 (1979): 325.

Finds O'Neill's sea plays inferior to Conrad's and
Hughes' sea stories. Notes O'Neill's cliches--the
shanghaied sailor, death at sea. Thinks the production
is good, but "unfocused."

Jones, Simon. Review. Plays and Players 26.8 (1979):
    24, 29.

Says that O'Neill's romanticism, anarchism, mysticism,
and acute grasp of social reality are all displayed, as
well as are his tendencies toward sentimentalism and
melodrama. Praises this production for its fidelity to
the original, even if it is a little ponderous. Says
Yank and Olson are especially well portrayed.

Taylor, John Russell. "London." Drama: The Quarterly
    Theatre Review 136 (1980): 41-43.

Review of productions of Voyage, Hughie and Iceman at
the Cottesloe. Voyage and Hughie are like dramatic
versions of O. Henry stories--anecdotes with a twist,
not great art but proficiently put together. The small
stage is used efficiently to conjure up a sense of
confinement in the below decks episodes.

84 The Long Voyage Home -- played with Zone, no. E137.

    Spectrum
    277 Park Avenue South

    Spring 1979 in repertory

    Dir. Norman Morrow

85 The Long Voyage Home -- A Revival, see no. E183.

    National Theatre Company
    Cottesloe Theatre
    London

        Fender, Stephen. "The Fatal Destiny." Times Literary
            Supplement 4008 (18 Jan. 1980): 62.

    Finds the representation of fate "a bit on the grand
    side" for such short plays. In O'Neill's longer plays
    speeches can produce an iornic distance between the

characters' public and private selves. In the shorter
plays such speeches become "isolated moments of rather
puzzling beauty."

---- The Long Voyage Home -- see Six Plays of the Sea, no. E240.

E186 The Long Voyage Home

        M.I.T. Drama Shop
        Kresge Little Theater
        Cambridge, MA

        4 - 6 Oct. 1984

        Dir. Robert N. Scanlan

>   Connolly, Thomas F. Review. EON 8.3 (1984): 35.

---- The Long Voyage Home -- see Sea Plays at Monte Christo, no. E237

E187 Marco Millions

        Playmakers Repertory Company
        Chapel Hill, NC

        16 Mar. - 2 Apr. 1978

        Dir. Tom Haas

E188 Marco Millions

        Sharon Playhouse
        Sharon, CT

        1-5, 8 - 12 Aug. 1978

E189 A Moon for the Misbegotten

      Mermaid Theatre
      London

      6 Sept. - Nov. 1973

      Dir. David Leveau

      Ian Bannen, Alan Devlin

E190 A Moon for the Misbegotten

      Lester Osterman - Richard Horner Production
      Morosco
      NYC

      Opened 29 Dec. 1973; recessed 13 July 1974.
      Reopened 3 Sept. 1974 for a total of 314 performances.

      Dir. José Quintero
      Set & Lights - Ben Edwards

      Josie Hogan - Colleen Dewhurst
      Mike Hogan - Edwin J. McDonough
      Phil Hogan - Ed Flanders
      James Tyrone, Jr. - Jason Robards
      T. Stedman Harder - John O'Leary

          Anon. Review. Playboy Apr. 1974: 42, 46.

          The production is a "restoration of a classic." The
          play's place in the O'Neill canon was uncertain until
          this production. The Dewhurst-Robards pairing is
          "symbiotic."

          Barnes, Clive. A Moon for the Misbegotten. New York
              Times 31 Dec. 1973: 22.

          Hails the production as a "landmark," calls the cast
          "ideal." Comments on the non-judgmental nature of the
          play and on the pieta suggestions: Dewhurst as the
          Virgin earth-mother, Robards, as the suffering Tyrone,
          and Flanders, as the sprightly Phil Hogan, get
          unqualified raves.

> Barnes, Clive. Review. London Times 10 Jan. 1974:
>   11g.

Speaks only in superlatives--it is a "landmark
production." Says the play is one of the four that made
O'Neill "one of the great playwrights of the modern
theatre."

> Clurman, Harold. Theatre. Nation. 19 Jan. 1974:
>   92-93.

Enthusiastic endorsement of the "best production of the
season." Applauds the Robards and Dewhurst performances
as well as Flanders', and Quintero's direction.

Gill, Brendan. "Views of Home." New Yorker 14 Jan.
    1974: 58.

Says the revival is "superb." Commends Dewhurst for
giving the "performance of her life," but says Robards
was uneasy in his role.

> Gottfried, Martin. The Theatre/"A Moon for the
>   Misbegotten." Women's Wear Daily 2 Jan. 1974;
>   NYTCR 1973: 121.

The staging is listless, the roles have little
dimension. Dewhurst gives Josie as much as can be given
the thin-ness of the character. The blocking on the li
of the stage make the production seem like a reading.
In this play "O'Neill's writing is at its clumsiest in
terms of literacy and boozy philosophizing."

> Harris, Leonard. WCBS-TV 11 Jan. 1974; NYTCR 1973:
>   122.

The play is a "masterpiece." The production
"magnificant."

> Holder, Geoffrey. NBC-TV 29 Dec. 1973; NYTCR 1973:
>   121.

Refers to the "great O'Neillian" director and to the
acting by "two great American actors" one of whom is
"pure brilliance," the other exhibiting "amazing
emotional power."

Hughes, Catharine. "The Performance is the Thing."
    America 19 Jan. 1974: 33.

Hails the production, although she is less enthusiastic
about the play itself. Says she will explain why the
production is so good, but doesn't--simply appreciates
the casting.

Kalem, T. E. "O'Neill Agonistes." Time 14 Jan. 1974:
    42.

Says that at the Morosco "power, beauty, passion, and
truth command the stage." Calls the production an
"unmitigated triumph" and that Quintero has
"beautifully orchestrated" the effort. Lauds Robards'
performance as "a touchstone for all actors to measure
themselves by" and says of Dewhurst that "no woman was
ever big enough for the part before."

Kerr, Walter. "It's a Rich Play, Richly Performed."
    New York Times 13 Jan. 1974: II 1.

Is "possibly O'Neill's best." Kudos for Colleen
Dewhurst--says she's particularly effective with the
unfinished lines in the text. Ed Flanders' performance
is "stunning." Robards begins "brilliantly." Kerr
Suggests that the impossibility of a relationship
between James Tyrone and Josie Hogan not be disclosed
until the fourth act.

Kauffmann, Stanley. "Stanley Kauffmann on Theatre."
    New Republic 26 Jan. 1974: 22, 34.

Dewhurst was ill-cast, as was Flanders, but Robards was
"superb."

Kroll, Jack. "Review of Misbegotten." Newsweek
    14 Jan. 1974: 83.

The review is almost all praise. The "most Irish" of
O'Neill's plays with an ambiance of Irish Catholicism,
puritanism, profanity, love, lust, "sense of
self-corruption," "polluted idealism."

> Melloan, George. The Theater/"A Dread Secret Unfolds o
    a Moonlit Porch." <u>Wall Street Journal</u> 2 Jan.
    1974; <u>NYTCR</u> 1973: 119-20.

"A great production, brilliant performances." Quintero
works "magic." The play is a rich "fabric of Irish wit
and subtle meanings." Notes that the O'Neills were
knights in Ireland and "the sense of tragedy of kingdom
lost" is deep in their consciousness.

> Miller, Jordan Y. Review. <u>Kansas Quarterly</u> 7.4 (1975)
    103-05.

Impressed that O'Neill's status has become such that a
commercial network would do <u>Moon</u> on prime time. Also
thinks the performances are of the highest quality, but
is still displeased with the play itself. Says Jamie
has no tragic stature and characters are always
retracting what they say.

> Nathan, Ben. Letter. <u>New York Times</u> 20 Oct. 1974:
    7.

Finds a "frail, weak-kneed work" in which O'Neill does
not make clear "what he had on his mind" until the last
act.

> Sanders, Kevin. WABC-TV 29 Dec. 1973; <u>NYTCR</u> 1973:
    122.

A bleak, dismal story of miserable people set in "Ma an
Pa Kettle country."

> Simon, John. "Theatre Chronicle." <u>Hudson Review</u> 27
    (1974): 265-66.

Mixed response. Finds Quintero's directing uninspired
but Dewhurst, Robards, and Flanders marvelous. Censur
O'Neill for "uncertain language, with its terrible
built-in obsolescence."

Watt, Douglas. "A Moon for the Misbegotten." Daily News
31 Dec. 1973; NYTCR 1973: 118.

"Stunning revival." The first act "almost pure
O'Casey."

Watts, Richard. Theater/ A Moon for the Misbegotten.
New York Post 31 Dec. 1973; NYTCR: 118.

"A superb play, superbly done." Notes the humor amidst
the tragedy. Josie and James Tyrone, Jr., are "among
O'Neill's most brilliant creations." Dewhurst is "right
for the role and looks very beautiful;" Robards is
"perfect;" Flanders "splendid."

191 A Moon for the Misbegotten

Guthrie Theatre
Minneapolis, MN

Opened 8 June 1977, on tour 1978

Dir. Nick Havinga

Jim - Peter Michael Goetz
Josie - Sharon Ernster
Hogan - Richard Russell Ramos

Eder, Richard. "Review of Moon for the Misbegotten."
New York Times 21 July 1977: C 19:1.

Says that "In this theatre the stage becomes an actor:"
that Director Havenga uses its thrust to act as a
"barometer of Josie's mercurial strength and
vulnerability" (She moves forward when she feels
strong, back when she feels weak).

Voelker, Paul D. "A Full Moon in Indianapolis."
EON 1.3 (1978): 15-17.

192 A Moon for the Misbegotten

Oregon Shakespeare Festival Association at Tao House
Danville, CA

24 & 25 Sept. 1977

E193 A Moon for the Misbegotten

        Intiman Theatre Company
        Seattle, WA

        Closed 15 Oct. 1977

        Dir. Margaret Booker

E194 A Moon for the Misbegotten

        Cohoes Music Hall
        Cohoes, NY

        31 Dec. 1977 - 28 Jan. 1978

        Dir. Tom Greunewald

E195 A Moon for the Misbegotten

        Foothills Theatre Company
        Worcester, MA

        11 - 29 Jan. 1978

E196 A Moon for the Misbegotten

        Playmakers Repertory Company
        Chapel Hill, NC

        16 Mar. - 2 Apr. 1978

        Dir. Tom Haas

E197 A Moon for the Misbegotten

        Berkeley Repertory Theatre
        Berkeley, CA

        21 Apr. 1978 - 28 May 1978

        Dir. M. Leibert

198 A Moon for the Misbegotten

> American Stage Festival
> Milford, NH
>
> 25 - 30 July 1978
>
> Dir. Stanley Wojewodski, Jr.

99 A Moon for the Misbegotten

> Lyric Stage Company
> 54 Charles St.
> Boston, MA
>
> 3 Jan. - 10 Feb. 1979
>
> Dir. Sue Bowlin

00 A Moon for the Misbegotten

> GeVa Theatre
> Rochester, NY
>
> 26 Jan. - 18 Feb. 1979

01 A Moon for the Misbegotten

> The Nassau Repertory
> The County Theater (in the Social Services Building)
>
> 30 & 31 Mar. 1979
>
> Dir. T.J. Barry
> Setting - Ken Hollamon
> Lighting - Victor En Yi Tan
>
> Josie - Caroline Sidney Abady
> Hogan - Tom Bahring
> James Tyrone, Jr. - James Gallagher
> With Steve Connor and John Little
>
> > Klein, Arvin. "Theater in Review." New York Times
> > 25 Mar. 1979: XXI 11.
> >
> > Finds the attempt at doing such a difficult play,
> > considering the company's resources, "foolhardy," the
> > performance "ineffectual and woe-begone."

E202 <u>A Moon for the Misbegotten</u>

        Monomoy Theater
        Chatham, MA

        1 - 4 Aug. 1979

E203 <u>A Moon for the Misbegotten</u>

        Troupe Theatre
        335 W. 39th St.

        13 Dec. 1979 - 5 Jan. 1980

        Dir. Geoffrey Sadwith

E204 <u>A Moon for the Misbegotten</u>

        Meadow Brook Theatre
        Rochester, MI

        3 - 27 Jan. 1980

        Dir. Charles Nolte

E205 <u>A Moon for the Misbegotten</u>

        New England Repertory Theatre
        Worcester, MA

        1979-80 Season, closed 9 Mar. 1980

        Dir. Jon Knowles

>   Wilkins, Frederick C. Review. 4.1-2 (1980): 26-28.

E206 <u>A Moon for the Misbegotten</u>

        Portland Stage Company
        Portland, ME

        Closed 18 May 1980

        Dir. Susan Dunlop

207 A Moon for the Misbegotten

        The Classic Theater
        NYC

        Closed 2 Sept. 1980

        Dir. Geoffrey Sadwith

208 A Moon for the Misbegotten

        Bergenstage (an Actors Equity Theater)

        The Laboratory Theater at Bergen Community College
        Paramus, NJ

        7 - 30 Nov. 1980

        Dir. Bing D. Bills
        Setting - Beeb Salzer
        Lighting - Susan Dandridge

        Josie - Nora Chester
        Phil Hogan - Vince O'Brien
        James Tyrone, Jr. - Kelly Fitzpatrick
        T. Stedman Harder - Kevin Gilmartin
        Mike Hogan - D. Peter Moore

            Catinella, Joseph. "Theater." New York Times 23 Nov.
                1980: XI 23.

            Notes that the production stresses the "twisty humor and
            jagged poetry of the play." Approves of the production
            except for Kelly Fitzpatrick (Jamie), who was miscast.

209 A Moon for the Misbegotten

        Old Globe Theatre
        San Diego, CA

        18 Jan. - 22 Feb. 1981

E210 A Moon for the Misbegotten

        Main Street Theater
        White Plains, NY

        Before 1 Mar. - 15 Mar. 1981

        Art Dir. Stephen Rosefield

        James - Frederic Coffin
        Josie - Suzanne Collins
        Hogan - Ian Martin
        Mike Hogan - Michael Mantel
        T. Stedman Harder - William Meisle

>   Frankel, Haskel. "Theater." New York Times
               1 Mar. 1981: XXII 16.

           Observes that there are repetition, monotony, and tedi
           in Misbegotten as in Journey, but there is "a dramatic
           sense" to them, adding to the texture of the plays.

E211 A Moon for the Misbegotten

        The Academy Theatre
        Atlanta, GA

        In repertory Feb. - May 1981
        Tour of the Southeast ended 3 Oct. 1981

        Dir. Frank Wittow

E212 A Moon for the Misbegotten

        StageWest
        West Springfield, MA

        12 Feb. - 7 Mar. 1981

        Dir. Robert Brewer

E213 A Moon for the Misbegotten

        Germinal Stage
        Denver, CO

        9 July - 2 Aug. 1981

        Dir. Ginger Valone

214 A Moon for the Misbegotten

        Woodstock Playhouse
        Woodstock, NY

        15 - 19 and 21 - 26 July 1981

215 A Moon for the Misbegotten

        McCadden Theatre Company, American Theatre Arts Conservatory
        Los Angeles, CA

        Fall 1981

        Dir. Henry Hoffman

            Hansen, Eugene K. Review. EON 6.1 (1982): 45-48.

16 A Moon for the Misbegotten

        Theatre Project Company, U of Missouri
        St. Louis, MO

        18 - 21 Feb. 1982

        Dir. F. Syer

17 A Moon for the Misbegotten

        Barton Square Playhouse
        Salem, MA

        26 Feb. - 3 Apr. 1982

        Dir. David George

            Connolly, Thomas F. Review. EON 6.1 (1982): 43-45.

18 A Moon for the Misbegotten

        2nd Story Theatre
        Newport, RI

        9 Mar. - 25 Apr. 1982

E219 <u>A Moon for the Misbegotten</u>

Playmakers Repertory Company
Chapel Hill, NC

27 Oct. - 14 Nov. 1982

Dir. Gregory Boyd

E219 <u>A Moon for the Misbegotten</u>

Theatre Calgary
Calgary, Canada

Fall 1982

Dir. John Murrell

Phil Hogan - Edward Atienza
Jim Tyrone - Eric Schneider
Josie - Janet Wright

>   Czarnecki, Mark. "the Endless Quest for Love."
           <u>Macleans</u> 8 Nov. 1982: 52+

      Applauds the director's "judicious" cutting of a half
°   hour of text.

E221 <u>A Moon for the Misbegotten</u>

Lyric Stage
Boston, MA

9 Feb. - 13 Mar. 1983

Dir. Polly Hogan

>   Connolly, Thomas F. Review. <u>EON</u> 7.1 (1983): 22.

E222 <u>A Moon for the Misbegotten</u>

Riverside Studio
London

June 1983

223 A Moon for the Misbegotten

       Steppenwolf Theatre
       Chicago, IL

       11 May - 5 Jun. 1983

       Dir. Jeff Perry

           Tuck, Susan. Review. EON 7.2 (1983): 23-26.

224 A Moon for the Misbegotten

       Dorset Theater Festival
       Dorset Playhouse and Colony House
       Dorset, VT

       21 - 30 July 1983

       Dir. John Morrison

25 A Moon for the Misbegotten

       American Repertory Theatre
       Cambridge, MA

       9 Dec. 1983 - 29 Jan. 1984

       Then the Cort Theater
       NYC

       Opened 1 May 1984

       Dir. David Leveaux

       Josie Hogan - Kate Nelligan
       Jim Tyrone - Ian Bannen
       Hogan - Jerome Kilty

           Kroll, Jack. "Courage of Their Convictions." Newsweek
              23 Jan. 1984: 69.

           The play "mixes blarney, melodrama and . . .
           sentimentality in an improbable fusion of emotional and
           spiritual power." Kate Nelligan acts "with a savage
           sophistication . . . beautiful to behold" and the
           performance has a "splendid dynamic variety and lyric
           intensity."

E226 A Moon for the Misbegotten

Tarragon Theatre
30 Bridgman Ave.
Toronto

Opened 8 Oct. 1985

Dir. Martha Henry

Josie – Clare Coulter
Jim Tyrone – Michael Hogan

E227 Moon of the Caribbees

WPA Theater (off off Broadway)

1974-75 Season

E228 Moon of the Caribbees

American Theater Arts
133 MacDougal St.
NYC

9 – 26 Nov. 1978

---- Moon of the Caribbees -- see The Long Voyage Home, no. E183.

---- Moon of the Caribbees -- see The Sea Plays of Eugene O'Neill,
no. E238.

Long Wharf Theatre
New Haven, CT

9 Mar. – 9 Apr. 1979

Dir. Arvin Brown

229 Moon of the Caribbees -- double-billed with Hughie, no. E122.

       Studio Theatre Productions
       Washington Square, NYU
       NYC

       27 - 30 Jan. 1982

       Dir. Rob Mulholland and Harold Easton

          Jiji, Vera. Review of Caribbees and Hughie. EON 6.1
            (1982): 48-49.

--- Moon of the Caribbees -- see Six Plays of the Sea, no. E240.

--- Moon of the Caribbees -- see Sea Plays at Monte Cristo, no. E237.

230 More Stately Mansions (British premiere)

       Greenwich
       London

       19 Sept. - 12 Oct. 1974

       Dir. David Giles
       Design - Kenneth Mellor

       Deborah - Elisabeth Bergner, replaced by Dorothy Reynolds
       Sarah - Frances Cuka
       Simon - Gary Bond

          Wardle, Irving. Review. London Times 20 Sept. 1974:
            8f.

          Instead of characters the people of the play are masks
          covering the pained opposition of "assailant-victim,
          peasant-gentry, mother-whore." "The play is fired with
          sexual contempt and the idea that men are corrupted by
          female greed." Deborah is a "dry-run" for Mary Tyrone.

231 More Stately Mansions

       U of Wisconsin
       Madison, WI

       15 Dec. 1980

       Dir. Ronald Miller

E233 More Stately Mansions

       Irish Rebel Theatre
       Irish Arts Center
       NYC

       Through 31 May 1981

E232 Mourning Becomes Electra

       Circle in the Square - Joseph E. Levine Theatre
       NYC

       Opened 15 Nov. 1972 for 53 performances

       Dir. Theodore Mann
       Setting - Marsha L. Eck
       Lighting - Jules Fisher

       Seth Beckwith - William Hickey
       Amos Ames - Hansford Rowe
       Louisa Ames - Eileen Burns
       Minnie - Jocelyn Brando
       Christine Mannon - Colleen Dewhurst
       Lavinia Mannon - Pamela Payton-Wright
       Hazel Niles - Lisa Richards
       Capt. Peter Niles - Jack Ryland
       Capt. Adam Brant - Alan Mixon
       Brig. Gen. Ezra Mannon - Donald Davis
       Josiah Borden - Hansford Rowe
       Emma Borden - Jocelyn Brando
       The Rev. Everett Hills - William Bush
       Mrs. Hills - Eileen Burns
       Dr. Joseph Blake - Daniel Keyes
       Orin Mannon - Stephen McHattie
       Chantyman - John Ridge
       Abner Small - William Bush
       Joe Silva - Daniel Keyes
       Ira Mackel - John Ridge

Loeb Drama Center
Cambridge, MA

20 - 31 July 1983

Dir. Jonathan Magaril

>Wilkins, Frederick C. Review. EON. 7.2 1983): 26-29.

ON

---- The Movie Man -- see <u>Three Lost Plays of Eugene O'Neill</u>, no. E244

        Lotus Theatre Group, Playhouse 46

        4 - 20 Nov. 1982

        Dir. Michael Fields

---- The Rope -- see <u>Six Plays of the Sea</u>, no. E240.

---- The Rope -- see <u>Sea Plays at Monte Cristo</u>, no. 237.

E237 <u>Sea Plays at Monte Cristo</u>: Caribbees (19 Sept.), Cardiff (Sept. 26), Voyage (3 Oct.), Zone (10 Oct.), Ile (24 Oct.), Cross (7 Nov.), and Rope (14 Nov.)

        "Monte Cristo"
        305 Pequot Ave.
        New Haven, CT

        Between 26 Sept. and 14 Nov. 1985

E238 <u>The Sea Plays of Eugene O'Neill</u> ["S.S. Glencairn"] Caribbees, Zone, Cardiff and Voyage

        Long Wharf Theater
        New Haven, CT

        Opened by 28 Mar. 1978

        Dir. Edward Payson Call
        Artistic Dir. - Arvin Brown
        Setting - John Jensen
        Lighting - Ronald Wallace
        Music - Robert Dennis

CREW OF THE S.S. GLENCAIRN

Driscoll - Robert Lansing
Smitty - David Clennon
Cocky - Emery Battis
Ivan - Peter Iacangelo
Yank - Beeson Carrol
Davis - Frederick Coffin
Max - Owen Hollander
Scotty - Lance Davis
Lamps - Bob Harper

he Donkeyman - William Swetland
lson - William Newman
addy - Richard Jamieson
aul - Dick Sollenberger
irst Mate - Edwin J. McDonough
aptain - Victor Argo

                    THE ISLANDERS

ella - Carol Jean Lewis
earl - C. C. H. Pounder
uzie - Shirley Martelly
iolet - Helen Chivas Hatten

                    THE LONDONERS

ɔe - Owen Hollander
ick - Lance Davis
ag - Le Clanche du Rand
reda - Marlena Lustik
ate - Nora Chester
vo Stevedores - Bob Harper and Richard Jamieson

        Eder, Richard. New York Times 30 Mar. 1978: C 15.

        Says the production does not succeed in taking the plays
        "out of mothballs." The set is good, the actors try
        hard but the plays are too difficult to do effectively.
        Dir. Edward Peyson Cale "has imposed a somnolent rhythm
        on all four plays." Caribbees is the "most clumsily
        performed" and slightest play. Zone is not much better.
        Cardiff has two actors. Voyage is poorly directed, but
        William Newman as Olson is good.

        Wilkins, Frederick C. Review. EON 2.1 (1978): 14-15.

39 Servitude

        Coppertop Theatre
        U of Wisconsin
        Center-Richland, WI

        14 - 16 Nov. 1981

        Dir. Paul Voelker

E240 <u>Six Plays of the Sea</u> -- comprising <u>Cardiff</u>, <u>Voyage</u>, <u>Zone</u>, <u>Ile</u>, <u>Rope</u>, <u>Cross</u>

      Apple Corps Theatre Company
      NYC

      Closed 2 May 1982

      Dir. Skip Corris

---- <u>S. S. Glencairn</u> -- see no. E238.

E241 <u>Strange Interlude</u>

      Duke of York's Theatre
      London

      6 April 1984

      Then Nederlander Theatre
      NYC

      21 Feb. - 5 May 1985

      Dir. Keith Hack
      Design - Voytek with Michael Levine
      Costumes - Deirdre Clancy
      Incidental Music - Benedict Mason

      Nina Leeds - Glenda Jackson
      Charlie Mardsen - Edward Petherbridge
      Ned - Brian Cox
      Sam Evans - James Hazeldine
      Madeline - Caitlin Clarke (in NYC only)

>   Gelb, Barbara. "Strange Interlude Returns to Broadwa New York Times 14 Feb. 1985: I 1, 24.

>   Kelly, K. Review. Boston Globe 22 Feb. 1985: 21.

>   Nightingale, Benedict. "Glenda Jackson Grapples with O'Neill's Everywoman." New York Times 14 Feb. 1 II 1, 6.

Rich, Frank. Review. <u>New York Times</u> 22 Feb. 1985: C 3.

Richards, David. "Enduring the Inerlude." <u>Washington Post</u> 22 Feb. 1985: E 6.

Simon, John. Review. <u>New York</u> 4 Mar. 1985: 110.

242 <u>Thirst</u>

Experimental Theatre
U of Wisconsin
Madison, WI

12 - 15 Apr. 1978

Dir. Edward Amor

Wilkins, Frederick C. Review. <u>EON</u> 2.2 (1978): 16-17.

243 [<u>Three Lost Plays of Eugene O'Neill</u>] -- comprising <u>Breakfast</u>, <u>Wife</u>, <u>Cross</u>

Nameless Theater
125 W. 22nd Sstreet
NYC

Closed 19 Jan. 1978

244 <u>Three Lost Plays of Eugene O'Neill</u> -- comprising <u>Wife</u>, <u>Movie Man</u>, <u>Web</u>

Lotus Theatre Group, Playhouse 46
423 W. 46th St. (at St. Clements Church)
NYC

4 - 20 Nov. 1982

Dir. Michael Fields

Wilkins, Frederick C. Review. <u>EON</u> 6.3 (1982): 24-26.

E245 A Touch of the Poet

>
Hartford Stage Company
Hartford, CT

Opened 31 Mar. 1974

Dir. Paul Weidner
Setting - Marjorie Kellogg
Lighting - Peter Hunt

Mickey Maloy - Daniel Snyder
Jamie Cregan - Jack Murdock
Sara Melody - Tana Hicken
Nora Melody - Maureen Quinn
Cornelius Melody - Paul Sparer
Dan Roche - Bernard Frawley
Paddy O'Dowd - Jerry Reid
Patch Riley - David O. Petersen
Deborah Harford - Barbara Caruso
Nicholas Gadsby - John Leighton

> Barnes, Clive. Review. New York Times 31 Mar. 1974:
53.

Endorses the production. Notes that the play is
typically American--unlike other later O'Neill. Says
Paul Sparer is impressive as Con Melody as were Tana
Hicken as Sara and Maureen Quinn as Nora.

> O'Connor, John J. Review. New York Times Apr. 25,
1974: 79.

Finds the production "cumbersome," and "somewhat
laborious," but still "solid and intelligent."

E246 A Touch of the Poet

Manhattan Theater Club (off off Broadway)

1974-75 Season

247 A Touch of the Poet

>York Players (off off Broadway)
>NYC
>
>17 Feb. 1976

248 A Touch of the Poet

>Irish Rebel Theater (off off Broadway)
>NYC
>
>Nov. 1976

249 A Touch of the Poet

>Helen Hayes Theatre
>NYC
>
>Opened 28 Dec. 1977 for 141 performances.
>
>Dir. José Quintero
>Decor and lighting — Ben Edwards
>Costumes — Jane Greenwood
>
>Mickey Maloy — Barry Snider
>Jamie Cregan — Milo O'Shea
>Sara Melody — Kathryn Walker
>Nora Melody — Geraldine Fitzgerald
>Cornelius Melody — Jason Robards
>Dan Roche — Walter Flanagan
>Paddy O'Dowd — Dermot McNamara
>Patch Riley — Richard Hamilton
>Deborah (Mrs. Henry Harford) — Betty Miller
>Nicholas Gadsby — George Ede
>
>>Anon. "Dear Valentine 'On Stage: Blarney and Bluster.'"
>>New Leader 30 Jan. 1978: 25-26.
>>
>>Too long, repetitive and indigestible. Is impressed
>>with Quintero's direction, but not with Robards'
>>performance.

> Barnes, Clive. Theater/"Touching Portrayal of Poet by
      Robards." New York Post 29 Dec. 1977; NYTCR
      1977: 97.

  "Too many words . . . too many flat words at that."
  O'Neill "wanders" and "blurs" but has a "vision." Rate
  production, acting, directing high. The performance
  gets to the play's "bitter, cynical core."

> Beaufort, John. Theater Reviews/"Outside Poet Tops New
      York Openings." Christian Science Monitor 5 Jan.
      1978; NYTCR 1977: 102.

  All superlatives, although some "judicious cutting" was
  in order.

> Clurman, Harold. Theatre. Nation 21 Jan. 1978:
      60-61.

  Objects to Quintero's direction of saying that he
  doesn't seem to understand the play fully. Also says
  Jason Robards isn't right for the part. Says that Con
  Melody's downfall is only meaningful if he isn't a
  phoney.

> Eder, Richard. "A Touch of the Poet Staged by Quintero
      on Broadway." New York Times 29 Dec. 1977; III
      13; NYTCR 1977: 99.

  High praise except for Robards' portrayal (or it may
  have been Quintero's direction) of Con in the first pa
  of the play.

> Gill, Brendan. "Overkill." New Yorker 9 Jan. 1978:
      59.

  Says that it was written in O'Neill's prime, yet it is
  clumsy. Says that the play cannot be enjoyed for
  itself.

> Gottfried, Martin. "The Cult of the Second-rate."
      Saturday Review 4 Mar. 1978: 41.

  Says the play is second-rate O'Neill and that neither
  Quintero's direction nor Robards' acting compensated
  the play's deficiencies.

Kalem, T. E. "Dream Addict." Time 9 Jan. 1978: 68.

Touch is "like a tidal wave that seems to purge almost
every defect of the play." The Robards/Quintero
pairing seems "attuned not only to O'Neill's text but to
his troubled soul."

Kauffmann, Stanley. "Stanley Kauffmann on the Theatre."
    New Republic 28 Jan. 1978: 24-25.

Emphasizes that O'Neill was fundamentally concerned with
the conflict of cultures: "Irish Catholic versus
American Protestant or American godless is at the base
of his great dramas." Says that Quintero and Robards
fail to discern this, in so they think of Con Melody as
acting grand: there is no tragedy if he is just acting.
Unimpressed with directing and acting--except with
Geraldine Fitzgerald.

Kerr, Walter. "Vintage O'Neill--But with the Crucial
    Ambiguity Missing." New York Times 8 Jan. 1978:
    II 5.

Says that the meaning of the play has escaped Quintero
and Robards: that although men with a touch of the
poet may be fools, they are "ambiguously fools."
Quintero and Robards fail to suggest that "there is
anything to be salvaged from the fantasist's inventive
brain." Approves most of Geraldine Fitzgerald and
Kathryn Walker.

Kroll, Jack. "Symphony of Despair." Newsweek 9 Jan.
    1978: 71.

The acting early in the play is "fussy," but improves.
The play is generally slightly below the great O'Neill
works.

Lape, Bob. WABC-TV 28 Dec. 1977; NYTCR 1977: 102.

"Scorching, searing theatre." Robards and Quintero are
a "formidable force."

> Oliver, Roger W. Review. EON 2.1 (1978): 11-12.

> Sharp, Christopher. The Theatre. Women's Wear Daily
>   30 Dec. 1977; NYTCR 1977: 98.

"Exotic poetry" but over-written, "a study in blarney."
"A bit self-conscious" of its historical setting.
Despite a slow start for the play, Robards is "at his
best," and the rest of the cast is "outstanding."

> Simon, John. Review of Touch. New York 16 Jan. 1978:
>   57-58.

Says the play is not great but does command our
attention. Notes the differing points of view by which
we know Con Melody and says this production is not
worthy. Compliments Kathryn Walker's Sara, says
Geraldine Fitzgerald is satisfactory, but objects to
Robards as Con and to Quintero's direction.

> Watt, Douglas. Theater/"Superb Touch of the Poet."
>   Daily News 30 Dec. 1977; NYTCR 1977: 98.

Lesser play than Misbegotten but still "grand enough an
fascinating." All superlatives.

> Williams, Gary Jay. "Theater in New York: Jason and
>   the Guilt Fleece: A Touch of the Poet." Theater
>   9.2 (1978): 147-48.

Maintains that the ambiguities of the historical setti
and the unbiographical characters give richness to the
play and spare us the near self-lionizing of Journey.
Robards is badly cast until his performance at the end
when the play becomes interesting.

> Wilson, Edwin. The Theater/"Robards Connects Again wi
>   O'Neill." Wall Street Journal 30 Dec. 1977; NYT
>   1977: 100.

Observes the usual O'Neill faults in the play but find
the production sterling.

250 A Touch of the Poet

U of Calgary
Canada

7 - 11 Feb. 1979

Dir. Richard Hornby

251 A Touch of the Poet

Ionia Summer Theater
New Rochelle, NY

Summer 1979

252 A Touch of the Poet

Actors Theatre of St. Paul
St. Paul, MN

7 Feb. - 1 Mar. 1980

Dir. George C. White

253 A Touch of the Poet

Lyric Stage
54 Charles St.
Boston, MA

20 Feb. - 22 Mar. 1980

Dir. Polly Hogan

Wilkins, Frederick C. Review. EON 4.1-2 (1980):
29-30.

254 A Touch of the Poet

Centralia College
Centralia, WA

28 Feb. - 8 Mar. 1980

Dir. Deborah Kellar

E255 A Touch of the Poet

> Library Theatre, St. Peter's Square
> Manchester, England
>
> 1 - 6 Jun. 1981
>
> Then Neptune Theatre
> Liverpool, England
>
> 8 - 13 Jun. 1981
>
> Dir. Roland Jaquarello

E256 A Touch of the Poet

> Intiman Theatre Company
> Seattle, WA
>
> 8 - 26 Sept. 1981
>
> Dir. Margaret Booker

> Pattin, Deborah Kellar. Review. EON 5.3 (1981):
> 20-21.

E257 A Touch of the Poet

> ANTA Presentation at Springfield College
> Springfield, MA
>
> 8 - 10, 15 - 16 Jan. 1982
>
> Dir. Gini Andrewes

E258 A Touch of the Poet

> The Whole Theatre Company
> Montclair, NJ
>
> 12 Oct. - 7 Nov. 1982
>
> Dir. Arnold Mittelman

259 A Touch of the Poet

        Roberts Theater, Rhode Island College
        Providence, RI

        11 - 14 Nov. 1982

260 A Touch of the Poet

        The American Stage Company
        St. Petersburg, FL

        24 Feb. - 27 Mar. 1983

        Dir. Kevin Coleman

261 A Touch of the Poet

        The Concord Players
        Concord, MA

        22 Apr. - 7 May 1983

        Dir. Dorothy A. Scheckter

            Brooks, Marshall. Review. EON 7.1 (1983): 22-25.

262 A Touch of the Poet

        Yale Repertory Theatre
        New Haven, CT

        3 - 21 May 1983

        Dir. Lloyd Richards

            Wilkins, Frederick C. Review. EON 7.1 (1983): 22-25.

E263 A Touch of the Poet

      Equity Library Theater
      NYC

      12 - 29 April 1984

      Dir. Yvonne Ghareeb
      Set - Dennis Bradford

      Con Melody - Gerald J. Quimby
      Nora - Helen-Jean Arthur
      Sara - Kay Walbye

E264 A Touch of the Poet

      Berkeley (CA) Repertory Theatre
      Berkeley, CA

      14 Sept. - 2 Oct. 1984

      Dir. Steven Schachter

---- The Web -- see Three Lost Plays of Eugene O'Neill, no. E244.

E265 Welded

      Academy Arts Repertory
      330 E. 56th St.
      NYC

      Closed 23 Apr. 1978

E266 Welded

      No Smoking Playhouse
      NYC

      Closed 10 Nov. 1979

      Dir. Irene Horowitz

267 <u>Welded</u>

Presented by the Summer Session and the Center for Theater
Studies at Columbia U

Horace Mann Theater of Teachers College
NYC

10 June - 5 July 1981

Dir. José Quintero
Setting - Quentin Thomas
Lighting - Michael Valentino

Michael Cape - Philip Anglim
Eleanor - Ellen Tobie
John - Court Miller
Woman - Laura Gardner

Brooks, Marshall. Review. <u>EON</u> 5.2 (1981): 18-19.

Gussow, Mel. "In a Sea of Symbolism." <u>New York Times</u>
        18 June 1981: C22.

Pans both the play and the production. Says this play
would have buried a lesser playwright. Objects to "sea
of symbolism" and the "over wrought language." Adds
that Quintero's "heavy-handed" direction is not helpful.

Hinden, Michael. Review. <u>EON</u> 5.2 (1981): 17-18.

Simon, John. "Theater." <u>New York</u> 29 June 1981: 39.

Says that although the actors were all professionals,
the play came off as a drama school amateur production.
It contains "clumsy plotting and elephantine language."

268 <u>Welded</u>

725 Broadway
NYC

Closed 12 Feb. 1984

Dir. Gregg Brevoort

E269 Where the Cross is Made

             Harvard Summer Repertory Theatre
             Loeb Experimental Theatre
             Cambridge, MA

             6 - 8 July 1978

             Dir. George Hamlin

>   Wilkins, Frederick C. Review. EON 2.2 (1978): 17-18

---- Where the Cross is Made -- see Sea Plays at Monte Cristo, no.
      E237.

---- Where the Cross is Made -- see [Three Lost Plays of Eugene
      O'Neill], no. E243.

---- Where the Cross is Made -- see Six Plays of the Sea, no. E240.

---- A Wife for A Life -- see [Three Lost Plays of Eugene O'Neill],
      no. E243.

---- A Wife for A Life -- see Three Lost Plays of Eugene O'Neill, no.
      E244.

FOREIGN LANGUAGE PRODUCTIONS AND REVIEWS

JLGARIA

Luna dli͡a pasynkov sud'by [Misbegotten]

> Teatr "Sofii͡a"
> Sofia
>
> 1977
>
>> Li͡ubimova, E. "Samyĭ i͡unyĭ v Sofii." Teatr zhizn 6
>> (1977): 21-22.
>>
>> Shamovich, E. and Shvydkoĭ, M. "Gastroli.--76." Teatr
>> 6 (1977): 116-26.

[Desire]

> Dramaticheskom teatre
> Sofia
>
> c. 1977

[Desire Under the Elms]

> Vratsa
>
> c. 1978

Luna dli͡a pasynkov sud'by [Misbegotten]

> Gabrovo
>
> c. 1979

NA

Andi [Anna]

> Theater of the Central Academy of Dramatic Arts
>
> Beijing
>
> 16 - 21 Oct. 1984
>
> Dir. George C. White

CZECHOSLOVAKIA

F6   [A Moon for the Misbegotten]

        Petr Bezruč Theater
        Ostrava

        1978

F7   [Anna Christie]

        Olomouc

        Feb. 1979

F8   [Long Day's Journey into Night]

        Cinoherni klub
        Prague

        c. 1979

        Dir. Ladislav Smocek

F9   [The Long Voyage Home]

        Prague

        c. 1979

FRANCE

F10   Le long voyage vers la nuit [Journey]

        Théâtre de l'Atelier
        Paris

        Mar. 1973

        Première en hommage à André Barsacq

        Mise en Scène - G. Wilson

11   Marco Millions

        Théâtre Montparnasse
        Paris

        1973

        Mise en Scène - M. C. Valène

12   Une lune pour les déshérités [Misbegotten]

        Odéon
        Paris

        1973

        Mise en Scène - J. Rosner

13   Le deuil sied à Electre [Electra]

        Paris

        Feb. 1974

        Adapted by Maurice Cazeneuve

                Walter, Georges. Article on Part I of the production.
                Le Figaro 20 Feb. 1974: 29.

                Walter, Georges. Review of Part II of the production.
                Le Figaro 28 Feb. 1974: 29.

14   Marco Millions

        La Gaité Montparnasse
        Paris

        31 July - 14 Sept. 1974

                Anonymous. Article on Marco Millions at La Gaité. Le
                Figaro 31 July 1974: 12.

                Gautier, J. J. Review. Le Figaro 14 Sept. 1974: 23.

                Olivier, J. J. "Etrangers au Montparnasse." Review.
                Le Figaro. 14 Sept. 1974: 15.

264   FOREIGN LANGUAGE PRODUCTION

F15   Une lune pour les déshérités [Misbegotten]

         Théâtre de l'Odéon
         Paris

         Feb. 1975

         Dir. Jacques Rosner
         Adapted by - Jacqueline Autrusseau

         James - Jacques Destoop
         Josie - Françoise Seigneur
         Hogan - Michel Aumont

>   Marcabru, Pierre. Review. France-Soir 22 Feb. 1975:
                  19.

F16   Le deuil sied à Electre [Electra]

         Théâtre d'Ivry
         Paris

         3 Mar. 1975?

>   Marcabru, Pierre. "Eschyle corrigé par Strindberg."
                  Review. Le Figaro 9 Feb. 1975: 21.

>   Gautier, J. J. Review. Le Figaro 1 Mar. 1975: 46.

F17   Le Marchand de glâce est passé [Iceman]

         Théâtre de la Commune d'Aubervilliers
         Aubervilliers

         c. 1975

         Mise en scène - Gabriel Garran

F18   Le long voyage vers la nuit [Journey]

         Théâtre de l'Atelier
         Paris

         Mar. 1979

>   Gautier, J. J. Review. Le Figaro 21 Mar. 1979: 29.

19   Le deuil sied à Electre [Electra]

         Théâtre des Quartiers d'Ivry
         Ivry

         1980

         Then Le Studio d'Ivry
         Paris

         5 Feb. - 9 Mar. 1980

         Mise en Scène - Stuard Seide
         Adapted by - Louis Lanoux

20   Le deuil sied à Electre   [Electra]

         8 - 22 Nov. 1981

         TV FR 3

         Dir. Maurice Cazeneuve

         Lavinia - Anna Deleuze

             Rebeix, Viviane. Section/ Télévision. Interview with
             Anne Deleuze. France-Soir 21 Nov. 1981: 22.

             Says that Mme Deleuze has played Electra in various
             productions since 1972.

21   De l'huile [Ile] and Marque d'une croix [Cross]

         Comedie de Caen
         Caen

         1983

         Mise en Scène - Claude Yersin

22   Le long voyage vers la nuit [Journey]

         Centre Théâtral du Maine
         Maine

         1983

         Mise en Scène - André Cellier

F23   Le long voyage vers la nuit [Journey]

       Théâtre Eclaté d'Annecy
       Annecy

       Jan. 1984

       Then Théâtre 13
       Paris

       3 Feb. 1984 and into March

       Mary - Nelly Borgeaud
       Tyrone - Jean-Marc Bory
       Edmund - Jean-Ives Chatelain

>   Marcabru, Pierre. Review. Le Figaro 27 Feb. 1984:   33

>   Rebeix, Viviane. Review. Section/Spectacles.
           France-Soir 13 Mar. 1984:   20.

F24   Une lune pour les déshérités [Misbegotten]

       Maison des Arts André Malraux
       Paris, France

       10 - 28 Jan. 1984

GERMANY

F15   Einer langen Tages Reise in die Nacht [Journey]

       Deutsches Schauspielhaus
       Hamburg

       27 Apr. 1975

       Prod.-Dir. Rudolf Noelte
       Designer - Ute Meid

       Mary - Maria Wimmer

>   Wertheim, Albert. Review. Educational Theatre Journal
           28 (1976): 122-24.

           The production turns the play into a character study of
           Mary considering her effect on others. Script cuts
           eliminate the Catholicism, and the references to the

> Virgin Mary and the convent days. The characters' main
> concern is curing Mary Tyrone. Such "slanting . . .
> need not . . . necessarily do the original disservice."

F26   [A Touch of the Poet]

> Rostock
>
> c. 1978

GREECE

F37   [Strange Interlude]

> Bretania Theatre
> Athens
>
> Spring 1985

HUNGARY

F28   Marco Polo millioí

> Nemzeti Színház
> Pécs
>
> 1973

F29   Egy igazi úr [Touch]

> Katona József Színház
> Kecskemét
>
> 1974

F30   Vágy a szilfák alatt [Desire]

> József Attila Színház
> Budapest
>
> 1974

F31 [A Touch of the Poet]

      Hungária Chamber Theatre
      Sokonai Theater
      Debrecen

      Spring 1975

F32 Boldogtalan hold [Misbegotten]

      Katona József Színház
      Kecskemét

      1975

F33 Hosszú ut az éjszakába [Journey]

      Pesti Színház
      Budapest

      1977

F34 Különös közjáték [Interlude]

      Nemzeti Színház
      Budapest

      1978

F35 Hosszú ut az éjszakába [Journey]

      Vígszínház
      Budapest

      1978

F36 [A Touch of the Poet]

      Hungarian Chamber Theater
      Debrecen

      Spring 1979

      Dir. Antal Rencz

NORWAY

F37   Mone for Livets Stebarn [Misbegotten]

          Bergen International Festival of the Arts
          Oslo Nye Theater

          15 May 1976

          Dir. José Quintero

          Josie - Liv Ullmann
          Jim - Toralv Maurstad
          Hogan - Espen Skjonberg

>   Waal, Carla. Review. Educational Theatre Journal 28
                     (1976): 557-58.

                     The audience focused its attention on the relationship
                     between Josie and Hogan. Although the production was
                     energetic and interesting, it was "difficult to follow
                     as a whole."

POLAND

F38   [Long Day's Journey into Night]

          Six productions between 1972-78.

F39   [Desire Under the Elms]

          Two productions between 1972-78.

F40   [The Iceman Cometh]

          Teatr Dramatyczny
          Warsaw

          Opened 16 June 1976

F41   [Long Day's Journey into Night]

          Wroclaw

          1977-78

F42   [Long Day's Journey into Night]

          Polish TV

          Spring 1978

ROMANIA

F43   Fire de Poet [Touch]

          Bucharest

          c. 1978

RUSSIA

F44   [Long Day's Journey into Night]

          Referred to in an article of 1973

F45   [Desire Under the Elms]

          Leningrad (?)

          Referred to in an article of 1975

F46   Liubov' pod viasami [Desire]

          Omskiĭ dramaticheskiĭ teatr
          Omsk

          1975

>   Dumma, G. "Strasti pod viasami. Omskaia pravda
              20 Dec. 1975.

F47   Desire/Liubov' pod viasami

          San Francisco Touring Company

          Various places in Russia

          June - July 1976

          Simultaneously in English and (through earphones) Russian

> Damidov, M. "O'Nil i Uaĭlder segodnîa." <u>Lit. gaz.</u>
> 9 June 1976.

> Kachalov, N. "Ne tol'ko vesel'e." <u>Sov. Kultura</u>
> 1 June 1976.

> Līubimova, E. "Osmyslenie proshlogo." <u>Teatr zhizn'</u>.
> 18 (1976): 28-29.

> Mikhaĭlova, N. "Liubov' i nenavist'." <u>Ogönek</u>
> 25 (1976): 29.

> Tsimbal, I.S. "Smeshnoe i tragicheskoe." <u>Leningr.</u>
> <u>Pravda</u> 13 June 1976.

> Fridshteĭn, Îu. "Amerika smeîushchaîacîa i
> stradaîushchaîa." <u>Teatr</u> 2 (1977): 115-18.

748 <u>Lyubov pod vîasami</u> [Desire]

Len Soviet Palace of Culture
Leningrad, USSR

Production referred to in an article dated 5 Sept. 1976

749 <u>Traur--uchast' Elektra</u> [Electra]

Ivanovskom dramaticheskom teatre
Ivanovo

1976

> Tarshish, N. "Imitatsiîa tragedii; Pravda zamysla i
> ispolneniîa." <u>Rabochiĭ krai</u> [Ivanovo] 29 May and
> 11 June 1976.

F50   Dusha poêta [Touch]

      Moskovskiĭ dramaticheskiĭ teatr na Maloĭ Bronnoĭ

      1977

>   "Dusha poêta." Teatr. zhizn' 8 (1977): 2-3.

>   "Dusha poêta." Vech. Moskva 20 Jan. 1977.

>   Garibova, O. "Dusha poêta." Teatr 5 (1978): 25-27.

>   Ryzhova, V. "Dusha poêta." Vech. Moskva 16 Feb. 1977.

>   Suknanova, T. "Takie raznye sud'by." Teatr. zhizn'
            2 (1978): 6-7.

MISCELLANEOUS: ADAPTATIONS, TV AND RADIO PRODUCTIONS,
AUDIO AND FILM RECORDINGS, AND FICTIONAL REPRESENTATIONS
OF O'NEILL'S LIFE

:1 O'Neill, Eugene. The Iceman Cometh. Dir. With Lee Marvin.
      Caedmon, TRS 359, 1973.

            Four discs Stereo, 33 1/3 rpm. The original sound track
            recording of the AFT film of Iceman. Duration: 228
            minutes.

:2 The Iceman Cometh

            The American Film Theater

            Dir. John Frankenheimer

            Hickey - Lee Marvin   The Capt. - Martyn Green
            Hope - Fredric March   Mott - Moses Gunn
            Slade - Robert Ryan   McGloin - Clifton James
            Parritt - Jeff Bridges   Jimmy - John McLiam
            Oban - Bradford Dillman   Chuck - Stephen Pearlman
            Kalmar - Sorrell Booke   Rocky - Tom Pedi
            Margie - Hildy Brooks   The Gen. - Geo. Voskovec
            Pearl - Nancy Juno Dawson   Moran - Bart Burns
            Cora - Evans Evans   Lieb - Don McGovern

                Canby, Vincent. "The Iceman Cometh Too Close." New
                    York Times 30 Oct. 1973: 36; and 11 Nov. 1973:
                    1, 3.

                Does not compare favorably with Lumet's Journey or the
                TV version of Iceman. March is "superb" but Lee Marvin
                is lacking as Hickey.

                Cocks, Jay. Review. Time 12 Nov. 1973: 122-23.

                The production is "worthy." Special commendation to
                Ryan as Slade. Lee Marvin lacks the "necessary bravura"
                for the role.

                Kael, Pauline. "Moments of Truth." New Yorker
                    5 Nov. 1973: 149-52.

                "Straightforward and faithful." Robert Ryan brought a
                new dimension to the character of Larry Slade, but Lee
                Marvin's performance was "acting on [only] one level."

> Kauffmann, Stanley. "Stanley Kauffmann on Films." New
  Republic 17 Nov. 1973: 24, 35-36.

  Jeff Bridges "does very well" as Parritt; Ryan is
  "sterling;" March is good as Hope; but Marvin "was bor
  to play Hickey." Sees the play as more suitable to fil
  than Journey.

> Zimmerman, Paul D. Review. Newsweek 12 Nov. 1973:
  119-20.

  A "great movie of a great play." Ryan provides the
  tragic dimension.

G3 Long Day's Journey into Night

    National Theatre Production
    ABC-TV

    8:00 - 11:00 pm est

    10 March 1973

    Tyrone - Laurence Olivier
    Mary - Constance Cummings
    James - Dennis Quilley
    Edmund - Ronald Pickup

> O'Conner, J. J. Review. 14 March 1973: 86.

  Thought the commercials "disastrous" to the play's
  atmosphere.

G4 O'Neill, Eugene. The Emperor Jones. Dir. Theodore Mann. With
    James Earl Jones. Caedmon, CDL 5341, [1974].

    Two cassettes. One-track mono. Duration: 93 minutes.

G5 A Touch of the Poet. By Eugene O'Neill. Dir. Stephen Potter.
    With Fritz Weaver, Nancy Marchand, Roberta Maxwell, and
    Carrie Nye. PBS. 24 and 25 Apr. 1974.

36   The Hairy Ape. By Eugene O'Neill. Adapted for radio: Yuri
        Rasovsky. With Danny Goldring. 1974.

            Chicago Radio Theatre production, broadcast 9 Dec. 1974,
            on WNIB, Chicago. Duration: 46 minutes, 16 seconds.

37   New Girl in Town -- A revival of the 1957 musical based on Anna.

        Equity Library Theater (the Roerich Museum on Riverside
        Drive)
        NYC

        9 Jan. 1975

        Music and lyrics - Robert Merrill
        Book - George Abbott

38   Moon for the Misbegotten

        ABC-TV Film

        27 May 1975

        Dir. Jose Quintero, with Gordon Rigsby

            Burke, Tom. "Ghost, Walk that Stage with Us." TV Guide
                24 May 1975: 12-17.

            Hendy, Valerie. Preview. National Catholic Reporter
                23 May 1975: 12-17.

            O'Connor, John J. Review. New York Times 27 May 1975:
                59.

            Says the play is not great but good--though good O'Neill
            makes the competition rather mediocre. "The characters
            are still another set of variations on compulsive
            O'Neill themes."

39   Beyond the Horizon. By Eugene O'Neill. Dir. Michael Kahn and
        Rick Hauser. With Richard Backus, Maria Tucci, Edward J.
        Moore, Geraldine Fitzgerald, James Broderick, John Randolph,
        and John Houseman. PBS. 14 Jan. 1976.

G10   Desire Under the Elms -- An opera based on Desire.

        Palmer Auditorium
        Connecticut College
        New London, CT

        10 and 12 Aug. 1978

        Music - Edward Thomas
        Libretto - Joe Masteroff

        Eben Cabot - Michael Best
        Abbie - Carol Todd
        Ephraim - William Fleck
        Peter - Sean Barker
        Simeon - Ken Bridges

G11   Mourning Becomes Electra

        PTV--WNET-TV's Great Performances Series

        Adapt. Kenneth Cavander

        Dir. Nick Havinga

        6 Dec. 1978 - 3 Jan. 1979

        Christine - Joan Hackett
        Lavinia - Roberta Maxwell
        Orin - Bruce Davison
        Ezra - Joseph Sommer
        Seth - Roberts Blossom
        Adam - Jeffrey DeMunn

>   O'Connor, John. New York Times. 6 Dec. 1978: C26.

>   Romano, John. Preview. TV Guide. 2 Dec. 1978: 23-2‹

G12   Emperor Jones--an opera, written 1932.

        Michigan Opera Theatre
        Detroit, MI

        Feb. 1979

        Composer - Louis Gruenberg

G13   Desire Under the Elms--an opera.

              Central City Opera
              Central City, CO

              Aug. 1980

              Music - Edward Thomas

              Libretto - Joe Masteroff

G14   Before Breakfast -- An opera based on Breakfast; part of a triple
      bill called An American Trilogy.

              New York City Opera
              NYC

              9 Oct. 1980

              Music - Thomas Pasatieri

              Libretto - Frank Corsaro

              Chor. - Zoya Leporski

              Mrs. Rowland - Marilyn Zschau

G15   Facets of Desire -- A ballet based on Desire.

              Pepsico Summer Fare '81 Arts Festival
              SUNY -- Purchase, NY

              25 July 1981

              Chor. -- John Butler

              Music core (woodwinds and strings) -- Alan Hoddinott

              Dancers - Kevin McKenzie/Martine van Hamel/Gary Chryst

G16   Wheeler, David. Here Before . . . Eugene O'Neill. EON 6.1
              (1982): 3-15.

      A one-person play spotlighting the character of Eugene O'Neill.

G17   Cheuse, Alan. The Bohemians: John Reed and his Friends Who Shook
      the World. Cambridge: Applewood, 1982.

              A novel, told from John Reed's perspective, about his
              life. Enter O'Neill as a drunkard.

G18   The Great God Brown--a story outline for choreography.

      1982

      Beatrice Laufer

G19   Roberts, Meade. Thornhill.

      Westbeth, NY

      Oct. 1983

      Prod. Fran Weissler
      Dir. John Casavetes

      With Ben Gazzara, Patti Lupone, Carol Kane

              A play developed in a studio-workshop.

G20   Take Me Along--an all-Black revival of the 1959 musical based on
      Ah, Wilderness!

      Richard Allen Center at Manhattan Community College
      NYC

      8 - 25 Mar. 1984

      Music and lyrics - Robert Merrill

      Book - Joseph Stern and Robert Russell

      Revised and adapted - C. T. Perkinson

      Dirs. Geraldine Fitzgerald and Mike Malone

G21   Wilkins, Frederick, ed. "Two Pen Portraits of Eugene O'Neill,
      Broadwayite." EON 8.2 (1984): 17-19.

                  Reprints two humorous sketches of O'Neill biography.
                  The first, "Eugene O'Neill, that Strange Interlude Man,"
                  by Samuel Marx, bears a striking resemblance to the

second, "The Great God O'Neill," by Sidney Skolsky.
Articles published in 1929 and 1930 respectively.

G22   Farrell, Herman Daniel, III.   <u>Dreams of the Son</u>.

West End Theatre
NYC

Opened 18 July 1984.

A play based on O'Neill's life.

G23   <u>Kejsar Jones</u> -- A chamber opera based on <u>Jones</u>.

Royal Opera
Stockholm

29 Sept. 1984

Music - Sven-David Sandstrom

Libretto and Direction - Lars G. Thelestam

Costumes and Masks - Sunniva Thelestam

Chor. - Stanislaw Brosowski

Jones - Kolbjorn Hoiseth

Tom J. A. Olsson. Review. <u>EON</u> 8.3 (1984): 33-34.

G24   <u>Take Me Along</u>--a revival of the 1959 musical based on <u>Ah,
Wilderness!</u>

Goodspeed Opera House
East Haddam, CT

12 Sept. 1984

Martin Beck Theatre

15 Apr. 1985. Closed after one performance.

EDITIONS OF PRIMARY WORKS

1 Three Plays. New York: Vintage, 1973.

   Includes Desire, Interlude, and Electra.

2 A Moon for the Misbegotten. New York: Vintage, 1974.

3 Return to Life. Ed. Robert Kastenbaum. The Literature of Death
   and Dying Series. New York: Arno, 1977.

   A reprint of Lazarus Laughed.

4 Four Plays/Eugene O'Neill. Franklin Center, PA: Franklin
   Library, 1978.

   A limited edition. Illustrated by Jerry Cosgrove. Contains
   Interlude, Electra, Misbegotten, and Touch.

5 Four Plays. Franklin Center, PA: Franklin Library, 1979.

   A limited edition. Illustrated by Fred Otnes. Contains
   Interlude, Electra, Misbegotten, and Touch.

   Selected Plays of Eugene O'Neill. Garden City: Doubleday, 1979.

   Includes Anna, Jones, Desire, Interlude, Electra, Touch, Iceman,
   and Misbegotten.

   Introduced by José Quintero.

   Eugene O'Neill: Poems: 1912-1944. Ed. Donald Gallup. New Haven:
   Ticknor and Fields, 1980.

   Publication of all 72 known poems by O'Neill. Sanborn and
   Clark's 1931 bibliography had published 30 of them.

   Four Plays/Eugene O'Neill. 1978. Franklin Center, PA: Franklin
   Library, 1980.

H9   Eugene O'Neill: Work Diary 1924-1943. Ed. Donald Gallup.
         Preliminary ed. 2 vols. New Haven: Yale UP, 1981.

     The Work Diaries, based on the "Scribbling Diaries," (all
     destroyed by O'Neill save for the one for 1925--here included in
     the appendix to vol. 2) are dated notes on when and where plays
     were produced, inspiration struck, work was done, and whatever
     seemed worth recording. The first volume covers 1924-1933; the
     second covers 1934-1943, Also included are various tables in
     which O'Neill charts the time he spent working and the time he
     spent abstaining from alcohol and tobacco.

H10 The Calms of Capricorn: A Play. Developed from O'Neill's scenari
         by Donald Gallup. New Haven: Ticknor and Fields, 1982.

     Includes a transcription of the scenario. The play was original
     to be the first then the third play of the Harford family cycle.
     Gallup corrects spelling, tries to integrate O'Neill's changes o
     plans, turns indirect speech into direct speech, and fleshes out
     what O'Neill "merely sketched." Perhaps the latter comprises
     15-20 percent of the play.

H11 Chris Christopherson. New York: Random House 1982. Foreword by
         Leslie Eric Comens.

     A three-act play, the precursor of Anna Christie, Chris
     Christopherson, opened in March 1920, its producer hoping to
     capitalize on the success of Horizon, but it folded the same
     month. This text is not the stage version, which is not extent,
     but it is from the transcript sent to the copyright office. It
     the only surviving produced O'Neill play that has never till now
     been printed.

H12 Hughie. New Haven: Yale UP, 1982.

H13 The Iceman Cometh. New York: Limited Editions Club, 1982.

H14 The Plays of Eugene O'Neill. 3 vols. New York: Random, 1982.

     1: Bound, Voyage, Lazarus, Zone, Ile, Cross, Rope, Dreamy,
        Fountain, Interlude, Caribbees, and Breakfast.
     2: Electra, Wilderness, Chillun, Marco, Welded, Diff'rent, Firs
        Gold.
     3: Anna, Horizon, Jones, Ape, Brown, Straw, Dynamo, Days, Icema

15   "Tomorrow." _EON_   7.3 (1983):   3-13.

     O'Neill's published short story, precursor of _Iceman_, is reprinted
     here.

16   _A Touch of the Poet_.   1957.   New York: Vintage, 1983.

TRANSLATIONS

Since a foreign language production presumes a translation, though
possibly unpublished, attention is called to F entries where relevant.

ARABIC

1 [Beyond the Horizon. Anna Christie]. Trans. Abdulla Motwalli.
   Kuwait: Ministry of Information, 1978.

2 Ragba tahta šagaratad-dardar [Desire]. Trans. Abdullah A. Hafez
   Mitwalli and Mohamed Samir Abdulhamid. Kuwait: Ministry of
   Information, 1979.

3 Al-yanbu [Fountain]. Trans. Salāh' Izz al-Dīn. Cairo: Maktabat
   Masr, 1980.

BULGARIA -- see Foreign Language Productions

CHINESE -- and see Foreign Language Productions

   Ch'ang yeh man lu t'iao t'iao [Journey]. Trans. George Kao. Hong
   Kong: World Today Press, 1973.

   [A Long Day's Journey into Night]. Taipei, Taiwan: Hsin Ya, 1976.

   Chinese annotations by Te-i T'an and others.

   Ta ti chih ai [Horizon] Trans. Ku Chung-i. Shanghai: Yung hsiang
   yin shu kuan, 1976.

   Reprint of a 1946 edition.

CZECHOSLOVAKIAN -- and see Foreign Language Productions

   Touha pod jilmy [Desire]. Trans. Milan Lukeš. Prague: Dilia,
   1976.

   Ach, divočina [Wilderness]. Trans. Jozef Kot. Bratislava: LITA,
   1977.

   Vel'ký boh Brown [Brown]. Trans. Jozef Kot. Bratislava: LITA,
   1977.

O Ach, ta léta bláznivá [Wilderness]. Trans. Eva Kondrysová.
   Prague: Dilia, 1978.

FRENCH -- see Foreign Language Productions.

GERMAN

J11 Trauer muss Elektra tragen: e. Trilogie (1:) Die Heimkehr (2-3:)
     Die Gejagten. Die Verfluchten [Mourning]. Trans. Marianne
     Wentzel. Frankfurt am Main: S. Fischer, 1971-76.

J12 Ah, Wilderness! Trans. Karl Goldmann. Frankfurt am Main:
     Hirschgraben-Verlag, 1973.

J13 Hughie: Stück in e. Akt. Trans. Ursula Schuh. Frankfurt am Main
     S. Fischer, 1973.

J14 Anna Christie: Schauspiel in 4 Akten. Trans. Sibylle Hunzinger.
     Frankfurt am Main: S. Fischer, 1975.

J15 Eines langen Tages Reise in die Nacht [Journey]. Trans. Ursula
     and Oscar Schuh. Stuttgart: Reclam, 1975.

J16 Ein Mond für die Beladenen: Drama in 4 Akten [Misbegotten].
     Trans. Marianne Wentzel. Frankfurt am Main: S. Fischer,
     1977.

J17 Marcos Millionen: Schauspiel. Frankfurt am Main: S. Fischer,
     1977.

J18 Seltsames Zwischenspiel: Drama in 9 Akten [Interlude]. Trans.
     Marianne Wentzel. Frankfurt am Main: S. Fischer, 1977.

J19 Fast ein Poet: Drama in 4 Akten [Touch]. Trans. Ursula Schuh an
     Oscar Fritz Schuh. Leipzig: Insel-Verlag, 1979. Reprint
     1957.

J20 Eines langen Tages Reise in die Nacht [Journey]. Ursula Schuh a
     Oscar Fritz Schuh. Stuttgart: Reclam, 1982.

GREEK -- and see Foreign Languge Productions

J21 O pagopolis erhetai [Iceman]. Trans. Marios Ploritis. Athens:
     Odysseas, 1979.

J22 Pothoi kato ap' tis ftelies [Desire]. Trans. Dora Volanaki.
     Athens: Dodoni, 1981.

UNGARIAN -- and see Foreign Language Productions

23 Drámák. Budapest: Európa Könyvkia, 1974. 2 vols.

Contents:
1. Jones Császár [Jones] and Vágy a szilfák alatt [Desire].
    Trans. Vajda Miklós. Különös Közjáték [Interlude]. Trans.
    Bányay Geyza. Amerika Elektra [Electra]. Trans. Ottlik
    Géza.

2. Egy igazi úr [Touch]. Trans. Vas István. Eljö a
    jeges [Iceman].Trans. Vajda Miklós. Utazás az éjaza kábá
    [Journey]. Trans. Vas István. Boldogtalan hold
    [Misbegotten]. Trans. Vas István. Terminal essay by Álmasi
    Miklos.

ITALIAN

24 Il lutto si addice ad Elettra [Electra]. Trans. Bruno Fonzi.
    Turin: G. Einaudi, 1974.

25 Lunga giornata verso la notte [Journey]. Trans. Bruno Fonzi.
    Turin: Einaudi, 1977.

26 Le Opere: La luna dei Caraibi. Il lungo viaggio di ritorno, etc.
    [Caribbees, Voyage, etc.] Trans. Bruno Fonzi. Turin: UTET,
    1978.

JAPANESE

27 Nire no Kokage no Yokubo [Desire]. Trans. Inoue Soji. Tokyo:
    Iwanamishoten, 1974.

28 O'Neill Meisaku-shu [Works]. Trans. Kishi Tetsuo, et al. Tokyo:
    Hakusuisha, 1975.

NORWEGIAN

29 Lang dags ferd mot natt [Journey]. Trans. Arthur Klaebo. Oslo:
    Det Norske treatet, 1976.

30 Hughie. Trans. Arne Skouen. Oslo: Norsk rikskringkasting, 1977.

31 Lang dags ferd mot natt [Journey]. Trans. Svein Selvig.
    Trondheim: Trondelag Teater, 1980.

POLISH--and see Foreign Language Productions

J32 Teatr. Trans. Kazimierz Piotrowski, Maciej Slomczýnski, Broniska
          Zielinski, et al. Warsaw: Pánstwowy Instytut Wydawniczy,
          1973.

     Contents:
     Jones, Ape, Chillun, Desire, Brown, Lazarus, Electra,
     Wilderness, Iceman.

PORTUGUESE

J33 Longa jornada noite adentro [Journey]. Trans. Helena Pessoa. Sã
          Paulo [Brazil]: Abril, 1980.

ROMANIA -- see Foreign Language Productions

J34 [Four Letters]. Petru Comarnescu. Scieri despre Teatru. Ed.
          Mircea Filip. Iaşi [Romania]: Editura Junimea, 1977:
          149-155.

     Dated 20 May 1938, 26 Nov. 1938, 8 Mar. 1939, 12 July 1945, the
     letters, to Comarnescu, are about translation and publication
     rights. In one O'Neill discusses critics' views of his work. T
     letters are in Romanian translations.

RUSSIAN -- and see Foreign Language Productions

J35 [Long Day's Journey into Night]. Three American Plays. Trans.
          and ed. E. Mednikova. Moscow: n.p. 9-127.

J36 "O tragedii" [?], "Strindberg i nash teatr" [Strindberg and Our
          Theatre], "Teatr i ego sredstva" [Theatre and its means (?)
          "Pis'mo v Kamernyĭ teatr" [Letter to the Kamerny Theater].
          Trans. G. Zlobina. Pisateli S. SH. A o Literature. Moscow
          n.p. 206-16.

J37 Traur, ucast' Elektry [Electra]. Trans. V. Alekseev. Moscow:
          Iskusstvo, 1975. Afterword by V. Malikov.

J38 Pred zajtrkom: igra v enem dejanju [Interlude]. Trans. Janko
          Moder and Dusan Tomse. n.p.: n.p., 1982.

SPANISH

39 Antes del desayuno [Breakfast]. Trans. Raul Blengio Brito.
      Montevideo [Uruguay]: La Casa del Estudiant, 1978.

40 Teatro escogido [selected plays]. Madrid: S.A. de Promocion y
      Ediciones Club Internacional del libro, 1982.

SWEDISH

41 Anna Christie. Trans. Sven Barthel. Helsinki: Yleisradio,
      1980.

THAI

42 Botlakorn plae ruang wai-wun [Wilderness]. Trans. Suchayadi
      Tantavanich. Bangkok: Praepitaya, 1976.

INDEX OF PLAYS

103662

Z
8644.5
.S6
1988

Smith, Madeline.
    Eugene O'Neill.

DATE DUE

SUSAN COLGATE CLEVELAND
LIBRARY/LEARNING CENTER
COLBY-SAWYER COLLEGE
New London, New Hampshire 03257

GAYLORD   PRINTED IN U.S.A.